Hackensack to Hollywood
My Two Show Business Careers

Hackensack to Hollywood
My Two Show Business Careers

From Krupa & Goodman
to *Mork & Mindy*

An Unauthorized Autobiography
By Gordon 'Whitey' Mitchell

Dedicated to Marilyn,
for all her love and support,
and to the memory of William
and Grace Mitchell, who I was
lucky enough to have as parents.

Hackensack to Hollywood: My Two Show Business Careers
From Krupa & Goodman to *Mork & Mindy*
An Unauthorized Autobiography
© 2007 Gordon 'Whitey' Mitchell. All Rights Reserved.

All illustrations are copyright of their respective owners, and are also reproduced here in the spirit of publicity. Whilst we have made every effort to acknowledge specific credits whenever possible, we apologize for any omissions, and will undertake every effort to make any appropriate changes in future editions of this book if necessary.

No part of this book may be reproduced in any form or by any means, electronic, mechanical, digital, photocopying or recording, except for the inclusion in a review, without permission in writing from the publisher.

Published in the USA by:
BearManor Media
P O Box 71426
Albany, Georgia 31708
www.bearmanormedia.com

ISBN 1-59393-121-2

Printed in the United States of America.

Book & cover design by Darlene & Dan Swanson of Van-garde Imagery, Inc.
Cover photographs by Marilyn Mitchell

Contents:

	Foreword	9
Chapter One	Star Day in Palm Springs	11
Chapter Two	Radburn ... I Show Up	14
Chapter Three	Ridgewood ... The Short Fat Kid with the Tuba	22
Chapter Four	Syracuse ... Higher Education?	28
Chapter Five	New York Part I ... Continuing Education	32
Chapter Six	Life's Ambition Realized ... Next?	39
Chapter Seven	The Worst Day of My Life! Suicide?	45
Chapter Eight	You're in the Army Now ... A Microcosm	50
Chapter Nine	New York Part II ... The Big Time Beckons	57
Chapter Ten	'Til Death (or some other reason) Do Us Part	62
Chapter Eleven	Make It Here ... Make It Anywhere	66
Chapter Twelve	We Love You, Eddie	79
Chapter Thirteen	Broadway, Rock 'n' Roll, Bar Mitzvahs ... and a Letter from Lenny	83

Chapter Fourteen	Welcome to LA . . . Sort of	105
Chapter Fifteen	New Career . . . Bye-Bye-Bassist	112
Chapter Sixteen	Mary Tyler Moore, Bob Hope and Beyond	121
Chapter Seventeen	Love & Marriage . . . This Time for Real	128
Chapter Eighteen	Movin' On Up	137
Chapter Nineteen	What's So Great About Norman Lear? I'll Tell You . . .	145
Chapter Twenty	Good Times . . . Keepin' Our Heads Above Water	164
Chapter Twenty-One	Me, Myself & I Versus Hollywood	176
Chapter Twenty-Two	Logan's Run . . . Hollywood Imitates a Movie	194
Chapter Twenty-Three	Big Changes . . . Ready or Not	205
Chapter Twenty-Four	The Little Town with a Heart	219
	Special Thanks	255
	Credits	256
	Heading Off into the Future	259
	Index	260

Foreword

I want you to know about two guys from Hackensack, New Jersey . . . because they're both me. I'm not a schizophrenic and I don't hear voices from God telling me to kill people, but I'm definitely two different guys with two different mind sets and abilities within the same cranium, and each guy has had a very rewarding and satisfactory career. Their careers have kept me totally anonymous and yet have allowed me to work at the heart of the entertainment world for (and sometimes against) some of the biggest names in show business. I've encountered the poor and the unknown as well as the rich and famous, including Benny Goodman, Gene Krupa, Andre Previn, Norman Lear, Buddy Rich, Frank Sinatra, Arnold Schwarzenegger, Carroll O'Conner, Jean Stapleton, Bob Hope, Charlton Heston, Lenny Bruce, Jack Benny, Eddie Fisher, Don Adams, Robin Williams and tons of others.

People are amazed when they learn about the two careers the guys in my head have had, although it doesn't seem the least bit amazing to me. I've been nagged for as long as I can remember to write a book about my lives and now I've finally caved, and here it is. The viewpoints are the sole property of the two guys from Jersey and, by the way, I'm never both of them at once. They have to take turns. When I'm playing jazz music, it's the greatest and when I'm writing, it's the greatest and if you ask me which guy I prefer, I don't have an answer.

Speaking as Gordon Mitchell, the writer, everything I've reported is exactly the way I remember it and I'd like to think it's pretty close to reality. I hope you find this book about the two guys from Jersey a feel-good, amusing account of my life because, let's face it, I'm a feel-good, amusing kind of guy. Whitey, the musician, adds "So am I"

Gordon 'Whitey' Mitchell
Palm Desert, California
September 1, 2007

Chapter One
Star Day in Palm Springs

February 20, 2006 was a perfect day in downtown Palm Springs ... bright sunshine, palm trees along the quaint historic main drag with a backdrop of the highest mountains in Southern California. For me, it was a day I'd anticipated and dreaded for several months. There was to be a dedication and unveiling of my star on Palm Springs' famous Walk of Stars, presented to me and sponsored by the Walk of Stars Board of Directors. To get one of these you have to be approved by the Board, plunk down $10,000 for the cost, and then wait a month or two for the whole process to be publicized and set into motion. But the big deal is to get that Board approval. You don't have to be a celebrity who doesn't wear undies while posing for crotch shots (although that helps) and then get bizarre tattoos, run over a few people with your car, marry bearded, riveted unkempt dudes and flee to rehab. But you should be outstanding in your field, whether you're an entertainer, radio/TV personality, actor, musician, writer, director, producer, philanthropist, humanitarian, Medal of Honor winner, or a former President of the United States. And you're supposed to be a person who has contributed to the charm and world prominence of Palm Springs. I qualified in the writer and musician categories, but I still have some work to do in the charm and world prominence of Palm Springs area.

But I'm a walking, talking, one-man band, Chamber of Commerce and huge fan of Palm Springs and the surrounding desert communities.

Especially since moving here twelve years ago after Hollywood declared me senile and drooling at age sixty-two. Of course, Hollywood will declare you senile and drooling long before you're forty if you're a television writer, but I'm getting ahead of myself.

Several hundred people had gathered around a roped off area on the sidewalk in front of the Plaza Theatre on Palm Canyon Drive. The theatre, home of the Fabulous Palm Springs Follies, has been a part of local history since its opening as a movie house in the early 1930s. Decades ago, it was home to the big-time network radio shows of entertainers like Jack Benny, Bob Hope and Bing Crosby.

My wife, Marilyn, the love of my life (who knows more about me than I've ever bothered to learn), produced this star dedication as well as a DVD of my life and two careers for the after-star party, and I'm still enjoying it more than a year later. She knew that I'd always admired from afar, but had never had a ride in a Hummer. And since her good friend, Carole, owned one…SHAZAM! I arrived at curbside in a brand-new, gorgeous (if a little effeminate) dark-red Hummer, chauffeured by Carole, after hanging out in a parking lot a couple of blocks away so as to get there at the exact moment Marilyn wanted.

The Hummer pulled up, I emerged from the rear passenger door and stepped out into the sunshine and into the crowd amid music, loud cheering and screaming from friends old and new, family members, dignitaries, fellow Board members, and a few people who were there by mistake, but liked what they were seeing. At that moment I had an inkling of what it must be like to be Brad Pitt. Except this happens to him if he just goes out for a Krispy Kreme.

Although nobody tries for this, some star dedications can get a little stuffy, overly long and tedious. Not Marilyn's production! Longtime friend and emcee of the event was writer/producer Allan Blye, who got things off to a perfect start when he said, "We're here today to honor a great man" and then mentioned the name of a talented but egocentric, pompous, and far-from-beloved local celebrity. When the laughter from that opening joke subsided (and it took a long while) the program blossomed into a warm, funny, sentimental affair that seemed to whiz by too quickly. Other speakers included a golfing buddy and kindred spirit, Patrick Evans, a CBS-TV2 local television personality, who was properly disrespectful, followed by Bob Hope's head writer and producer for thirty years, Mort Lachman, then eighty-eight years old, who made the trip from Los Angeles for the occasion. Or maybe for the party that followed. Mort just gets funnier as he gets older. Then came jazz pianist/singer Frankie Randall, a Frank Sinatra protégé, who got laughs just reading from my bio/resume and bitching the whole time that his name was nowhere to be found. I was hoping I'd be as funny as the other guys, and I'm told that I was. But what I was really hoping for was just not to throw up on my star.

But it wasn't all just laughs. My beautiful daughters, Lesley, Karen, and Michele, all said wonderful, heartfelt things that brought tears to my eyes, as did a surprise letter Marilyn arranged from my hero, Norman Lear, extravagantly praising my writing career. There were also letters from the President of the New York Musicians' Union Local 802, the President of the Writers Guild of America, and a Proclamation from Palm Springs' Mayor Ron Oden declaring February 20, 2006 as Gordon "Whitey" Mitchell Day! Quite a momentous day for a guy whose midwife-assisted birth in a log cabin on the Illinois plains seventy-some years earlier led to all of this.

Okay, I lied about the log cabin and the midwife and Illinois. It was a hospital in Hackensack, New Jersey, and the medical help was probably all licensed. But it started me thinking: maybe people would find it interesting that it's possible to be at the heart of show business in two successful careers and at the same time be virtually unknown. And maybe if this could somehow be captured in a book and written in a semi-amusing way, with lots of references to personal contacts with showbiz greats and not-so-greats, such a book might be welcome. But, where to start? Here's a thought: At the beginning.

Chapter Two
Radburn . . . I Show Up

As my parents took me home to Radburn, New Jersey from nearby Hackensack Hospital where I was born, the big story of the day was the bungled kidnapping and death of the Lindbergh baby. They were relieved that, since they weren't celebrities, they'd never have to go through such an ordeal. And since they weren't celebrities there was nothing in the paper about the birth of Gordon Mitchell, but they did notice an item about the birth of the newest Kennedy son, Edward M. Kennedy. It was news because of the prominence of the Kennedys and because Rose Kennedy was forty-two at the time, medically risky back in those days. Mom passed on the information to me that Ted Kennedy was born (in the same time zone) at the exact moment as I was, and I can't think of a more devastating argument against astrology.

I joined a family already in progress. Dad, William D. Mitchell, was an engineer who worked for AT&T in their New York City headquarters at 195 Broadway. Ma Bell took him right out of college and he had a steady, if not terribly enjoyable, job for the next forty-five years until mandatory retirement. He'd wanted to be in Research & Development because he was a creative guy interested in almost everything, but was stuck in Operations & Engineering, a less imaginative department. But he didn't really speak up or fight for what he wanted, was frustrated by his career in the company and paid a high price medically. It was a great lesson he inadvertently passed on to his sons: do what you're good at and what you have the most fun doing in life and speak up when the time comes. Dad may have been an engineer in O&E during the day, but in his off hours and in his soul, he was a singer, choir director, accomplished musician, and church organist with a self-designed classic pipe organ in our home.

Mom, Grace J. Mitchell, was a poet, a dreamer and a former newspaperwoman with a lot of spunk and the ability to speak up loud and clear. She more than made up for Dad and not many people put anything over the Mitchells and lived to brag about it. She had a lifelong love of words and every month we all had to endure the Readers' Digest Improve Your Vocabulary Test, or whatever it was called. It was usually humiliating and certainly improved my vocabulary as well as my hatred for tests. Although the gift of music was evident throughout her family, it had apparently bypassed Mom and she was, in fact, tone deaf. She was only able to recognize with any degree of certainty two melodies: "The Star Spangled Banner" and "Danny Boy," and she would promptly stand up with her hand over her heart if she thought she heard either one.

Me on the left, age two, with Mom and Keith.

My brother, Keith "Red" Mitchell, was four and a half years old when I arrived. He was a skinny kid with orange hair, freckles, prominent nose and teeth, and was extremely self-conscious about his looks. Later on in life the freckles took care of themselves and he did something about the nose and teeth, but as a kid he seemed to avoid mirrors. I was considered blond and good looking, and it didn't help brotherly love much that Mom's best friend kept referring to me as Little Lord Jesus.

I adored and admired Keith and spent at least half of my life trying to get closer to him, which never seemed to happen outside of family vacations. He enjoyed his own peer group and I was mostly outside looking in. His first conscious act was to pee all over the attending physician, and that set the tone for his lack of appreciation of authority throughout his life. His relationship with our parents was largely adversarial, something that puzzled me at the time and ever since. And so he became the difficult, rebellious kid and I became the nice kid who never gave them trouble. Well, hardly ever. Years later, when we managed to spend five minutes together alone, Keith (by this time he was Red and I was Whitey) said that he grew up thinking, a la the Smothers Brothers, that Mom and Dad always liked me best. I grew up thinking, sure, that's because I was nice to them. They may have liked me better, but they revered him. There was just something worshipful in their facial expressions at the mere mention of his name. I forgot to mention: he was a certified musical genius. More about Red later.

Radburn sounds like one of those names made up by real estate people, and I guess it was. If you'd just created America's first Planned Urban Development, you probably wouldn't want to call it Secaucus, for example. Every house had a garage, every neighborhood had a community swimming pool, and every kid could walk to a nearby school without crossing a street. That was unprecedented and was a big deal in the late 1920s. It's hard for me to imagine that my parents were ever hip and modern, but they were, and they bought a house in Radburn. By the time I came along the Great Depression was in full swing and the projected city population of 50,000 became frozen at around 5,000, and Radburn was eventually swallowed up by the large neighboring town of Fairlawn.

It was great growing up in Radburn. In the morning all the dads went into New York City on the train, and all the moms got their kids off to school and spent the rest of the day, presumably, much in the manner of *The Stepford Wives*. If there were bizarre extramarital activities or drug and alcohol orgies going on, it never trickled down to my innocent ears. Or to the ears of my even more innocent mom. I'm told that the wonderful vocal group The Modernaires, of Glenn Miller fame, lived in Radburn, although I didn't meet them until I played their act at the Paramount Theater with Tex Benecke & the Glenn Miller Orchestra about three decades later.

My long-term memory goes back to age two, but don't feel jealous. My short-term memory only goes back about twenty minutes. When I was three, my Grandfather Mitchell died in our house, where he'd spent his last months. It was carefully explained to me that although we wouldn't be seeing Grandpa around anymore, he was okay because his soul was on its way to heaven. I'm not sure if the concept of soul reached my three-year-old brain, because later that day I was outside in the yard with my playmates and noticed thin wisps of smoke curling up from our chimney and told the other kids with a degree of certainty that that was Grandpa's soul.

Saturday was Metropolitan Opera day at the Mitchells' home and Dad could sing along in French, Italian, or German while he heard his favorite arias on the radio as he (and sometimes we) worked on the pipe organ, which was a tunnel with no light at the end. Dad, never a rich guy, bought pipes made by European craftsmen from the previous century from torn down mansions on Fifth Avenue for pennies a foot, as well as other organ parts, and somehow got them to New Jersey and eventually into his home pipe organ. Some of the pipes were as much as thirty-two feet long, and so the household males were constantly digging under and around the house enlarging the chambers and making room for them. The digging and the opera are so connected in my memory that even today, if I hear opera music, my nose begins to twitch and I swear that I smell the distinct musty odor of deep earth tunnel excavation.

Mom and Dad were socially liberal, fiscally conservative, without any detectable prejudices, and were deeply religious people. But they didn't

Dad plays his first home pipe organ in Radburn.

beat you over the head with it. They simply lived the message that was too radical for the Mid-East 2,000 years ago and is still too radical today: love thy neighbor. They would have to be listed as Republican and Christian, though they would be appalled at what passes for either one today.

Keith started piano lessons at age five and in spite of kicking and screaming and resenting it, was quite accomplished as far back as I can remember. When it was my turn for lessons, I had a few until the teacher died and no replacement was ever named. So I played by ear, learned a couple of simple boogie-woogie pieces and left it at that. I thought music was no big deal and that everyone came from a house like ours where everybody was gifted and could play. I remember saving up for a clarinet that a neighbor had for sale for thirty dollars, a lot of money back then. Dad had established the concept of matching funds, so all I had to come up with was fifteen dollars. But they were hard-earned paper route dollars, since I was then way past the days of getting money just by being cute. So even if I didn't really play the piano, I could rattle off some boogie-woogie or toot the clarinet well enough for school shows and the clarinet came in handy when it came time to join the Fairlawn Junior High School Band.

Keith was in constant demand to play at parties and dances and even in his awkward teenage years was considered a catch. I recall one incident when perhaps the least attractive girl in his entire school invited him to be her date at some function and he was amazed/repelled and (in a pathetic attempt not to hurt her feelings) stammered a little and then begged, "Give me twenty-four hours to think it over." He called the next day to say "No."

Family get-togethers with the aunts, uncles, cousins, and favorite near-relatives were a lot of fun, with charades, music, jokes, and the highlight of the evening, The Finding Game. Sometimes called Camouflage (but not by us), the game consisted of searching for a long list of hidden ordinary household objects (pre-prepared by the evening's hosts), which were placed in plain sight but cleverly situated so as to blend in with the background. Whoever found the most objects was declared the winner, and children were playing on a level field in this game. We all used to dread the evenings Uncle Cuyler was the host because he hid things so well it bordered on sadistic behavior. After he gleefully hid a pencil lead from a mechanical pencil in a crack on a piece of antique furniture which could only be seen looking straight down on it with the help of a flashlight and a magnifying glass, there was mass Mitchell outrage and The Finding Game was put on hiatus, then quietly disappeared from the party agenda. But there was still plenty of fun, such as when Uncle Roy taught the children who were interested (the boys, of course) how to burp. I think the responsible adults present were relieved that that was the only disgusting bodily function wisdom coming from Roy that evening. I remember only two jokes from this era. One was my dad's and one was mine. Dad's joke: A guy named Franklin Delano Stink went to court to change his name. To Joe Stink. My joke happened when I was about four, and everyone around the table was naming his or her favorite vegetable. When it was my turn, I announced that my favorite vegetable was MEAT. Not a big joke, but a deliberate joke, and I got some bonus money just for being cute.

So it was a great childhood. But, of course, not everything was wonderful. Mom, who had a lifelong thyroid deficiency (which wasn't discovered until very late in her life), got into the hands of some up-to-the-minute Doctor Feelgood, who put her on amphetamines, which led to her spending a lot of time either crying in a dark room or being whacked out and eventually having psychotic problems, which led to a stay in a mental institution. Keith and I were farmed out to two different friends' homes and endured some cruel taunts from our peers while the little men in the white coats tried to figure out what was wrong with Mom. Lo and behold, as soon as her medication was stopped, so did the weird behavior. She was soon declared normal and allowed to come home. Dad's problem was duodenal ulcers, probably psychosomatic in origin (holding everything in, not speaking up), that required radical surgery when he was forty. He had two-thirds of his stomach removed, survived his less than fifty-fifty chance of making it, and went on to live twenty-five years past his retirement age. My turn. I almost lost my right eye in a stupid chemistry set accident, but luckily it was on a Saturday. Dad was home, gave me first aid and rushed me to the doctor ... who was also home and lived next door.

The Mitchell Family goes to war!

Other things must have gone wrong, including my mechanically ungifted mother's habit of wracking up the family car several times at one particular intersection, which came to be known as Gracie's Corner. But no big downers, except for World War II, and when that came along, the Mitchells pitched in. Dad was our neighborhood's Air Raid Warden, Mom was a Red Cross Volunteer, Keith was a Boy Scout, and I was a Cub Scout. We had the cellar set up like a bomb shelter, grew a Victory Garden, stored food and water, obeyed the rationing laws and, like most Americans of that era, joined in the war effort. It was an amazing time in this country's history never before (or since) seen.

With the house constantly full of words and music, hilarious family get-togethers (pay no attention to the two jokes I mentioned), vacations on Fire Island or long motor trips, or visits to a farm in New England, it was a great way for a kid to grow up, and I survived childhood with the firm conviction that life should be filled with music and humor and is supposed to be fun. I still believe that.

Chapter Three
Ridgewood ... The Short Fat Kid with the Tuba

All the contributions we Mitchells made for the war effort, such as saving cooking grease (used for explosives), recycling tin cans, growing our own veggies, blacking out the headlights on the family car, buying war bonds, etc., really paid off big time in the spring of 1945 and caused Germany to collapse and Hitler to die. By this time I was, in effect, an only child. Keith had left home for Cornell University the year before, then decided that the piano was more fun than the slide rule, and now was in the army.

Like *The Jeffersons* series three decades later, my parents decided it was time to be "Movin' on Up," and bought an old large house in Ridgewood, New Jersey, a few miles farther away from New York. Both parents had gone to high school there, had lots of relatives and friends around, and there were plenty of churches, all in need of choirmasters/organists. But the real reason, friends, was that there was no place else to dig for organ chambers at the Radburn house and endless room for excavation to accommodate Dad's ever expanding pipe organ in Ridgewood. And now that I was a teenager, the shovel was handed to me, further cementing my hostile relationship to opera music.

Among the first troops to occupy post-war Germany was big brother Red Mitchell. His dangerous army gig was to play piano and arrange music for a band and show unit which had lots of talented people in it, including

Anthony Benedetto, who later on became Tony Bennett. I don't know how it happened, but Red had suddenly discovered the joys of playing string bass, and soon wanted to do nothing else. With his lifelong connection to music he brought lots of musical knowledge, as well as ability and passion to the study of the instrument and soon became (and I'm not the only one who thinks so) the best jazz bass player ever. Of course this created giant footsteps for me to attempt to follow, but more about that and my career-long shadow dwelling later.

During his months in Germany, Red found a little old violinmaker who made him a bass from scratch with pre-war wood. The price? Fifteen cartons of cigarettes! With the black market running the way it was in those days, everyone figured Red was swindled. Those fifteen cartons, traded off judiciously, got the violinmaker an entire new machine shop. Some swindle! Red had paid seventy-five cents per carton for them at the PX. Soon after that the army, in its wisdom, changed the rules about buying cigarettes in the Post Exchange and when it came time to ship the bass home, the shipping crate cost much more than the bass.

When Red left for Cornell, at Utica, New York, then the Army, it still hadn't dawned on me that we'd never again be living under the same roof. I was always pretty good at writing funny letters and I sent him quite a few. But nothing came back from Utica except occasional cardboard suitcases full of dirty laundry which were addressed to Mom. Sometimes I'm a slow learner. It took years for me to figure out that I was never ever going to get a letter from Red, and neither was anyone else. It just wasn't his thing. But I was determined that, once and for all, he should send a letter to his kid brother. My final effort banked heavily on humor and involved a questionnaire and a stamped, self-addressed envelope. The questionnaire was a few frivolous and (I thought) funny questions, with multiple-choice answers. A no-brainer. All he had to do was check off a few answers, put it in the envelope and drop it in the mail. It never came back and for years I never tried again. Then I had some monetary crisis, which I described as a hopeless financial morass, and sent him a letter begging him to loan me "all available loot" so that I could survive the next month. About a month later I received a postcard from him, which started "Enclosed is all available loot" and ended with some insightful thoughts on hopeless financial morasses.

I didn't like high school. I was a year younger than my classmates, short, fighting weight and pimples, and getting anywhere with girls wasn't in the cards. Ridgewood girls were trained well by their mothers. They all wore invisible psychic chastity belts covering all-important parts of their bodies which were not penetrable or removable until their wedding night, give or take a day or two. Bear in mind this was cold northern New Jersey and years before the Sexual Revolution changed America's bedroom habits forever. By the way, the Sexual Revolution is due to hit Ridgewood any day now.

But the biggest drag about high school was sitting in class after class waiting for the dumbest kid in the room to grasp the lesson of the day before we could move on. I have a low threshold of redundancy and used those wasted moments (while things were re-explained to the slow ones) to do my homework from that or some other class. I took pride in the fact that I never brought books home and never did homework at home. But never took pride in the fact that I ended up graduating about 315th out of a class of 350. I had some nice, patient teachers, including a wonderful English teacher who liked my sense of humor, encouraged my primitive efforts and saw to it that I wrote some humor pieces for the school magazine, which was fun and which foreshadowed half of my life. God bless you, Mr. Darby!

Then came a life-changing event. Suddenly the marching band was without a tuba player. I guess the kid who played it either quit or moved out of town. So somebody had to switch to tuba (actually, sousaphone, that tuba that wraps around your body) and fast. The bandmaster cast his beady eyes on me, Mr. Quickstudy, and even though I was perhaps the shortest, plumpest kid in the band who would look the most ridiculous climbing into a sousaphone, I agreed to play his damned white tuba . . . on condition that I could be taught to play string bass in the orchestra and learn both instruments at the same time. I'd always loved the sound of the bass and realized how musically important the bottom note of any chord can be. So I took some quick instruction on both instruments, and from then on I marched with the band at football games and played with the orchestra at their occasional concerts. I soon began to play weddings, parties, and dances with bands . . . for money. Sixty years later I'm still playing with bands for money. God bless you, Mr. Cook!

It's December of 1946, a few days before New Year's Eve, when Red shows up unexpectedly. He's out of the army now, and starting to have a career as a bass player. Seems he has a New Year's Eve gig in Paterson, New Jersey, he took a long time ago and would like to get out of, because a much better paying one had come along. He was delighted to learn that I'd started to play bass a few weeks earlier, and gave me his job. He didn't even have to make a phone call to find a sub. Poor Dad would have to drive both of us to both gigs, but he seemed to like the idea.

My first New Year's gig and professional debut was with The Irving Cohen Trio at The Halfway House in Paterson. I was not yet fifteen and may have been playing bass for only a few weeks, but trust me, I was the best player in the band. Irving's wife, who seemed to have far too many thumbs, played piano, if you can call it that, and Irving screeched away on a violin. There's no sound much worse than the sound of one violin in the wrong hands, and believe me, the hands of Irving Cohen were the wrong hands. I would have hidden my face in my hands, but they were both busy with the bass, trying to keep time and trying to play notes that might tie the whole thing together. But no. We were God-awful. After the first set, the owner came up to Irving and said, "I know I promised you guys eighteen dollars apiece for playing three hours, but if I paid you six dollars would you go home right now?" Irving quickly agreed, and I got the feeling that he must have received lots of offers like that in the past.

But thanks to the disappearing sousaphone player, I became a professional musician in high school and started my lifelong love affair with the bass. The painful teenage years were almost fun, once I was a bass player and I began to play with better and better musicians. I played a lot of my own high school proms with The Duke Edwards Orchestra for ten dollars a night, but unfortunately had to wear the jacket of the previous bass player, who was a lot older and bigger than me. And there were lots of Italian/Polish weddings (I still don't know why that was such a popular inter-cultural event) and I joined a Gilbert & Sullivan Operetta company orchestra, quietly dropping out of Mr. Cook's school bands (that's gratitude for you).

When I became a high school senior at sixteen, I still wasn't "Whitey" yet. I was either "Mitch" or "Satchel-Ass," depending on how well you knew me, and I wasn't a licensed driver yet. So, if you wanted to hire me for your band, you had to provide round-trip transportation from Ridgewood. I took it as a good sign that so many bandleaders were willing to do that. In the "Don't Try This at Home, Kids" category, I heard from my brother about a den of iniquity in Paterson called The Club Ely. They had B-Girls, ladies who would hustle drinks from would-be Johns that probably had no alcohol in them. If the bartender accidentally put booze in their drink, they would discretely spit it back. Also, there were actual hookers who operated

Playing bass at my own prom at age 15 with the Duke Edwards Band.

independently. The club had several nightly shows featuring a comic/emcee, a singer, lots of strippers, and, best of all, the band: Slim and his Trio. These were three beautiful black guys from New York who had played with everybody and were a little tired of the road and settled down at Club Ely for some steady (if low-profile) employment. They had piano, drums, and tenor sax . . . no bass. And when I first sat in with them after some dumb wedding gig, they welcomed even an inexperienced ofay bassist like me. By the way, "ofay" is a very old term used by some African Americans as a noun meaning "white person." It's simply Pig Latin for the word "foe," but Slim and his guys never called me that and Club Ely became my home away from home.

I'd "borrow" the family car after my parents were asleep, cruise over to Paterson and Club Ely and indulge in depraved sights and sounds that any sixteen-year-old red-blooded boy would appreciate and play music all night with terrific, experienced musicians. As a bonus, since we were playing by ear, it was always possible to sneak a peek at the strippers. I was working for free, but I was earning my BA in Jazz. I should have paid Slim, Herb and Gene for the privilege. They're the guys who started calling me "Whitey," by the way. It was to differentiate me from my brother whom they nicknamed "Red," when he'd worked with them a year or two earlier.

Chapter Four
Syracuse . . . Higher Education?

In 1949 I ran away from home at age seventeen. Well, I really didn't run away, I was driven . . . by Dad. He took me to Syracuse, New York, where I was to start at the university's excellent School of Communication. I didn't know at the time that I was leaving the nest for good.

We took a slight detour and drove to Rochester, New York, where Dad had a couple of long lost cousins he wanted to look up. We found them at a country club where one of them was the Head Pro. Two decades earlier the cousins were great golfers and used to win tournaments, breaking par and shooting scores in the sixties, which nobody did in those days, and were known as The Mitchell Boys. I'd love to meet them now, but was too dumb to be interested back then. The Golf Bug wasn't due to bite for another seventeen years and my head was full of be-bop.

A couple of years earlier when I was fifteen, Keith smuggled me into The Three Deuces, a jazz joint on New York's fabulous 52nd Street, to hear Charlie (Yardbird) Parker and Dizzy Gillespie and their combo. My brother had discovered them and wanted me to have the chance to appreciate them too. So we found an old suit of Dad's and a hat that could be pulled down over my eyes and into the city and into the Deuces we went. It was a mind-boggling experience listening to those geniuses of jazz and wonderful of Red to set the whole thing up. As I'm writing this, I'm remembering that he did a lot of other wonderful things for me . . . when he was around. I guess my chief complaint about my brother was his absenteeism. I always wanted to hang out more with him and he was forever not around. Including now. He never had a clue about how to live a healthy lifestyle and died much too young. Maybe it's time I got over it.

I was on my way to college mostly because my parents wanted me to have a college education, so I went along with it and applied to Syracuse, never dreaming I'd be accepted. My grades, except for English, were mediocre to horrible. But, like the Nearsighted Mr. Magoo, who bumbled through many of UPI's best cartoons stepping over and around potential disaster without ever seeing it or realizing it was there, I came along four years after the end of World War II, when the colleges and universities had all expanded in anticipation of a flood of veterans taking advantage of their G.I. Bill of Rights and seeking higher education. Apparently the flood warning was exaggerated, or the postwar bump had already subsided by the time I was available, and there were too many empty desks and not enough qualified students. So they went with non-college material like me. I can think of no other explanation.

Syracuse University was a disappointment. The School of Communications was brand new and state-of-the-art, and the campus was just what you'd imagine, but I was shocked when I found out that I couldn't live anywhere near there. Oh no! Lowly freshmen were shuttled off to Skytop, an abandoned World War II hilltop anti-aircraft battery emplacement and barracks on the outskirts of town. Skytop must have been successful for the military, because if I remember my history correctly, not one Nazi bomber ever got through to attack Syracuse. Skytop was nicely reconditioned and furnished, and a pleasant place to live if you didn't mind too much being completely cut off from civilization as we know it.

The lifestyle at Skytop would be considered pretty tame by today's standards. Sure, we drank beer and smoked, and bragged about non-existent sexual conquests. And we even managed to study from time to time. But there were no hard drugs and no macho drinking contests that, too often, go on until the first fatality. It never occurred to me at the time, but as I think back now, it seems very strange that, out of hundreds of freshmen that I either knew or saw daily, there wasn't one gay student. Not one. Which is statistically impossible. I guess, back then, people were going into the closet, not coming out. And, oh, yes ... another rule: freshmen were not allowed to own cars. Transportation to and from campus was accomplished by a few condemned surplus navy buses freshly painted in school colors. Coming down that hill was a lot like Mr. Toad's Wild Ride and more excitement than I cared to handle. I don't remember taking the shuttle more than once.

And so the No-Car Rule was destined to be broken and I broke it almost immediately, trading my ancient typewriter for an even more ancient car. It had no lights, no gas gauge, and was a putrid beige color with a bright orange "S" thirty inches tall painted on both sides. It came with a stick, which you could use to measure the gas, oil and water levels and pry open the hood, if necessary. But it got me to the campus and to the city, and I was suddenly much more popular in Skytop than I'd ever been in high school as the short fat kid with the tuba.

I slowly dropped out of the uninteresting classes, which meant pretty much all of them except for the rare and fun Radio/TV/Communications classes, which were my reason for being at Syracuse in the first place. I got the chance to combine my musical ability with writing for the first time (and maybe the only time) with a student half-hour TV show I created called *Recipe for Rhythm*, and it was about as dumb as it sounds. Fortunately, no videotape or recording of the series exists. As for the other classes, I remember them as being crowded, endless and just more high school reflux.

But I was busy with other stuff, like playing four nights a week at The Casablanca, a wonderful Italian restaurant and cocktail bar hangout that featured live jazz and was a magnet for local musicians. Since my car had no headlights, hanging out until dawn became the rule rather than the exception. So once again, as Mr. Magoo, I'd blindly stumbled into a good situation, and I was warmly welcomed. The Casablanca was owned by the Genovese family (yes, that Genovese family) and was the first of my many wonderful relationships with "connected" club owners. (I was told to say that.)

Syracuse was a fun year and a year of development. I discovered a couple of local radio guys who allowed me to hang out with them and participate in their shows, and attempt to make them funnier. I joined the local chapter of The American Federation of Musicians, and became a better bass player. Toward the end of the second semester, my parents got a letter alerting them to the fact that I'd missed three consecutive geology classes. In truth, I never found the geology class. It was in a temporary building that didn't seem to be on any map. By that time of the year I'd pretty much made up my mind that I wanted to do other things than live at Skytop and attend the few Radio/TV classes I was allowed to join. So I got rid of the car without taking too big a loss, packed up the new bass I'd bought, and said bye-bye to Syracuse. Then there was a huge sigh of relief . . . from Syracuse.

Chapter Five
New York Part I . . . Continuing Education

My parents were shocked when I left Syracuse and announced that I was going to be a professional musician. But then, they were easily shocked. They thought I was just copycatting Red, who by now was making a big name for himself with the Woody Herman band. At this point they'd never heard me play with a band, and I assured them I loved music, was good at it, and would be successful. And I was moving to New York as soon as I'd saved enough start-up money. My life's ambition at that time was to play with a big name band. For young people who may be reading this book by accident, that would be like appearing on *American Idol*, surviving the snide remarks, winning, and then being invited to appear on *Dancing with the Stars*. That's how big a deal it was in those days. But Mom and Dad were convinced I was just overcome with sibling envy, and would soon come to my senses. So when I packed my things and headed for the bus station, they came up with a deal: I could stay at home rent-free and save as much money as I wanted for the move to New York as long as I agreed to be tested. Tested?

I think I mentioned that, hard as it was for me to imagine, my parents were once young and hip. They'd heard about The Johnson O'Connor Research Foundation whose Human Engineering Laboratory gave exhaustive aptitude tests for career guidance. Over time, they'd tested thousands of successful (and unsuccessful) people in a variety of occupations, and had determined that all human beings possess seventeen specific aptitudes to some degree or other and that people who did well in various fields tended to have very similar-looking aptitude charts. They never claimed to be infallible, but they did maintain that, at the very least, they could steer people in the right direction, career-wise. I'd forgotten that when Red made a similar announcement a few years before, they sent him to Johnson O'Connor and he was tested. But, knowing what I knew about music and musicians of the day, and being aware that my ability was somewhere between Benny Goodman and The Irving Cohen Trio, and knowing that I was going to go into the music business anyway, I agreed.

So into the big city I went for two days of aptitude tests. The tests were cleverly designed to find out your various natural abilities and there's no way you could possibly study for them, even if you knew what they were. You either had finger dexterity or you didn't. (I didn't.) I vaguely remember putting together wiggly blocks, odd cubes, paper folding, word association, structural visualization and other tests. But the biggies were the three aptitudes involving music, and there's no way to fake these or cram for them: tonal memory, pitch discrimination, and rhythm memory. I was definitely better at those than wiggly blocks, and when the results were tabulated and the aptitude chart completed, the counselor said, "Well, I see we have a musician on our hands," as well as some mention of leadership qualities and something called foresight. And if that were true, I wouldn't have loaded up on Enron.

Mom and Dad believed my report of what the counselor said, especially after they looked at the completed aptitude chart. They dragged out Red's chart and compared the two, which were amazingly similar, with the three music aptitudes in the A+ category for both of us. But I didn't blame them then and I don't blame them now for making me jump through that hoop. They were just following the aptitude both of them had in abundance: Good Parenting aptitude.

I don't remember much of my life in a tiny rented room at the Radio Center Hotel in mid-town Manhattan in 1950, except that it was an exciting time of discovery, including the fact that I could look across the street

Inventory of Aptitudes and Knowledge
Johnson O'Connor Research Foundation
Human Engineering Laboratory

Standard Tests	FORM	SCORE	PERCENTILE	LOW	AVE
Visual Perception					
Graphoria (clerical speed)	380 AB	0.3201	47		
Divergent Thinking					
Ideaphoria (flow of ideas)	161 DA	248	C		
Foresight	307 AF	74	95		
Convergent Thinking					
Inductive Reasoning	164 FG + EE	175	93		
Analytical Reasoning					
Numerical					
Number Series					
Number Facility					
Spatial					
Structural Visualization	4 + 246	190	66		
Wiggly Block	4556	1.60	56		
Paper Folding					
Cube	246 BA	2.73	78		
Auditory					
Tonal Memory	498 AB	85	A+		
Pitch Discrimination	364 GB	86	A		
Rhythm Memory	366 AC	55	95		
Memory					
Memory for Design	294 VA	84	52		
Silograms (word learning)					
Number Memory	165 BE	84	78		
Observation					
Motor					
Finger Dexterity: RIGHT	16 DA	64	8		
LEFT	16 DA	66	10		
Tweezer Dexterity:					

	FORM	SCORE		
Personality 1ST MEASUREMENT	35 FP	14	78	OBJECTIVE
Word Association	35 FP + AH	32	65	OBJECTIVE
Red-Green Vision				

NAME GORDON BROWNELL MITCHELL DATE MAY 23 + 24, 1950 FOLD: 4-20

Maybe they were right.

and see the windows of the chorus girls' dressing rooms of the Winter Garden Theater, which on hot days were always open. Talk about a room with a view! I loved never knowing what was coming next, living from hand to mouth, going to jam sessions at all hours of the day and night, living on one or two bucks per day. On one-dollar days it was the Nedick's hot dog stand, period. In a short time I was an accepted member of the music community, and began getting low-paying jazz gigs in Jersey, Brooklyn, and in Nyack, New York, at Sonny's Paradise, where I got to play with great black musicians. Looking back, I don't know how I got there or how I got the gig, since I had no phone and no car, but it somehow worked out. In those days, way before the civil rights movement was even thought of, I was welcomed at black clubs like Sonny's Paradise, and learned a lot about how to play jazz music. And the name "Whitey" was never said in a denigrating way. In fact, I sometimes felt as if there were some kind of sign stuck on my back reading: "Okay to hang out with this ofay."

One of the musicians I met was a brilliant guitar player named Mundell Lowe, who was fast making a great reputation for himself and on his way to becoming a top studio musician, jazz player, recording artist, and composer/arranger for television and film. Mundell had heard me play somewhere and hired me for a weekend gig in Suffern, New York, to play for an off-Broadway tryout of a new musical called *The Wind Blows Free*, written by Stephen Sondheim and Alex North. Guitar and bass ... that was the entire orchestra. I remember thinking that the show was clever and would be too hip for Peoria, and might even be a little too artsy-fartsy for New York, and perhaps I was right. I don't think it ever got to Broadway. But Stephen Sondheim certainly did. But my clearest, most cherished memory of that weekend was that we had rooms at a nice hotel and that Mundell had arranged for two user-friendly star-struck ladies from Yonkers (let's face it: nymphomaniacs) to join us for the weekend. My kind of bandleader! That weekend raised the bar (among other things) for entertainment and more than made up for years and years of rigid frigid Ridgewood girls.

Back in The Apple I began to get busier and there were fewer and fewer one-dollar days at Nedick's. About the time I started to feel I really belonged in Manhattan, it was time to leave. A bass player I'd met wanted to get out of a long road trip he'd signed up for and recommended me as a replacement. It was with the Elinor Sherry Quartet, which I'd never heard of, and they had an extensive cross-country tour coming up which would take them, basically, everywhere. I was reluctant to leave Nedick's and New York, and it meant that I'd have to sing harmony parts and learn a lot of pop tunes I didn't know, but the idea of a check every week was certainly a temptation and, who knows, we might even play Yonkers. So I jumped aboard.

It was a great introduction to life on the road, which can be a lot of fun when you're young and single and stupid and not carrying a lot of baggage. But I noticed how the older guys in our band and others we ran into felt. To the traveling musicians with families back home, the idea of living like a permanent gypsy gets old real quick and booze and drugs sometimes become the inadequate replacement for a normal family life. I never forgot that lesson, and about eight years later, when I'd become a family man with a house in the 'burbs and a couple of young kids, I had no trouble at all turning down offers from Louis Armstrong (fifty consecutive weeks on the road each year), Duke Ellington (similar commitment) and Woody Herman (forever on the road and not a living wage).

But back to Elinor Sherry. It was a pleasant gig, not musically inspiring, but educational, especially in terms of where we went: down South and out West. I'd heard of segregation, but seeing it firsthand was shocking to me. Up North if you had anti-minority feelings it wasn't cool to brag about it, and so there was less overt discrimination, although I'm sure it was there.

I was unprepared for the beauty of the West, particularly the desert, and on many occasions we'd drive all night to get to the next gig and experience daybreak in the desert. It made me think about a career as a poet, but, fortunately, when the sun finally came up and it became 120 degrees in the shade that idea melted away. We played a lot of less-than-four-star places and a few military bases and, as the youngest kid on the band, I had a lot to learn and began to learn it. I always valued older musicians (and later on, older writers) and tried to absorb whatever social or musical wisdom they might pass along. When the tour was over, I was glad for the experience and happy to reconnect with the New York jazz world.

There were more gigs in New Jersey and Sonny's Paradise in Nyack and a ton of jam sessions and sit-ins, one of which led to an actual well-paying gig: the bass player with Shep Fields asked me to sub for him at a show and dinner/dance at one of the larger hotels in Brooklyn. He also made noises like he was expecting an offer from Tommy Dorsey and wanted to leave the band. Shep Fields & His Rippling Rhythm was a big name in those days. It was a commercial orchestra (musicians referred to bands like that as "Mickey Mouse") in the Lawrence Welk vein, but this was before Lawrence became a household word. This was late in 1950 and back then, the Welk band was a "territory band." That is ... nine guys who lived in a bus, never saw daylight, never checked in anywhere, never had a day off, and traveled incessantly through the Midwest for terrible money. Shep Fields, whose style Lawrence would soon be copying, would be a giant step up for a guy like me, a couple of months away from his nineteenth birthday. So I jumped at the chance to play with that band, knowing that it was probably an audition.

Shep and the guys in the band couldn't have been nicer to me, and I enjoyed playing with a big band (I still do), reading their arrangements, and playing the show. The entertainment consisted of a few variety acts, a big-time opera singer named Jan Peerce and an unknown young comic named Lenny Bruce. Lenny, at this point in his career, hadn't found his niche yet and was trying to be just another Catskill Mountains Borscht Belt Comic of the "Take my wife ... please!" variety. So I don't remember his act. Just his music folders.

All performers have to have their own music, and it can easily be one of their biggest expenses. Special music, special arrangements, original music, all of which has to be orchestrated for different-sized groups from combo to big band and hand copied by professional copyists. It can cost a bundle. So the acts usually don't spend a lot on music folders to pass around to the various musicians (drums, trumpet, alto sax, whatever) containing the music that each instrument is supposed to contribute to the overall sound of the orchestra. The folders are usually cardboard, with the name of the performer neatly printed, as well as the particular instrument whose music is inside.

Lenny's folder was different.

First of all, comics in those days didn't have folders or even special music. The band would play them on by faking (playing by ear) some showbiz tune like "Fine and Dandy," and then when the funnyman reached center stage, maybe a chord. Then the band would either sit there and pretend to laugh (musicians have heard all of the jokes) or leave the stage. So a few eyebrows were raised when Lenny solemnly passed out his music folders, which were luxuriously bound in sculptured leather and embossed with 24-karat gold lettering. Inside, on the right-hand side was a single sheet of music paper on which was written in crayon, "Play me on with 'Fine and Dandy.'" And on the left-hand side was a provocative picture of a totally naked lady!

Chapter Six
Life's Ambition Realized . . . Next?

Apparently, the big gig in Brooklyn went well, because I was offered the job with Shep Fields. The guy whose place I took auditioned for Tommy Dorsey, but wasn't hired. I saw him around New York for many years trying to make a name for himself until drugs ended his career. Meanwhile, I'm not yet nineteen and I've already fulfilled my life's ambition. What to do now? Find another life's ambition, you idiot! It took two years and being drafted into the U.S. Army before I was able to come up with another life's ambition . . . to get out of the army.

But in the meantime I really enjoyed playing with a name band. I was making eighty-five bucks per week and couldn't spend it all. It doesn't get any better than that. Except it did. After a tryout period of a month or two, Shep raised me to full salary: $105 a week. Shrimp cocktail and steak every night!

A few words about Shep Fields. He was a pleasant old man, maybe forty when I came along, who'd been a household name since he was twenty-one. He'd lost a bundle on a musically far-out all-saxophone band, took his beating and was now back in safer territory with his very commercial Rippling Rhythm Orchestra. He loved music and musicians and treated us great. I became the driver of his car and got to know him pretty well. I admired the way he handled his successes and his failures, and I learned my first words of Yiddish from Shep Fields (nee Sol Feldman), which came in handy years later in Hollywood during my second career as a writer in meetings where, if you didn't speak Yiddish, you had to at least nod and understand. I had a nice, if brief, reunion with Shep toward the end of his life when he was working as an agent with ICM with his younger brother Freddie Fields. I really liked the guy.

When we played the Statler in New York, a very prestigious hotel, formerly The Pennsylvania, one of Glenn Miller's stomping grounds ("Pennsylvania 6-5000"), I knew it would be a good chance for my parents to actually hear me play, perhaps for the first time. They thought it was a good idea too, and said they'd show up. On stage, with the lights shining directly on the bandstand, it was tough to make eye contact with anyone in the darkened candlelit room, but I knew Mom and Dad were there when, during a momentary break in the music, I clearly heard my dad's shocked voice questioning the menu: "$1.35 for a chicken sandwich!" After the Statler experience (I mean seeing me play, not their brush with inflation), my parents never again questioned my career choice.

My nearly two years with Shep and the guys were full of firsts, for me at least. Such as my first recording sessions, which were in a sound studio in the Merchandise Mart in Chicago. They were called "transcriptions" and were destined not to become records sold in a music store, but listening music played over speakers as atmosphere in public places, sort of like Musak, which was a new thing then. The standards weren't very high and there were no retakes. We just started with arrangement number one, Shep's theme song, and went through the whole library, song by song. Three hours later it was over and we packed up and left. It was really music-by-the-pound elevator music, repetitious and non-challenging, like so-called smooth jazz, which may be smooth, but is definitely not jazz. Kenny G., I'm told, is an excellent jazz player, but chooses to make his living with smooth jazz. That is, playing the simple melody over and over again with few variables, backed by a studio orchestra playing a sweet arrangement. If you're not careful, you can easily go into insulin shock.

Another first for me was doing live network television at NBC when Shep Fields & His Rippling Rhythm was featured on *The Kate Smith Hour*.

Life's Ambition Realized... Next?   41

The Shep Fields Orchestra on the *Kate Smith Show* on NBC, 1951.

Kate Smith, an immensely popular singer of sentimental American songs since the 1930s, almost worshipped by people of my parents' generation, had her own talk/music show and would frequently invite name bands to perform. The memorable event of the show that I recall was not the music. It was Kate, waiting in the wings during the warm-up, as her announcer/sidekick was introducing her to the studio audience, who accidentally dropped her handkerchief. Kate Smith in 1951 was a middle-aged lady with a lifelong weight problem, which seemed to get worse year after year. By this time she had reached perhaps three hundred pounds, was rigidly corseted from head to toe, couldn't really move, and couldn't possibly even see the handkerchief, let alone stoop to pick it up. The scramble to retrieve the handkerchief quickly as if nothing had happened was intense among nearby members of her staff, with the winner and sycophant-in-chief being her announcer/sidekick Ted Collins.

It was great running into other bands, which were either following us or preceding us at a given venue or working a different location in the same large city. Following Jimmy Dorsey's band into a large ballroom somewhere between the Hudson River and the Mississippi and putting our stuff in the band room, or at least, attempting to put our stuff in the band room, was impossible. There were so many empty beer and liquor bottles piled around the room there was not one plane surface available anywhere to put something down on. If we were in rural areas and had a day off, Shep would treat us to a barbecue at the nearest middle-American small town if they had a park. (I told you he was a nice guy.) In the big cities we pursued our own agendas.

We worked some really prestigious venues, like the Muehlebach Hotel in Kansas City, the Peabody in Memphis and the Edgewater Beach in Chicago, as well as some weird venues like the Sam Houston Auditorium, where we appeared with the extremely funny, but totally insane legendary entertainer Lord Buckley, whose bizarre humor had us in stitches. Lord Buckley quickly latched onto the band, did some drugs with (and hit on) some members of the band. But we were outa there before any harm (or arrests) occurred, and all I know is that I'd never heard far-out, original material like that of His Lordship before. Or since.

We also played in beautiful Biloxi Beach, Mississippi, which was recovering from a hurricane, as well as Congressional crime hearings in Washington, which were focusing on gambling in America, and which had temporarily (everyone thought) shut down illegal gambling casinos in the South. I was too young and too naive to realize that gambling casinos were large supporters of name bands, and that the writing was already on the wall: Big

Bands Are Doomed. At the hearings it was revealed that Frank Costello, a big-time mafia godfather of the day, lived in a large penthouse atop the Majestic, a luxury apartment complex on Central Park West, and the building where Shep lived. As soon as we got back to New York for a hiatus, Shep joined his fellow renters, shared their umbrage, and signed a petition to the building management asking for the removal of Mr. Costello from the premises. The petition was denied . . . mainly because Mr. Costello owned the management company as well as the building! And as a symbol of his displeasure, Frank quickly raised all the rents about 20%. Shep wasn't laughing, but the story was pretty funny twenty-five years later when it became the basis for an episode of *The Jeffersons*.

Being on the road for seemingly endless one-nighters wasn't all work. Some guys brought their golf clubs along if they noticed any gaps in the itinerary, and got to play wherever there was a nearby golf course. I wondered at the time, "What can they possibly see in that?" Ask me now. But in my spare moments I began to take flying lessons, usually a half-hour at a time, and always in small airports. I accumulated twelve hours of flying time and was about ready to solo, when fate stepped in and changed everything.

In Newburgh, New York, during a month-long Shep Fields hiatus, I was working a nightclub I can't remember anything about, and the reason I can't remember the nightclub was because Donya, the exotic dancer, was on the bill. She was a Russian-American, she was blonde, blue-eyed, petite, gorgeous, and she became my first love. Donya was very graceful on the stage, and once she was on, you couldn't take your eyes off of her. And who would want to? She had several different routines which came under the heading of "exotic dancing" during which she'd remove clothing here and there, all carefully timed to very elegant pieces of music like "Slaughter on Tenth Avenue," "Rhapsody in Blue," and "Manhattan Towers." I gave up trying to define exotic dancing and would usually answer inquiries by saying, "It's kind of like stripping, but with much better music."

I don't know why she noticed me when she could have had the pick of the band as well as most of the male population of Newburgh to choose from. But we began to hang out, and I learned her story and current plight: she was trying to get rid of an aggressive would-be boyfriend who wouldn't leave her alone, and she thought he might be dangerous. He was Mickey Spillane, the author of best-selling shoot-'em-up detective novels. He suspected that something was going on between Donya and one of the guys in the band, but before the great detective novelist could figure out it was the bass player (the least likely suspect), the gig was over and I left town. Later, I hooked up with the unharmed Donya when we were both back in New York, and I more or less moved into her nice fourth-floor walk-up apartment on Eighth Avenue and 47th Street. The reason I'm very clear that it was on the fourth floor . . . have you ever tried to carry a bass fiddle up four flights? You'd tend to remember that. And the reason I said "more or less moved in" is that I had no worldly goods to speak of. Mostly just my clothes and my bass. No stereo, no books, no television and, of course, no furniture. So, moving in was easy. So was moving out, as I discovered to my horror many months later.

I was twenty and Donya said she was twenty-three, but somewhere along the way I sneaked a peek at her driver's license, which said she was thirty-one. Whatever. I was young and brainless and, for the first time in my life, in love. It became tougher for me to leave the 47th Street love nest, and I began to identify with the married guys. But luckily, Donya had a good act and a good agent and she began getting herself booked in the cities where our band was playing, if it was a location for a week or more. I had given my parents the Disney version of my relationship with Donya, and they (or at least Mom) could never quite figure out the amazing "coincidence" that Donya and I would be in the same city at the same time and constantly run into each other. "How lucky!" Mom would write.

We pretended to be married mainly for the sake of an actually married couple on the band. But I don't think anyone really bought that. We went so far as to buy cheap wedding rings, which we'd flash while checking in someplace. That should give you an idea of how long ago that was. To nail the time period a little more precisely, a war hero named Eisenhower was running for President.

Chapter Seven
The Worst Day of My Life! Suicide?

The worst day of my life really began two days earlier and seventeen hundred miles away in Dallas, Texas. The Shep Fields road tour ended there on a Saturday night and we were all looking forward to a two-week break. But first we had to get back to New York. Part of my gig was to be the driver of Shep's big black Chrysler New Yorker, a great road car. I cheerfully looked forward to driving straight through so I could get back to my wonderful Donya and her love nest apartment at Eighth Avenue and 47th Street. The concept of a thirty-something-hour drive was okay with Shep, because he was an old man of forty-two and he knew he'd be asleep in the back seat most of the way. I knew I could drive for that length of time because I'd already done it, and without taking "bennies," which the other designated drivers on the band popped like M&Ms. Of course, when they got where they were going, their hearts would be racing and their eyes would be stuck on "open" for hours to come. So I would use the old slap-your-face, or maybe just stick-your-head-out-the-window techniques to stay awake.

There were no Interstates in 1952 and only a piece of the Pennsylvania Turnpike was open, so it was a grueling trip through every city along the way, but the reward at the end of the journey was to get to my first love and see if we could break any records, sexually speaking, during the next two weeks. Somehow, magically, the long drive was over, and there I was at Eighth Avenue and 47th Street, exhausted, but eager. Shep had been delivered to his luxury apartment on Central Park West, and I was ready for my reward for thirty-plus hours of sleep deprivation.

To this day I don't recall what the fight was about, but I'd guess it was one of those George and Weezy fights based on a misunderstanding that propelled so many episodes of *The Jeffersons* twenty-five years later. But there I was on the sidewalk after a huge row with lovely Donya that somehow got out of hand and turned into the end of our relationship. I was groggy, depressed, angry, and standing there with my bass, my suitcase, my Shep Fields uniform in a dry cleaners' see-through bag, and my few pathetic belongings. What to do? I ruled out the idea of falling asleep on the spot, even though it was tempting, because New York being New York (even way back then), I'd wake up with everything missing, especially the bass. Then it dawned on me that I really had no choice. I had to crash at my parents' house in Ridgewood until I could get some sleep and think of a plan. Big macho Whitey, on my own since age eighteen, having to sleep at Mom and Dad's place! I was much too tired to argue with myself and the Port of Authority Bus Terminal was only a few blocks away.

I don't know how I made it those few blocks with all that stuff, but I also don't know how ancient Egyptians were able to construct the great pyramids without using giant cranes, or how even more ancient people were able to schlep those stones over great distances and create Stonehenge. My little trip is certainly less of a mystery, and I probably moved and guarded my possessions in bunches, a few feet at a time. Anyway, I somehow got all that stuff and myself on a bus to Ridgewood, and an hour or two later I arrived at my parents' house in Ridgewood and headed for the living room sofa and some much needed oblivion.

But Mom, always glad to see me, was actually expecting me, since it was the day I was scheduled to have a chest X-ray. A chest X-ray? I never knew that and if things had only gone a little differently at Donya's pad, I would have been there at that moment, and well on the way to a new world's record.

My brother also happened to be at our parents' home that day for one of his rare visits. He was on his way to the West Coast with the Red Norvo Trio, and had a few days off. He'd contracted tuberculosis a few years earlier doing one-nighters with Woody Herman and his Third Herd and had spent an entire year recuperating at Bergen Pines, a nearby sanitarium. Since then, every family member was supposed to be regularly X-rayed, but I was never around for that. When Red volunteered to drive me to Bergen Pines for my X-ray, I figured I could stay awake for another hour and it would be a good chance for us to catch up, so I said yes.

If you showed me a picture of Bergen Pines along with a dozen other similar places, I couldn't pick it out of the line-up. And I don't remember anything about the X-ray, which was apparently "unremarkable" (doctor talk for "okay"). But I wasn't okay. I was tired, depressed, and in dire need of sleep. All I wanted to do was get outa there! But Red, Mr. Congeniality in every situation, except perhaps at home with his family, decided to have fun visiting with some of his buddies with whom he'd shared his incarceration. So we had to go through a lot of doors to meet them all. To the library, to the music room, to the cafeteria, to the therapy rooms, all the places for which he was suddenly nostalgic, before we could get to the door I wanted: the door marked EXIT.

We almost got there. In fact, I had my hand on the knob when a faint, raspy voice called out "Hey, Red!" We went backwards a few feet to the last room in the corridor and there on the bed, weighing in at about sixty pounds, was a yellowish-looking nearly dead person, smoking a cigarette in a long, filtered holder, who stopped coughing long enough to greet his long-lost pal. I'm not at all certain Red even remembered him, but he feigned enthusiasm for this reunion and the man, who I'll call Mr. Cadaver, started unbuttoning his hospital gown, while wheezing and sputtering "Yeah . . . they took out my lung yesterday." As he continued to unbutton, I saw the top of what appeared to be a very long crimson scar with Frankensteinian stitches trailing down and ending who-knows-where. It's the last thing I remember about Mr. Cadaver. Red said later he thought I was bending down to tie my shoelaces (even though I was wearing loafers). What I was doing was leaving Bergen Pines my way . . . by passing out.

 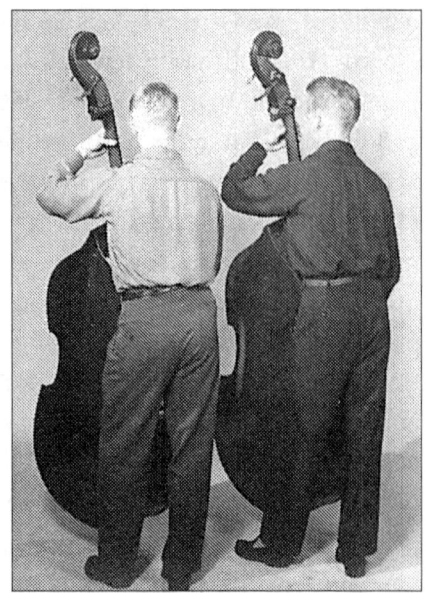

Red and me. Double double-basses.

I woke up on the operating table with bright lights in my face and the nauseating smell of ether, being bombarded with questions I couldn't answer, such as "Do you know who you are? Do you know where you are? Do you know what day it is?" and other toughies like that. In hitting the floor face first I'd lost one front tooth, damaged the other beyond repair, and cut myself from nose to chin. I was stitched up with unsubtle stitches much like Mr. Cadaver, black and blue and bandaged here and there.

When Red finally got me back to our parents' home, Mom took a look at me and screamed. I wanted to scream too, but was only able to manage a very weak, "Now can I sleep?" and headed for the sofa. I was only seconds away from dreamland when Mom told me I'd gotten a letter in the morning mail. "Here? I haven't lived here for two years! Who'd write me here?" It was a letter from the government, which began "Greetings from the President of The United States . . ."

There was something going on I'd heard about called the Korean War and that was my draft notice. Just before I blacked out, thoughts of suicide crept into my brain. Hara-kiri? Too messy. Jump from a building? I'm afraid of heights. Gun to the head? Nobody I know owns one. Pills? But by then I was out.

Fast forward to the pre-induction physical a couple of months later. Shep Fields had contacted congressmen, senators, federal judges, and all the biggies he knew, but none of them agreed with him that playing Rippling Rhythm was more important to our country than stopping communist aggression in Asia. So there I was, reporting for my army physical and hoping I would flunk. I knew some musicians who went to great lengths pretending to be gay or on drugs and who managed to avoid serving, but who'd want to live with that the rest of their lives? Besides, I was pretty sure my flat feet would keep me out. Nope. I passed every test they could throw at me. The final stop was just an interview with a guy behind a desk (who, with greater wisdom years later, I decided must have been a psychiatrist) asking me questions about life, girls, drugs, politics, and so forth (just two guys hanging out) as he made notes without really looking at me. When he finally looked up and noticed my not-quite-healed scars and apparent extensive dental work he asked, "How'd you get that?" I told him of my ill-fated trip to Bergen Pines, he made a quick note, shook my hand, and said "You're in! Report to Fort Dix on 10 September."

There's a real O. Henry ending to this story. You'll find it in the next chapter.

Chapter Eight
You're in the Army Now...
A Microcosm

Fort Dix was the processing center for draftees from the Greater New York area and I remember seeing Willie Mays there as well as Wynton Kelly, the brilliant jazz piano player. We were given a million shots, asked to "cough!" far too often, issued our basic clothes, boots, poncho, helmet, stuff like that, all of which had to fit into a large duffel bag. The poncho was at the bottom, since it was issued first, and the other items crammed in on top. After signing for our gear, we were ordered by the sergeant in charge to "fall out and fall in," which we guessed meant to line up in some kind of ragtag order. Then he ordered us to get out the ponchos, because it looked like some weather was headed our way. I looked up, saw nothing threatening, and like everybody else, just milled around for a couple of beats figuring I'd take a chance on the weather. When we lined up again there were maybe three ponchos in sight, out of a potential two hundred. The sergeant noticed this and chided us in his own colorful way, "I hope it rains like a cow pissin' on a flat rock!" And, sure enough, it did.

Then I was shipped off to Fort Lee, Virginia, home of the Quartermaster Replacement Training Center. It was an old post with World War I-era barracks, and a ton of World War II-era cans of C-Rations and K-Rations that it was our destiny to consume every Thursday. Those who could afford to ate off post, and Thursday became bonanza day for all the area restaurants.

Before basic training began I was interviewed by the 392nd Army

Band, but there were no vacancies. Not for a bass player, anyway . . . especially a professional. Seems the band's commanding officer had been reassigned and no replacement designated, so the band was run by the First Sergeant, whose roommate and buddy (read into this whatever you want) was a half-assed bass player who was playing string bass at all the parties and dances and other paying gigs himself. No need for another bass player! Case closed. So basic training suddenly became more important. If my life was going to be endangered in FECOM (Far East Command . . . Korea), and it was, I wanted to know everything I could about being a soldier.

Back then I wasn't exactly Rambo, but I wasn't a fairy fart-blossom either, as our drill sergeant suggested. I was just a young musician who'd never been in a fight and who'd never fired a weapon more lethal than my boyhood Red Ryder BB gun. Turning me into a killing machine in only eight weeks of basic infantry training would be a challenge for the army, not to mention me.

My twenty-year-old brain was apparently brain-washable, because I took to the soldiering. I threw the grenades, I bayoneted the dummies, I became a marksman on the M-1 Garand rifle, which I learned never to call a "gun." It was a "piece," and forgetting that was worth twenty-five instant push-ups. I learned how to take the weapon apart in the dark and then put it back together again in a few seconds, just like everybody else in H Company. It's amazing what you can endure if two hundred of your peers are going through the same experience at the same time. Like running for two miles with helmet, rifle, and full field pack. If we had an outdoor lecture on some phase of warfare training, it would be for fifty-five minutes with a five-minute break. Unlike my mother and brother, who both had lifelong sleeping problems, I escaped that curse and was able to go to sleep on command, and I would plop to the cold, hard ground and snooze for those five minutes. I felt sorry for the G.I.s who never seemed to be able to sleep when they were supposed to, and had a tendency to doze off in the middle of a lecture on, say, proper mortar trajectory. The instructor would invariably notice them nodding off and would then quietly write on the blackboard "Disregard the following verbal command!" step back and call out "Attention!" Only the sleeping soldiers would snap to attention, followed by laughter and humiliation and push-ups.

In eight short weeks I became a killing machine ready to pull the trigger and kill gooks (sorry, but that was the word back then) to save my own life or that of my buddies. So I was ready, the day after basic, to take whatever the army had in store for me. We were all lined up with gear fully packed and looking pretty sharp, when our drill sergeant, in his usual subtle and charming way, announced: "All you motherfuckers is goin' to FECOM! Right face! Forward march!" As we obeyed and marched off he had an afterthought: "Not so fast, Mitchell! Report to Headquarters Company." I was stunned. The rest of the guys went on without me, and many of them never came home from Korea. All I had to do was walk half a mile away to Headquarters Company.

I was still a little disoriented, no pun intended, when I reported to my next assignment and learned what was in store for me: the job of writing the official correspondence for the Commanding Officer. I would write letters, commendations, AWOL notices, letters of sympathy to the families of deceased soldiers, letters advising parents to turn in their AWOL sons or daughters, or anything else the Commanding Officer had in mind. There was a style book and previous correspondence to look at, so it wasn't much of a problem learning to get the feel of army communication. I'd be living in a brand-new brick barracks with state-of-the-art furnishings, a nice comfortable dorm, a day room with billiards, TV and other comforts. And I'd be working normal business hours, Monday through Friday, which meant the possibility of playing music on weekends.

I took to the job and the comfortable surroundings, and especially the weekends off. It wasn't long before I bought a junk car and started playing music in Richmond, about thirty-five miles away, as well as in local joints nearer the base. I met hundreds of attractive, willing, sexy southern girls of all ages in Richmond, and I'd like to thank them all and apologize to all of them at the same time for my shallow, male chauvinist pig days which lasted, well, for the whole two years I spent at Fort Lee.

I finally landed a steady weekend gig in Richmond at a supper club and was able to put together a decent combo which included a very good saxophone player named Wendell Decker who was a Second Lieutenant,

You're in the Army Now . . . A Microcosm

PFC Mitchell at work. Pay no attention to those cigarette butts.

courtesy of college ROTC, and shouldn't have been hanging around with lowly enlisted men like PFC Mitchell. Wendy was by no means a soldier, let alone an officer, and the term for guys like that was 90-day wonder, referring to their total military training in college. One weekend Wendy was missing in action at the supper club, and I later learned the reason why. He was taking his turn as Officer of the Guard at Fort Lee, misread his orders, and sent home some sentries three hours early, and the post was basically unguarded for three hours. He was off to FECOM faster than you could say "Oops!" I never heard from him and worried that he might have become cannon fodder. Years later, whenever I was on the road with bands, I would try to look him up when I got near his hometown, but no luck. Nothing in the phone book and no help from the local Musicians' Union. Several years ago we hooked up, thanks to the internet, and we exchanged pictures, updates and CDs. He's alive and well and still playing great in Lansing, Michigan, his hometown, which I had incorrectly remembered as Detroit, a frequent destination in the jazz days.

I felt very lucky to be in Headquarters Company, and to be considered a writer of sorts by the army, which allowed me to live in comfort out of harm's way, go out at night and play music and break female hearts. At my day gig in the office I had access to certain service records which I needed in connection with writing letters about missing, wounded, or dead soldiers, and among the service records available to me was the file on PFC Gordon Mitchell, which was right next to that of the deceased Mitchell I was looking up. Curious, I checked out my own records, and was shocked to notice, under the category: PHYSICAL CLASSIFICATION-----1-C, UNFIT FOR COMBAT, and nearby was the space: EXPLANATION------FAINTING SPELLS. Fainting spells, plural, based on my sleep-deprived visit to Bergen Pines. It turned out that the worst day of my life might very well have saved my life!

A pianist friend of mine at Headquarters Company wanted me to be part of a combo he was putting together for a possible weekend in New York via an appearance on an ABC television show called *Arlene Francis' Talent Patrol*, a variety show involving service personnel who were performers. When he mentioned the date of the show, I realized that Red would be playing in New York that month, so I agreed to be part of the group, even though I didn't think his group was top-notch. Apparently the producers of *Talent Patrol* disagreed with me, and we were booked on the show.

It was a nice weekend, but weird. One of my southern belles showed up on her own to cheer us on at the TV studio and to cheer me on for the rest of the weekend, which was great. The weird part was that, despite playing phone tag with Red between rehearsals and the show, I never really got in touch, and couldn't quite figure out where he was working or where he was staying. The messages that he left were very vague and incomplete, and a classic case of an unplanned failure to communicate. Except that it wasn't. It was a deliberate plan not to communicate on his part, which I didn't learn about until twenty years later. But you only have to wait until we get to Chapter Nineteen for the explanation.

And just when things were going great at Fort Lee, they got even better. I got a call from the 392nd Army Band: Please, oh please ... join our wonderful band. We have a warrant officer in charge of the band now, and that sergeant and his greedy half-assed bass player buddy have shipped out. We need a real bass player to play with the band at the Officer's Club every Saturday, the NCO Club Thursdays, the WAAC Headquarters on Fridays, plus lots of parties, dances, and cocktail hours. It sounded like a good way to spend my second year of service, and though I didn't know it at the time, the army, in its wisdom had divided up my term of service exactly as life did ... half writer, half musician. A perfect microcosm. So I agreed ... with certain conditions, because I could tell they were desperate: no guard duty, no KP, no parades, no funerals, and absolutely no sousaphone. They didn't like it, but they went along with it, and so I left the comfort of the brand-new brick building and moved into the World War I-era barracks that housed the 392nd Army Band. I no longer needed to travel to Richmond for my weekend gig. All the work was either on the post or in nearby Hopewell or Petersburg, just minutes away. An additional bevy of warm and friendly beauties was now available, and I'd like to extend my apologies to them also.

It was a good band and we did concerts and TV shows, as well as the paying gigs. The Officers' Club on Saturday night was my favorite. It was a big band, not a combo, and we'd play "Army Blue," a sentimental drinking song from West Point which would bring tears of nostalgia to the eyes of older Regular Army officers. All of America embraced the song a few years later when someone named Elvis recorded it with new lyrics as "Love Me Tender." It was interesting pretty much every Saturday night watching drunken generals dancing with and groping their subordinates' wives and those ladies handled the situation gracefully, considering the sword of Damocles known as FECOM was over their husbands' heads and only hanging by a thread at all times.

In the previous year during my Headquarters Company days, I'd learned to speak Pentagonese, or at least understand it enough to read the army circulars, which were official notices that came down regularly from the powers that be and were posted on the company bulletin board. A real winner showed up in the spring of 1954 that caught my eye. The war in Korea was winding down and the army started offering early discharges of up to ninety days to those enlisted people who had the opportunity to accept a summer job of a cyclic nature or attend an accredited summer school. It was called a Discharge at the Convenience of the Army, and I didn't have to read it twice.

I wangled a forty-eight-hour pass to New York, enrolled in the Manhattan School of Music's summer session, returned to the base and applied for an early discharge. All of this was unknown to my buddies, most of whom were drafted before me and were constantly bragging that they'd be outa there way ahead of me.

My request was granted, and I was discharged exactly ninety days early. I left my amazed (and slightly pissed off) buddies behind as well as all my uniforms neatly hung, my boots polished, my bunk area spotless, and my footlocker open and ready for inspection. (I had forgotten to say "no inspections.") The Officers' Club band was once again without a bass player.

Up until then it was the smartest move I'd ever made in my short life.

Chapter Nine
New York Part II...
The Big Time Beckons

I appreciated the army's rebate of three months of my life, and I used them well. During that summer I joined Local 802 of the Musicians' Union, worked in Birdland with genius-level clarinetist Tony Scott and his group, recorded an LP with upcoming (and unrelated) pianist/composer Bobby Scott, and met hundreds of musicians at the place they all hung out...Charlie's Tavern, a saloon on Seventh Avenue and the center of the jazz world. In Charlie's you could find food, drink, comradery and, best of all, employment. Charlie had a heart of gold and a soft spot for musicians, particularly those who paid their tabs, but he had no love for junkies. If Charlie found out you were using, he'd 86 you, and there was no ACLU around to take up your cause. One day as I was heading there, I noticed a well-known jazz trumpet player standing just outside the door. Between his tears he explained that Charlie had just busted him for drug use and thrown him out for good. "What am I gonna do?" he cried. "I'm banned from bars and barred from bands!"

My summer session with the Manhattan School of Music lasted one day. There was nothing in the army circular about cyclic employment or summer sessions that said either one had to be completed. It was a long, boring bus ride from my cheap pad in Greenwich Village uptown to the school, and I had something important to do the second day and the day after that and just never came back. Things were happening in the Apple so fast for me, why spend endless hours studying harmony, theory and composition, when I was learning from the masters every time I played Birdland?

I don't know which was more important to me, Charlie's or Birdland, because both places were great to make contacts and further your career. Probably the nod should go to Charlie's because it was open longer and anybody who was anybody could be found there at any time of day or night. Case in point: Kai Winding, the great Stan Kenton trombone player, had come to New York to put together a twenty-piece jazz orchestra for Pete Rugolo, the marvelous orchestrator and creator of the so-called "Kenton Sound." There would be recordings for Capitol Records, some concerts, a long run in Birdland, and an eight-week tour in the fall with a musical extravaganza called *The Biggest Show of '54*. Kai hired me and I helped him put together a swinging rhythm section. That summer jazz was at the highest peak it ever reached in terms of public acceptance, and I'd gotten to New York just in time to catch the wave.

I found myself playing right next to some of the biggest names in jazz in Pete Rugolo's orchestra, and we played Birdland and did an album for Capitol Records as promised. When rehearsals for the fall tour started, I was thrilled to be on the same stage with some of my idols, like singers Billy Eckstine and Peggy Lee, and comic/impersonator George Kirby, all outstanding performers of the day. Then a strange thing happened shortly before the buses pulled up and we all got in and headed out. The producers added one more act to the show for insurance, they explained, possibly reacting to soft advance ticket sales. It was four guys singing street corner harmony that had no music, no uniforms, and, near as I could tell, no act. But they did have a record out there that was a big hit in certain cities. It was The Drifters, with whom I'd do many, many, record dates in the years to come, including some you may have heard of, depending on your age group: "Spanish Harlem," "Save the Last Dance," "Under the Boardwalk" and "On Broadway" come to mind.

The Biggest Show of '54 was hurt by the fact that there were a lot of similar shows out there that year all hustling for the same audience. Had

The Big Time Beckons 59

With Pete Rugolo's 20-piece band at Birdland, New York, 1954.

the producers just gone out with their ragtag rock group they might have been better off, because the times they were a-changin', and The Drifters became the de facto stars of the show. When I noticed that, a flashing red warning light should have gone off in my head, but it didn't. Besides, the show was hurt by other things than tepid audience response and changing cultural tastes. There was a major, devastating hurricane that closed in on the East Coast about the same time and in about the same places as our show was destined to go. The producers scrambled for alternate venues and alternate dates, but it became an impossible situation and it was very obvious that the show was in trouble. The producers finally pulled the plug after six weeks and, to their eternal credit, Billy Eckstine and Peggy Lee did not press for their salary guarantees so that the other acts and the band could be paid without litigation. Pete Rugolo realized that this wasn't exactly the right time in entertainment history to launch a twenty-piece orchestra, so he went quietly back to the West Coast to resume his career as a very successful film and television composer. The band went back to

New York and, with a little more money and a little more prestige, I picked up work as if I'd never been away.

Local 802 of the musicians' union had a rule in place that prohibited new members from accepting steady work until they'd lived in the jurisdiction for at least six months, I guess to protect their current members from an onslaught of immigrant musicians showing up from the sticks. I'd heard that you could bribe your way around the six-month rule if you knew the right people, but I never had the corporate mentality you'd need to have to carry that off, let alone the bribe money, which was around a thousand bucks (a lot of money in those days), so I just sweated it out finding work in Connecticut with Mundell Lowe, and other friends in New Jersey, like teenaged jazz pianist Frankie Randall who one day would be Frank Sinatra's friend and protégé, and occasional one-night-stands in Greenwich Village jazz clubs or in Birdland.

If you worked in Birdland you had to cope with the Maitre d'-Announcer-Greeter, a very tiny, very loud African-American dressed like a bellboy from Madagascar named Peewee Marquette, whose gig it was to bring on each band for each set while the theme song "Lullaby of Birdland" was being played. If he screamed your name on mike over the sound of whatever band was onstage, his piercing voice would definitely reach everybody in the room as well as some passersby on 53rd Street. I was told he had a new scam going and now expected to be tipped at the rate of two dollars per week per musician, and when I asked what for, the answer was: so he'll pronounce your name right. It sounded a little like blackmail to me (no pun intended) and I didn't go along with the alleged scam until I heard myself being introduced as "Whitey Marshall on bass" for the first two sets. Not really wanting that name to catch on, I convinced myself to get two dollars together and put them into his greedy little hands. It's amazing how his memory cleared up after that transaction, and soon he was screaming "On bass... Whitey Mitchell!" His malaprops were legendary and I can recall his Erroll Garner intro: "Birdland proudly present... the man for whom the piano were invented for... Erroll Garner!" And he outdid himself bringing on Dizzy Gillespie after one of his world tours:

"And here he is just back from Pakistan and Iran and Afghanistan and . . . and all them Scandinavian countries . . . Dizzy Gillespie!"

I began doing better and better work, even though there wasn't a single call from the Irving Cohen Trio and, by the end of the year and my six months prohibition, I was ready to settle down with a steady gig at some good hotel or club. So, of course, it was time to go, in the words of Willie Nelson, on the road again. This time with the great Charlie Ventura and his quartet. Charlie had Dave McKenna on piano and Sonny Igoe on drums, the same two guys my brother had worked with on Woody Herman's band years ago, and it was definitely a step up for a twenty-two-year-old kid. It was also a life changing career move, as I'll explain in:

Chapter Ten
'Til Death (or some other reason) Do Us Part

Charlie Ventura was one of my favorite bandleaders. He was not only a superb musician, he was inventive, flashy, and great at creating commercially acceptable jazz. Dave McKenna and Sonny Igoe were a pleasure to work with, and both are included today in my short list of favorite jazz players. It was a growth experience for me, not yet twenty-three when I joined that excellent group. At the time I didn't have a religious, sociological, or political thought anywhere in my brain, because there was no room. It was crammed full of be-bop.

Charlie took us to all the jazz venues I'd ever heard of, like the Rendezvous in Philadelphia, just down the street from a legitimate theatre where I saw a pre-Broadway matinee performance of *Tea and Sympathy*. I felt I was making enough money with Charlie to buy a car, and I was paid mileage to transport my bass and me from gig to gig. Don Palmer, Charlie's manager for over twenty years, was a smooth operator and the whole Charlie Ventura deal was well-run, without glitches, honest and above-board. When we got new uniforms they were more expensive than the stuff I was used to and, because I was a little stretched from buying the car, Don convinced Charlie that an expensive Italian suit was temporarily beyond my means, and that it would be okay if he deducted a little money each week from my check to pay off the threads.

Pittsburgh, Detroit, Chicago . . . there were jazz clubs everywhere and,

With Charlie Ventura and drummer Sonny Igoe, on tour in 1955. Dave McKenna on piano, not seen.

although there were fewer and fewer big bands, combos were the rage, and more suitable to jazz anyway. When we got to Chicago, we worked the Blue Note and stayed where all the bands had always stayed ... at the Croydon. I don't know if it's still there, but it was terrific in the mid-fifties. Dave McKenna and I were having a bite in the coffee shop when Stan Kenton appeared in the doorway, spotted us, came over and joined us. I'd never met Stan, who had the best band on the West Coast for years, and when Dave introduced us, Stan, always a lavish, extravagant and generous man when it came to words, said, "So this is the young genius I've been hearing about!" I'm sure he had heard of me either through the trades, the grapevine, or through his pal Pete Rugolo, and before I could finish savoring the moment, Dave quickly put an end to it by saying quite positively, "No, you must be thinking of his brother." I would have been permanently hurt by that if it weren't so amusing, both to Stan and me, and I quickly forgot about the whole incident. Sure.

So life was great, the band was great, the money was great, and the prospects were healthy for a long-running, musically satisfactory gig. Until we got to Minneapolis and played The Flame, where two guys in the band fell in love and, surprisingly, one of them was me. I met a sweet young girl whose friend was the publicist for the club and almost immediately strange alien thoughts of marriage and cottages with picket fences, which had never even come close to showing up before, started flooding into my otherwise empty brain. Those thoughts just wouldn't go away until eleven days later when we were married by a Justice of the Peace in Ames, Iowa, which was Minneapolis' favorite elopement destination, with both town drunks from the nearby park as our witnesses.

In my twenty-three years of life I had never been much interested in organized religion. I had never paid attention to the word "fundamentalism," and had never heard of the extreme evangelical sect Assemblies of God, two things very much in my bride's background. When I met her, she was in the nightclub we were playing, smoked occasionally, and was not averse to an alcoholic beverage or two. She was apparently in remission from what must have been a life of bible-thumping brainwashing.

But I learned quickly about fundamentalism as soon as I met her parents and extended family. I was immediately challenged by a cousin, who asked if I'd made my peace with Jesus. My response that I didn't know we were at war didn't go over well, and I was a marked man from that moment on. I learned later that my instant father-in-law became incommunicado, went into a deep depression, stayed in a darkened room, and was on suicide watch for about three days after he heard that his only child had married a jazz musician, an unbeliever from Sodom and Gomorrah or New York or one of those places. Which might explain why he worked ceaselessly, even after three children were born, for the breakup of the marriage, which took twelve years to accomplish. This same man might down a three-egg ham-and-cheese omelet, steak, cottage fries, French toast, juice, fruit, sweet rolls, coffee with sugar, and perhaps a parfait for dessert, then lumber off somewhere with his three-hundred-pound frame and lecture on "temperance." I'd like to belatedly thank my late Minneapolis ex-father-in-law for the privilege of knowing him, which came in very handy about eighteen years later, when I was writing the Archie Bunker character on some *All In*

The Family scripts. I'd also like to thank him for helping me reach a philosophical conclusion that's been with me ever since: Religion is mankind's oldest mental illness.

Charlie Ventura, the other guy who fell in love in Minneapolis, went nuts over the hatcheck girl/vocalist with the house band and when the gig at The Flame was over, after making sure he deducted the rest of whatever I still owed on the Italian suit, he simply disappeared with her and headed for an undisclosed location in an undisclosed continent. He abandoned his manager Don Palmer, his wife and children, all future engagements as well as the ones he'd already signed onto and, lastly, we his musicians. Don Palmer, hoping that Charlie might only be temporarily insane and would show up somewhere in the short term, pulled a rabbit out of a hat and saved the four one-week gigs we had that would take us back to New York, by booking four different big-name saxophone players to sub for Charlie while he was "ill."

I left my bride in Minneapolis because we hadn't quite had time to work out an exit strategy, and she needed time to explain to her family her own temporary insanity. So she gave notice where she worked, and I worked my way back to New York playing with some jazz giant guest stars along the way, including Coleman Hawkins, Ben Webster, and Bud Freeman. I never saw Charlie Ventura again.

Chapter Eleven
Make It Here . . .
Make It Anywhere

Now a semi-well-known jazz musician and a married man, I knew I had to take the bull by the tail and face the situation. If I didn't want to be on the road forever, I had to learn how to make a living in town, and I proceeded to do that. The bubble of good work that followed over the next few months was shattered by an offer from Gene Krupa, the father of modern jazz drumming, to join his group. Gene held out the promise of lots of steady, great gigs, not all of them out of town, culminating in an appearance with Jazz at the Philharmonic, the *crème de la crème* of jazz concerts, known throughout the world. It was to be the ultimate tour: forty-nine cities in forty-nine days. It would pay twice as much as I was earning and, with a baby now on the way, it seemed like the right thing to do.

Bobby Scott was the piano player, Eddie Shu played sax and trumpet and the three of us would travel in the same car and I was the driver. Gene would go from gig to gig by himself in some more elegant manner. Bobby, no longer content to be just a be-bop piano player, was thinking of being a singer and was affecting a "black" sound. He'd sit in the back seat and practice his new act, which was God-awful. We finally told him to shut up. But he got the last laugh a couple of years later when he recorded his big hit record, "Chain Gang," with that same fake voice, and it sold a million copies. He later wrote a Broadway musical called *A Taste of Honey* with his partner, lyricist Ric Marlowe, and made a ton of money. He passed

The Gene Krupa Quartet at the State Theatre in Hartford, Connecticut.
Eddie Shu, me and Gene. Bobby Scott on piano, not seen.

away at a relatively young age, and I never heard why. All I know is, when we were roommates, I found myself in the awkward position of having to play dumb about his nighttime whereabouts when his wife would call and Bobby was out hitting on ladies somewhere.

After a decent amount of time playing with Gene Krupa, I boldly

Putting on the Four Aces, also on the bill, their picture behind us.
The Gene Krupa Quartet backstage 1955. Bobby Scott, Me, Gene & Eddie Shu.

asked for some billing. After all, I was an up-and-coming bass player (at least according to *Down Beat*) and it wouldn't hurt Gene to give my career a little PR boost. Brother Red was all over the place in the trade magazines and I was becoming more of a shadow dweller week by week. Gene kept his word about giving me some billing and sure enough, when we got to Cleveland, our next town, we drove past the club where we were to appear and there was a nice big sign in the window: GENE KRUPA QUARTET–FEATURING RED MITCHELL.

Jazz at the Philharmonic was all it was promised to be, and more. Coast to coast with one of the greatest shows ever assembled. We had Dizzy Gillespie, Roy Eldridge, Lester Young, Flip Phillips, Illinois Jacquet, Oscar Peterson, Herb Ellis, Ray Brown, Buddy Rich, Ella Fitzgerald, and the Gene Krupa Quartet. We actually did the forty-nine cities in forty-nine days, traveling mostly by commercial airlines. I'd have to bluff my way onto each plane early with the elderly and the handicapped so I could find someplace safe in the cabin for the bass and strap it down. Airline companies weren't very sophisticated back then, and I was never charged for an extra ticket, which is what happens these days. We played to sold-out concerts wherever we went and because we almost always went by air, we had a decent amount of time in every city. On the planes I'd just relax or maybe play chess with Gene or Dizzy, and I'd never been on such a first-class tour. And I haven't been on one since.

One of our trips wasn't exactly wonderful. We were flying from Oklahoma City to Denver at night, after the gig, on an older two-engine chartered plane. I was awakened by a loud engine noise, and noticed that Ray Brown, the father of modern jazz bass playing, across the aisle from me, was gesturing at something outside his window. In view, highlighted by the pilot's spotlight, was the left engine, which had failed. The propeller wasn't turning and wasn't even feathered (rotated for least wind resistance) and was vibrating badly. The aircraft's remaining engine was straining mightily to maintain altitude, and wasn't making it. We were slowly heading downward. We heard PING! PING! PING! from the plane's intercom as the pilot summoned the flight attendant to his cabin. She raced up the aisle,

On tour with Ella Fitzgerald and Jazz at the Philharmonic, 1955.

deathly white, went in briefly, then emerged a different color: nauseous green. She started sputtering incoherent instructions involving removal of sharp objects from pockets, putting head between knees, returning seats to normal position, and so forth, but not in an understandable way. I learned later it was her first (and maybe her last) flight. Ray Brown and I both got busy strapping down our basses, which was a little like the old cliché of changing deck chairs on the *Titanic*.

Everyone on the plane was awake by now, and our one functioning engine seemed to be straining louder and louder as we continued to pitch downward through the blackness. The Captain turned out all but the reading lights and de-pressurized the cabin, and the water in the galley turned to steam. So we had an old-fashioned plane with just the reading lights on, heading earthward in a steam-filled cabin, and it looked like one of those airplane disaster movies from the '40s. At this point Flip Phillips started whistling the theme from *The High and the Mighty*, a recent airplane disaster movie, and Ella Fitzgerald, who was busy hugging her maid-assistant, cried out, "That's not funny . . . that's *not* funny, Flip!"

I really thought we were going to die and I fantasized the headline in the Ridgewood Herald-News: RED MITCHELL'S BROTHER DIES IN FIERY CRASH! I looked out into the darkness once again and thought I saw a string of white Christmas lights on the ground a couple of miles ahead and as we got nearer, I saw that it was not my imagination. The "Christmas Lights" looked more and more like a landing strip in the middle of nowhere, and we were definitely heading in that direction. Apparently, we'd reached a twenty-four-hour weather station in Garden City, Kansas, with a guy on duty who was able to light up the short landing strip. We only had one crack at hitting it and the pilot brought us down perfectly. I think I forgot to thank him. Is it too late?

Ray Brown, who'd been Oscar Peterson's bass player almost forever, was making noises like a guy who wanted to get off the road and settle down in town and do studio work, sort of like me, only his town was L.A. He realized that his bowing technique on the bass left something to be desired, and so he brought some exercise books on the road with him to try to improve his skills. These books, beginners' books actually, had some bass duets in them, and since my bowing technique was also something south of mediocre, I accepted when he asked if I wanted to play some duets. I agreed providing we could find someplace private where no one could hear us. Backstage one afternoon, when we thought we were alone, we set up two music stands, got out the basses and the bows, rosined up, and began scraping through Exercise #1. It sounded pathetic, but we kept going anyway. Out of nowhere came the wonderfully creative jazz genius, saxophonist Lester "Prez" Young, who was walking along minding his own business. He stopped long enough to listen for a few seconds, cocked his head, then ventured his opinion: "My, my, Schoolboy Row." Prez, who had named Billie Holiday "Lady Day," and had nicknames and double entendres for almost everyone and every occasion, had done it again. I didn't know anything about baseball at the time (still don't) and didn't realize that Schoolboy Row was the nickname of a famous ballplayer, as well as a good description of the level of proficiency that Ray Brown and I had reached. I don't remember any further duet sessions with Ray Brown after that zing.

A regular feature of the Jazz at the Philharmonic concerts was the so-called "Battle of the Drums"... this year between Gene Krupa and Buddy Rich. After an opening chorus of some standard jazz tune, the drummers, side by side, would try to outplay each other in a series of four-, eight-, or sixteen-bar solos. Although Buddy Rich was the acknowledged best drummer who ever lived and could play rings around Gene (and did every night), showman Gene Krupa would get most of the applause. In Montreal we had a stopover, and I had an opportunity to read the morning papers, which were unanimous in their condemnation of the crowd-pleasing "Battle of the Drums." Critics used words like "jungle noise," "cacophony," "tedious," "repetitious," and worse. I was having breakfast when I saw Buddy buy all three papers, go right to the reviews, read them, make a face, and discard them. Later that day, on the short train trip to the next city, Buddy was bothering Gene during a nice chess game we were having and, to give him a little needle, I asked if he'd read the reviews of last night's show. He said, "Kid, I learned a long time ago ... never read the reviews!"

When we got to Norfolk, Virginia, a young sailor came backstage after the show looking for me. He was a high school friend and the drummer in a kid band we'd had together in junior high school and he desperately wanted to meet Buddy Rich. I told him exactly what gate we'd be using when we left the airport later, and warned him that Buddy Rich wasn't always in a great mood and might react in a salty or hostile way, but that he'd enjoy meeting Gene Krupa. I met him at the gate and we awaited the arrival of the two most famous drummers in the world. Gene appeared first. He looked weary as he slumped along, perhaps with a beverage or two under his belt. As he headed through the gate toward our waiting plane,

I stopped him and said, "Gene, I'd like you to meet Bob Graham. He's a drummer and we once had a kid band together, back in . . ." Gene said, "Very good. Very good," waved, and went through the gate and onto the plane without missing a beat. Then Buddy, lower lip protruding and looking angry, came into view with a definite "Don't bug me, I'm busy" look on his face. Fearlessly, I stopped him and said, "Hey, Buddy . . . I'd like you to meet Bob Graham. He's in the service right now, but when we were both kids he played drums in our garage band." Buddy stopped and shook hands with Bob. "You play drums, huh? What kind of sticks do you use?" As I looked on in astonishment, Buddy and Bob had a drummer-to-drummer few minutes together, which ended with Buddy giving him his drumsticks and an autographed picture. Go figure!

Jazz at the Philharmonic was really the highlight of my jazz career, and playing Carnegie Hall at age twenty-three with Gene Krupa still sounds pretty good. But when the tour ended it was time to say bye-bye to the road in general and, regrettably, bye-bye to Gene Krupa, my absolute favorite bandleader. I found a nice apartment in Jackson Heights, a few minutes from mid-town New York by subway, awaited the birth of my first child, and immersed myself in the New York scene. I subbed for the bass player on the old *Tonight Show* with Steve Allen, playing for Steve and Eydie and Andy Williams with Skitch Henderson's band, did some one-nighters with a few other bands and found steady gigs in nightclubs, and occasional record dates.

A wonderful call came from Hollywood, and it was composer/jazz pianist Bobby Troup, then boyfriend and later husband to Julie London, who had just recorded a big hit record called "Cry Me a River," and was coming to New York for her nightclub debut. Would I like to join legendary guitarist Al Viola and play for her at The Cameo? Would I!

The Cameo was an elegant East Side supper club and Julie was a smash hit, which began just as soon as people took a look at her. She didn't know a lot of tunes and almost had to be begged into performing, she was so shy. She didn't have any music, so I'd had to listen to her LP and memorize the bass parts, which was no big deal, because the accompaniment on the album was just bass and guitar. After Julie came the great Mel Torme and I stayed on

Two thirds of my trio at The Cameo, New York.
My piano player is the great, late Bill Evans.

at The Cameo for his engagement. Then the ancient and outrageous Frances Faye showed up with her terrible home-made piano playing, which she more than made up for with her bawdy hilarious routines, her orange hair, and her over-the-top Jewishness. If you didn't know any Yiddish, you did after an evening with Frances Faye. During one of her shows I was onstage and was about to do a bass solo, but she stopped the music and said, "Put down that bass and go home, you schmuck! You just became a father!"

My first gorgeous daughter Lesley's birth thus became part of the show at The Cameo, which turned into a steady job. I stayed on and became the leader of the house band with my own trio, and hired jazz genius Bill Evans when he was just a great piano player and before he became a jazz genius. Other acts showed up like Vegas favorite Buddy Greco and jazz singer Morgana King. Morgana had a great career which all began at the Club Ely in Paterson, New Jersey, when she was fifteen. I can identify with that. The Cameo gig finally ended, perhaps not like the way the writers of *The Sopranos* might have conjured up. I came to work one night and all the wires from the five phone booths in the foyer had been cut and were hanging down onto the floor like berserk spaghetti. Seems the boss, who was running a bookie joint right out of the club, and whose marital infidelities were well known to everybody within ten blocks of The Cameo, had been busted by his wife (who actually owned the joint) for having a quickie with a hat-check girl, and she ratted him out to the police. The place was immediately "closed for remodeling" (sure) and never reopened.

Jazz was still alive and well in the late fifties and, operating out of a comfortable apartment in Jackson Heights, I found my share of good gigs, Birdland, Basin Street, The Embers, and so on, working with wonderful players like Bobby Hackett, Urbie Green, Joe Puma, and everybody good who was around. ABC Paramount wanted me to do a jazz LP with my own group, so I rounded up Neil Hefti to do the arrangements, and six of my favorite players and we went into the studio and recorded some of my favorite jazz tunes, plus my original tune called "Lesley Leaps In," named after my baby girl. Because I'd had the wisdom to hire saxophonist Steve Lacy before anyone else had heard of him and he'd become a cult hero to soprano saxophone fans, that LP is now a remastered CD called *Steve Lacy: The Complete Whitey Mitchell Sessions*.

My wife's roommate from Minneapolis showed up in New York as a Talent Coordinator on a hit Goodson/Todman show called *To Tell the Truth*, in which a minor celebrity and two imposters answer questions from the panel (made up of real celebrities) whose job it was to figure out who was telling the truth and who was bluffing. The Talent Coordinator thought I might make a

At least I fooled one panelist, Johnny Carson, on *To Tell the Truth*.

good contestant and I agreed to do the show mainly as an exercise in terror. I wasn't very good in front of an audience in those days unless I had my bass to hide behind, and my three goals were: don't shake visibly or faint, try to get a laugh out of panelist Johnny Carson and, most importantly, don't throw up on camera. The guy my fellow imposter and I were supposed to be was Will Jones, a humor columnist from Minneapolis whom I knew slightly and who had written a funny bachelor's cookbook called *Wild in the Kitchen*.

I wasn't great, but I accomplished my three goals, including getting more than one laugh out of Johnny Carson, who was the only panelist I fooled and who voted for me. We were to be paid the magnificent sum of two hundred forty dollars for each incorrect answer, which we'd split three ways. So my end was eighty dollars ... which was exactly what the record date I'd given up to do the show would have paid.

Work was steady and always moving upwards with more and more record dates, everything from a Guy Lombardo album to *Jackie Gleason With Strings*, and an occasional gig like appearing with Andre Previn on the pres-

With Andre Previn on NBC's prestigious Bell Telephone Hour. Don Lamond on drums.

tigious NBC show *The Bell Telephone Hour*, situated in the midst of a gorgeous sixty-five-piece orchestra and having them accompany us. When my mother heard about this, she said, "I'm going to get you some publicity!" and what she meant was she'd plant a little item and picture in the *Ridgewood Herald News*, the successor to the paper she worked for as a young woman, which was published every other Thursday. When the paper came out there was the story, along with a charming photo not of me, but of my brother Red. So we furnished them with a group publicity shot which included me, Andre and several executives from AT&T, and no Red Mitchell in sight. Two weeks later, which is now long after the event, the paper reprinted the paragraph Mom had given them along with an apology and a nice photo of Gordon Mitchell, except that the guy pictured was perhaps sixty-two years old and was a Vice-President of AT&T. Two weeks after that, having weathered another identity crisis, I was happy to see they finally got it right, and by this time it had become a quarter-page story explaining about the two brothers who were in the same business and were often confused for one another. Well, not really. But it was shortly after that that I had some business cards printed up which just had a giant "YES" in the middle of the card and on the bottom, in teeny-tiny lettering, "I am Red Mitchell's brother."

Andre Previn was invited back on *The Bell Telephone Hour* one more time and hired me and great drummer Don Lamond again, but this time I was careful not to ask for any publicity from Mom. And this time I couldn't help but notice the first chair (principal) bassist, a wonderful, classically-trained musician named Homer Mensch, who had played in Toscanini's NBC Orchestra, and I approached him about teaching me correct classical bowing and fingering techniques. I knew that I needed to be a lot better in that area if I were to do Broadway shows, and that's where the money was (and still is) for New York musicians. Homer accepted me as a student and I had to start from scratch, which was roughly the sound I was getting whenever I tried to bow the bass. He was a wonderful, patient teacher. I progressed quickly with him and became a decent player. And I'm still trying to perfect his teachings forty-some years later.

About a year ago I noticed an inspiring piece in *Time* about nonagenarians who were still working, and was very pleased to see that there was a full story on Homer Mensch and a photo of him and his picture-perfect technique, bowing happily on his two-hundred-year-old bass. Homer helped me to get to the musical level I needed, technique-wise, and I was soon a good enough legitimate player to start getting Broadway shows, and I did a bunch of them.

One show in particular stays with me because it was so untypical and extraordinary that it deserves its own chapter.

Chapter Twelve
We Love You, Eddie

In the early sixties Eddie Fisher had a pleasant voice, lots of hit records, and something you can't get at Julliard: charisma. So it was a big deal when he played the Winter Garden Theatre. It was a smaller deal for me . . . just another high paying theatre gig. Having just lost Elizabeth Taylor to Richard Burton, Eddie had the sympathy of America as well as the normal adulation of his motherly fans, which inhabited the balcony, and who would scream down at first sight of him, "WE LOVE YOU, EDDIE!" as well as "TURN THE DRUMMER DOWN," a suggestion nobody ever acted on.

The first part of the evening's performance included Juliet Prowse and Dick Gregory, whose acts we played from the orchestra pit with a smaller group and then Act Two . . . Eddie himself, on stage with a forty-piece tuxedoed orchestra providing lavish accompaniment as he struggled to get through his own act without a musical train wreck. Not known to the public or the screamers in the balcony, but well known to musicians everywhere, was the fact that Mr. Fisher was rhythmically challenged. In other words, he had trouble keeping time. For anything more complicated than "Happy Birthday to You," he couldn't sing it all the way through without losing the meter of the piece, either adding bars or skipping bars, (no one ever knew which was to come) and ending up in a different place than the orchestra. I was told that years earlier, when he did his live TV show, the producers would hire a guy to stand just off camera and mouth the words to the song Eddie was singing so he would know when to come in, and when to go out and keep in sync with the orchestra.

No such device would work on the stage of the Winter Garden. Instead, the music director provided the rhythm section (piano, bass, guitar and drums) with earphones. When Eddie would wander off to the wrong place in a song, the conductor would wave the orchestra out. They'd just sit there not playing while the rhythm section would scramble around, figure out where Eddie was and go there. Then the conductor would whisper the approaching correct bar number and the orchestra could be brought back in safely with the hope that singer and musicians would all end up on bar #168 at the same time, as the arranger intended.

A big hunk of Eddie's act was the "Jolson Medley," a tribute to Al Jolson, who in past years had had many triumphant engagements at this same venerable theatre and, in fact, had been honored by the city of New York, which renamed a portion of the street outside as "Al Jolson Way." The medley was an overlong and cumbersome concoction of about twenty of Jolson's hits all strung together with musical bridges, transitions, tempo changes and key changes…a formula for disaster, given Eddie's shortcomings. At the first rehearsal, I knew that the "Jolson Medley" would affect the length of that rehearsal when the orchestra played it perfectly the first time through and Eddie couldn't get through more than one and one-half tunes without driving off the road and crossing the center line into oncoming traffic. The rest of the rehearsal went well. Juliet Prowse . . . no problem. Dick Gregory . . . no music, no problem. The rest of Eddie's act? He'd been trained to get through portions of it without obvious trouble and it was 90% okay. But the "Jolson Medley" was a disaster and I overheard Eddie questioning the line-up of tunes and asking things like, "Can't we go from 'Climb Up on My Knee, Sonny Boy,' right into 'I'm Alabammy Bound' and then do 'Toot-Toot-Tootsie,'" which implies a complete disinterest in such things as tempo changes, key changes, instrument switches, not to mention arranging and music copying, and I knew we were headed for trouble.

I was right. On the second day's rehearsal we now had two "Jolson

Medleys," each the bulk and heft of a Manhattan phone directory and the new one was called "Jolson Medley Revised." We were to keep both mega-arrangements handy and would be told in plenty of time which would be the medley *du jour*. Opening night we played the "Jolson Medley Revised" and there were train wrecks in the usual, as well as new places, with the orchestra waved out, the rhythm section waved in and many out-of-sync endings.

Surprise! There was to be a rehearsal the following day, even though the show had already opened and the only entity needing rehearsal was Mr. E. Fisher. So orchestra members had to rearrange their lives, cancel record dates, other gigs and family responsibilities, so they could once again rehearse the dreaded "Jolson Medley." New York Local #802 of the American Federation of Musicians, in a weak moment, had provided Broadway producers with additional rehearsal time, should it be needed, after a show opened, at ridiculously low rates and without any ending date. So, theoretically, we could be kept all day every day at that theatre, employed at coolie wages, and giving up our lives during the entire run of the show.

Yet another day of rehearsal and another surprise! "Jolson Medley Revised Transposed" . . . the same music played down one-half tone. Apparently, all the music copyists in New York had been up all night making fresh sheets of manuscript paper, accomplishing the slight key change and had pasted together our third medley. This didn't go well either and, of course, for all the same reasons, which led to:

Another day of rehearsal and yet another "Jolson Medley." This time, the original medley, but transposed one whole tone down. It must have taken all the music copyists of New York, New Jersey, and Connecticut all night to come up with this beauty, the "Jolson Medley Original Transposed." Now we had four telephone directories to deal with. As tough as that is for a bass player, who has to hold the bass with one hand while dealing with hand-copied arrangements with the other, I felt sorry for the reed players, who now had to go from oboe to bassoon, to clarinet, to piccolo, to saxophone and back, all in a split second with no chance to moisten a reed or do any kind of prep. The atmosphere at this latest rehearsal was a little like what it must have been in the hold of a slave ship a couple of hundred years ago . . . seething.

That day I had the only tantrum I've ever had in either of my two show business careers. It wasn't bad enough that we were never told which goddamned "Jolson Medley" was up until about the time the tympani was rolling and Eddie was being announced and the curtain was rising. But at this particular rehearsal Eddie was still complaining about not being able to reach certain notes and not liking the line-up of tunes, something that should have been nailed down months ago, and he still wanted to change things. He still didn't grasp all that was involved. He conveyed his latest thoughts to his pianist/conductor, who listened, nodded, pondered for a beat, then turned to the orchestra, saying something like, "Fellas . . . here's what I want you to do: on Bar #147 of the 'Jolson Medley Revised Transposed,' make a cut to Bar #68 of the 'Original Jolson Medley,' play up to the first Del Segno, then take the Coda and tacit while I play a musical bridge which will get us back to . . ."

Nobody heard the rest. I screamed like a demented banshee and threw all four "Jolson Medleys" high up into the air, from where pages and pieces and inserts floated downwards all over the stage for the next four or five minutes. I calmly put the bass down and strode off the stage. End of rehearsal for me. As I passed Eddie and his conductor, I heard Eddie's puzzled voice: "What's the matter with him?"

That night and every night thereafter there was one "Jolson Medley" (the original, I believe) on the music stands. And there were no more rehearsals for the rest of the engagement. One other note: because Eddie had complained to the producers that "the band stinks," they flew in conductor Colin Romoff from the West Coast, where he'd been doing Andy Williams' television show, and paid him $5,000 to stay for a week and try to figure out what was wrong with the orchestra. What they got for their five-grand was Colin's only suggestion: that the saxophone players in the front row should pull up their black socks!

Chapter Thirteen
Broadway, Rock 'n' Roll, Bar Mitzvahs ... and a Letter from Lenny

This is just my opinion, but in the late fifties and early sixties music took a terrible turn for the worse from which it has never fully recovered. Rock 'n' Roll significantly lowered the bar in popular music, and suddenly any garage band could sound as good as any professional recording, which I ought to know, because I'm on hundreds of them. As my dream of becoming a higher paid studio player began to come true, the music got less and less interesting to play. There were some memorable dates like *Jackie Gleason With Strings* (with a large studio orchestra) or a similar couple of sessions with a very young, but very professional Barbra Streisand, recording her *My Name Is Barbra* album. But more and more, unknown street corner singers recorded never-to-be-heard-from non-hits. And if by chance, they made it onto the charts soon enough after the date that I could remember them, I'd buy the record and put it on my home office wall. It's the only way I have even a faint recollection of what I was recording. And it's a paradox ... that stuff sounds better to me now than what they're doing today. I was first-call bassist for some wonderful people, including Capitol Records, Atlantic Records, and great musicians/songwriters like Lieber & Stoller and Burt Bacharach. One of the hundreds of dates I did involved three hours spent on a two-minute song with four chord changes called "Stand by Me," which I still hear wherever I go.

1958 was a pivotal year for me. My son Brian was born, and just like older sister Lesley, he was born as I was on stage. This time at the Village Vanguard, where I was leading a combo. And, like Lesley, he was beautiful from day one. Talk about your Little Lord Jesus!

It was also the year I played the Newport Jazz Festival with Anita O'Day, which was filmed and turned into an award-winning documentary about the whole event called *Jazz on a Summer's Day*, available at Amazon. com. And it was the year Leonard Feather, noted jazz critic, pianist and producer, got the bright idea to record Red and me and non-related Mitchell, Richard "Blue" Mitchell, thereby having an LP featuring Red, Whitey, and Blue Mitchell, and Metrojazz Records agreed. Lots of LPs were produced based on a thinner premise than that and they were not nearly as patriotic sounding. I'm proud of that LP, which represents perhaps the only time Red and I ever worked together. We used Andre Previn and Frank Capp, who Red was working with, as well as Pepper Adams and Frank Rehak and it's called *Get Those Elephants Outa Here*, based on what my mother screamed one day when she came into the living room of her home in Ridgewood and found three or four basses (in their cases) cluttering up the place during a rare visit by both sons. It also features my original tune "Blues for Brian," named after my son, and carries on the tradition that every kid born near the planning stages of one of my albums gets a tune named after him or her. (Sorry Karen and Michele.) That LP was recently remastered and released on a CD in the *Leonard Feather Presents* series, *The Mitchells* and *The Joneses*' and is available from www.worldsrecords.com

Now, with Brian aboard, the apartment in Jackson Heights became too small, and it was time to buy a house in the 'burbs. It was also the year I met the man who was unwittingly responsible for my writing career in a weird, negative way. I somehow got hooked into working with society bandleader Lester Lanin . . . not on one of the twenty or thirty bands he'd put out on a weekend night, but with his band and him. He was possibly the least likeable person I'd ever met and after I got to know him, I began to regard him as some kind of pestilent gnome whose mission in life was to torture me. Lester only paid flat scale, but because his jobs were all "continuous" (the music never stopped) and lengthy and involved lots of travel-

With Anita O'Day at the Newport Jazz Festival, 1958.

ing, with per diem, mileage and cartage, the check at the end of the week was huge, which was especially welcome news to a new homeowner. On a "continuous" gig, if you asked to leave the bandstand to go to the john, he'd invariably reply, "You knew about this job three weeks ago!"

Lester would occasionally send a small unit to Charleston, South Carolina, which was a nice two-day getaway, and I made a few of those trips. The piano player was always Silvio, a good musician and a pleasant forty-something man with the I.Q. of a summer squash who lived with his parents. Silvio had once written a hit tune and it's what kept him alive financially, because everything he made from Lester went to his losing gambling habit. One morning at the airport, everyone was gathered and good to go except that Silvio hadn't shown, and the contractor/drummer was worried that something terrible had happened, because Silvio had never before been late to any gig, let alone missed one. Then one of the guys reading the paper noticed that it was opening day at the racetrack, and came up with a pretty good possible explanation. Silvio, with the understanding and the attention span of a gnat, had probably forgotten all about the gig and was making plans to go to the track, so the contractor called him. Silvio answered:

"Hello?"

"Silvio! Where the hell are you? You're supposed to be at La Guardia right now!"

A long beat, and then:

"This isn't Silvio."

"Then who is it?"

An even longer beat, then:

"This is my father."

Another player in the Lanin office was legendary jazz drummer Cliff Leeman, who would work with Lester's bands only when the jazz business got real slow. One night Cliff was heading out the door in his tux for a wedding gig on Long Island when the phone rang and it was the Lanin office. Seems the father of the bride had suddenly passed away and the wedding was on permanent hold. Cliff could have the night off. No money, just the night off. He said, "Great!" and asked his wife how quickly she could get dressed because they were goin' out on the town! She said she needed at least an hour and Cliff said okay, and that he'd mix up a big batch of martinis. By the time his wife was ready, the martinis had been consumed by Cliff, also a legendary drinker, and he was completely smashed. But out the door they went. Cliff hailed a cab, pushed his better half inside, and climbed in after her. When the cab driver asked "Where to, buddy?" Cliff's slurred response was "Take us someplace where we can get our corks soaked!" Or something like that.

But back to Lester. When I noticed a pattern of blinding headaches that began exactly at 9:00 p.m. (or whenever the first down beat occurred) each night that I worked with Lester himself, I put two and two together and came up with the plain truth. No amount of Lester Lanin money was worth the mental abuse and physical illness I seemed to be getting, so I quit, still filled with loathing and resentment. I found out that I could almost fill the financial void by doing "Jewish" work. That is ... weddings and bar mitzvahs mostly on Long Island (pronounced: Lawn Guyland) and mostly at a place called Leonard's of Great Neck, home to hundreds of affairs per week. The musicians were not only musical, they were nice, the money was good and my limited Yiddish was enhanced, which, unknown to me at the time, would come in very handy during my writing career in Hollywood. But I couldn't get Lester out of my mind.

He was extremely two-faced. A horrible Captain Bligh to his musicians, and a worshipful Uriah Heep to his wealthy clients, and in reality he cared about neither. I guess he wasn't really evil, which is a word I'll leave to judgmental religious types. Let's just call him nasty. But nasty can be funny (ask George Jefferson or Archie Bunker) and Lester, a bundle of neuroses topped off by paranoia, unconsciously said and did some very funny things. One night, facing the band with his back to the dancers, as he was castigating us for some imagined minor infraction, a client tapped him on the shoulder and Lester did his instant Mr. Hyde-to-Dr. Jekyll transformation, turned and almost knelt to the man, who was a little drunk, and who demanded to know "Are you Jewish?" Lester, who temporarily

All the happy faces under the baton of Lester Lanin.

couldn't remember if we were playing for the B'nai Brith or the Knights of Columbus, panicked, quickly looked around the ballroom for clues. Finding none, he stammered, "Not necessarily!"

For some reason Lester had become the darling of the super-rich upper echelon of New York society, and it was interesting to watch these millionaires fight over Lester Lanin beanies, which were cheap Coney Island felt hats with "Lester Lanin" stitched onto them in garish colors. If there were to be fifteen hundred guests at an affair, he'd bring fifty beanies, and when he started passing them out from the bandstand (usually when bucking for overtime) the shark beanie-feeding frenzy would begin, which sometimes led to torn shirts and bloody noses.

We played for the Fords, the Rockefellers, the Kennedys, and one fan in particular, Mrs. Gary Cooper, the wealthy wife of the movie actor. At a function in the upscale Hamptons section of Long Island, she hired Lester and his band to fly to the West Coast and play for a party she was planning in Beverly Hills. At least she agreed to enough money to fly the whole band out there, play the gig, stay over, and then fly back. But Lester had other ideas once the deal was made. He'd take his drummer and his lead trumpet player, Johnny Parker (who later became Arthur Godfrey's musical director), fly to the Coast, and have a "rehearsal" with fifteen of the top West Coast players, thus cheating Mrs. Cooper and saving thousands of dollars worth of those troublesome travel expenses for fifteen guys. During this rehearsal, he fantasized he'd teach them his style, which is a little like teaching a leopard to have stripes instead of spots.

Johnny Parker told me exactly what happened. At the so-called rehearsal in walked the best players in town: Stan Getz, Zoot Sims, Frank Rossolino, Maynard Ferguson, and other marquee musicians, who simply played the music they knew: jazz and blues, having nothing to do with Lester and his two-beat Mickey Mouse music. Now the famous Lester Lanin orchestra would sound exactly like what it was: a ragtag bunch of jazz musicians with no particular style playing zero danceable music. Mrs. Cooper would know she'd been had. At the hotel later, getting ready for the gig, Parker noticed that the door to Lester's adjoining suite was open and Lester was lying down in a near fetal position, eyes closed, mouth moving rapidly, with no sound coming out. He rushed over to Lester and asked if he was okay. Lester opened one eye and explained that he was just "praying to Almighty God to give me the wisdom and the strength to deal with those dirty cork soakers!" (Ask Cliff Leeman for the exact words.) The other Lester stories were equally funny, in a bizarre way, mostly appealing to musicians, and I couldn't help but mentally collect every single one I heard about or participated in.

One night at Nick's in Greenwich Village, where I was working with a Dixieland jazz band, we were hanging around during a break, and I began to tell "Lester stories" to wonderful response. A man I'd never met was there and seemed extremely entertained by them. He asked if I could write down some of these yarns for *Down Beat*, where he worked as an editor, and I said, "Sure. Who couldn't write this stuff down?" That weekend I dashed off a satirical piece on Lester, whom I named Julius Martinet, had a lot of fun at Julius' expense, got rid of some not-so-ancient hostilities, sent it in and forgot about it. I was amazed that the man's offer wasn't just party talk. *Down Beat* published the piece and a nice check, my first for writing, arrived. In those days fifty dollars was nice. And I was astonished when letters to the editor began to appear in subsequent issues, all praising that piece, including one from Lenny Bruce, who called me a genius! That got my attention. Here's the article and Lenny Bruce's response (with *Down Beat's* permission):

My First 50 Years With Society Bands
by Whitey Mitchell

It hasn't been easy for me, as a jazz player, to devote 50 years of my life to playing with society bands, especially since I'm 28. But if someone had kept track of all the choruses of "Lady is a Tramp" I've had to play; all the hours I've had to spend looking for private residences on unmarked, unpaved, and unlit streets in Nassau and Fairfield counties; all the dry chicken sandwiches I've choked down in one dismal country club kitchen after another; all the time spent in fellowship with musicians who know more about the Dow-Jones industrial average than the contents of a C7 chord; all the hours spent absorbing hysterical-emotional abuse liberally dispensed by tone-deaf baton-wavers under working conditions that would have interested Marx and Engels—then that someone could only conclude that an estimate of 50 years of servitude is a conservative one.

There seems to be a curious relationship between jazzmen and society music, and it is one that has existed for a long time.

Every successful society leader I know of depends on the ability of his band to play any tune at any time at any moment and without benefit of music. A surprising amount of jazz is required at society functions, and it's well known that not very much jazz can be produced by a lone man waving a stick. Hence society leaders are always ready to ensnare good jazz players, and Benny Goodman, Gene Krupa, Bobby Hackett, Urbie Green and scores of others, at one time or another have earned money playing society music.

I would like to offer illustrations of some of my experiences in society work, and I'll attempt to boil all of them down into one job, on one occasion and under the baton of one maestro, whom I shall call Julius Martinet.

On the union exchange floor, where musicians mill around like a mob of stevedores waiting to be hired for unloading a banana boat, Julius' contractor, Melvin, asked me if I had been hired yet for the following Sunday. Unfortunately, I couldn't say that I had, so I wrote down the directions and was hired for the Waltney party at the Sandtrap Country Club near Old Quogue on Long Island.

The occasion, as I understood it, was the first anniversary of the AT&T stock split. Saturday night at 9:05, in the ballroom of the Sandtrap Country Club, as the drummer finished setting up and as the other musicians applied resin or valve oil or adjusted their rugs, Julius was busy thinking up schemes for by-passing an intermission and trying to decide which members of the orchestra he would pick on during the evening.

Mr. and Mrs. Waltney were stationed at the entrance to the ballroom, waiting to greet their first guests. A car engine was heard, and the Waltney social secretary signaled to Julius that the first group was arriving. Julius started slapping his thigh at the approximate tempo we would be pursuing for the rest of engagement, and was screwing up his face trying to think of some appropriate music for the host and hostess, who are of Roman Catholic persuasion. Unable to think of an opening tune, Julius whispered to the band at large, "What do you play for Catholics?" and without missing a beat, the first trumpet player whispered back, "I'm Confessin'." Julius gave the down beat, and we were off.

After the medley had been in progress for an hour or so, a friendly waiter appeared at the bandstand with a full tray of gin and tonics for the band. Before Julius could utter his famous line, "My boys don't drink or smoke," one of the saxophone players pulled Julius' coattail and pointed significantly to the rear of the room.

Julius put on his glasses, turned around and peered into the crowd for about 15 seconds. Seeing nothing unusual, he turned back to the band, put away his glasses and scowled at the saxophonist who now was involved in a chorus of "Sweet Georgia Brown." Meanwhile, the tray of drinks had been looted, and a large cloud of tobacco smoke enveloped the brass section.

At about the two-hour mark, the party began to move into high gear, with emphasis on the word high. Julius sensed that the orchestra's e*sprit de corps* left something to be desired, so he flagged down a waiter and asked him to bring glasses of water for the musicians. By prearrangement with a certain bartender, some of these glasses were filled with the type of water that leaves one breathless, and to the amazement of nobody but Julius, the band began to rally.

Then it became time for the nightly contest between the brass and reed sections to determine which group could skip bars more gracefully than the other. At the high point of this meter-losing set, we established a new world's record by playing "St. Louis Blues" in five bars and two beats. Failing to get any satisfactory reaction from either Julius or the guests, the band turned eagerly to the bar-adding contest to see who most casually could add 8, 10 or 20 bars of music to a 32-bar song. For instance, Julius called "Tramp" and then turned around to sign a few autographs. The band took up the challenge and played:

I get too hungry for dinner at eight,
I like the theatre, but never come late,
I like the theatre, but never come late,
I like the theatre, but never come late,
I like the theatre, but never come late . . .

At this point, Julius whirled around, with a wounded expression, and the band continued:

I never bother with people I hate,
That's why the lady is a tramp!

Two grueling hours and three rounds of water later, Julius seemed to be inspired anew, judging from the semaphoric activity of his arms. He tripped over another of the many glasses of water that had been finding their way to the vicinity of his feet throughout the evening and complained to the rhythm section that the tempo was rushing. Possibly this occurred to him because we had just finished "California Here I Come" and now were attempting to play "My Funny Valentine" at the same tempo.

After a series of audible groans, which seemed to swell with each passing moment, Julius reluctantly fished out his watch, and after a secretive screening, announced it was five minutes to one and time for the "Good Night, Ladies" medley.

We all had our own watches, and they all said at least 10 after one, and we all knew that there would be at least two hours overtime, having been informed of this at the time we were booked, but everyone good-naturedly went along with the farce.

At the first strains of "Good Night, Ladies," those of us who didn't have horns in our faces began to moan, "No . . . no . . . no" without moving our lips. Soon the guests who were still coherent took up the cry, and Mrs. Waltney came rushing up to Julius and insisted that the band stay at least another hour. We went right into "Everything's Coming Up Roses," and Julius was so pleased that he forgot about finding out who the fink in the band was who had yelled "Hooray!"

An hour later the same stunt was employed. Only this time, the ratio of "no" to "hooray" seemed to be reversed. Julius had knocked over two more water glasses and was by now soaked to his knees. The band, too numb to care, played on.

During the third hour of overtime, one couple began dancing on the high diving board of the pool outside. Of course, they were soon pushed in, and as soon as they climbed out of the pool, they grabbed some of the curious onlookers and made participants out of them. It soon became more fashionable to be in the pool than out, and posses were formed to round up all the squares who were still dry. Julius had just asked Mrs. Waltney about the fourth hour of overtime when 12 husky dripping guests arrived and dragged her, screaming, into the pool. This left only the band dry, and after a chorus of "By the Sea," we departed in record time. Julius had to stay over in Old Quogue that night because he didn't have the nerve to ask anyone to ruin his car upholstery on his behalf. This may sound like a lot of fiction, but it's not. As they say on television…only the names have been changed to protect the innocent.

Besides, I'm still open Saturday.

Lenny Bruce's letter to the editor:
ORCHIDS FOR WHITEY That Whitey Mitchell is a brilliant writer. I laughed both times I read his article. A delightful talent to be able to be so "in" and "out" at the same time. He is a commercial writer—commercial along with Miles and Michelangelo and Philly Joe Jones and Bach. I don't know who gave that word a trite connotation. Commercial—"relating to a large group." That's my definition. Me, I like large groups; a session is no fun with just two guys ... As a reader, I am grateful for your selectivity. That rare talent that few editors have. As they say in letters to the editor ... let's have more of Mitchell. Miami Beach, Fla. Lenny Bruce

I became even more of a family man around that time with the arrival of beautiful daughter Karen, who had the wisdom to be born at a reasonable hour when I was not playing jazz in some den of iniquity. She was born in Hackensack Hospital, where I first saw the light of day twenty-nine years earlier, and her birth certificate was signed by the same lady (with the same neat signature) who'd signed mine. Our house in the 'burbs was in Hackensack, a town noted for its participation in the American

Revolution when the townsfolk threw rocks and rotten eggs at George Washington and his army, as they retreated from a disastrous battle on Manhattan Island. I think most of the Tories are long gone; at least they were in our part of town, a pleasant blue collar neighborhood, where all the dads would get in their cars and drive to work every morning. Except one. The neighborhood kids couldn't figure out why I was home many days of the week. One such day I was in my home office writing an arrangement for Cozy Cole's quintet. I heard a bunch of kids just outside my window asking the usual question: "How come your dad is home a lot?" Lesley, tired of this question' shot back, "Because he's a musician!" and after a beat, one of them asked, "Well, can you just get him to do one trick?"

Rock 'n' Roll didn't burst onto the scene, it just kind of sneaked in, one Doo-Wop after another, and I predicted that it would only last about six weeks. The last time I looked, I was wrong by about fifty years. But it wasn't all rock 'n' roll. Some of the sessions were actually fun because of the musicians involved, and singers like Jane Morgan, Anthony Newley and Jack Jones kept the business musically interesting.

I got to play for Jack Jones for his opening in the prestigious Persian Room at the Plaza Hotel. He'd just had some mega-hits such as "Lollipops & Roses" and "Wives and Lovers," and he was a class act. On opening night every important person from New York, as well as a few from the West Coast, filled the room and later jammed into Jack's dressing room, which he had kindly shared with his rhythm section.

So I was there when Jim Aubrey (Mr. CBS at the time) and Sheldon Leonard, former actor and now Executive Producer of *The Andy Griffith Show* and the new hit *Gomer Pyle* (as well as many other biggies I couldn't identify), came in to congratulate Jack. After things quieted down, Aubrey and Leonard began discussing their Jim Nabors dilemma. Here was the star of *Gomer Pyle* who had a deep, rich, baritone voice, and who could sing like an angel, but who was playing a kind of sweet unsophisticated hillbilly with a squeaky voice and the I.Q. of Forrest Gump. His singing voice was absolutely counter to his character as well as the premise of the series, and they'd been racking their brains trying to think of a way to work his music into the show. I spoke up with five words: "How about a dream sequence?" They all stared at me for a beat, with a how-did-that-cockroach-get-in-here expression until they realized that I was just the bass player and didn't deserve to be in the room, let alone in the conversation. Without considering my idea for a tenth of a second, they turned their backs and went on with their discussion but not loud enough to be heard. I was pleased to note about a year later that Gomer Pyle dreamed that he could sing, and it became a device they used more than once.

When he got to be about six or seven, my son Brian loved going into the city with me, and I loved his company. He was bright and well behaved and on a few occasions I brought him into the orchestra pit during performances of Broadway shows. He'd sit there in his little dark blue suit, eyes wide open in amazement and joy when the musicians would play. Or I would take him to the union, where I would pick up recording checks, book some club dates, or just hang out and have a hotdog from a street vendor with my peers. They all loved Brian, and he'd always have a great time.

We lived about fifteen minutes from the George Washington Bridge, the gateway to Manhattan, and one day, as we were pulling out of the driveway on our way to the city, Brian asked me, "Dad . . . what's a lead?" Before I answered, I realized it was a multi-purpose word, to say the least. As we drove, I began one of my too-much-information explanations, pointing out that, in music, the lead is the melody, and everything else is harmony. In electricity, the lead is the positive wire. In detective work, a lead is a clue that could point the way to discovery. In sports, the athlete or team that's in first place is said to be in the lead. On Broadway, the lead is the star, and so on. It took me about the same time it took the car to reach the bridge to explain every possible facet of the word "lead." When, finally, I'd run out of definitions, I asked him why he asked me that question and heard, "Because there's this neat movie called *Twenty Thousand* Leads *Under the Sea*."

By the early sixties big bands were almost over. A few well-known leaders could still book gigs and put together bands that could play their music, then return to New York and wait for the phone to ring again. I played with a lot of groups like that, such as Les Elgart, Boyd Raeburn,

Skitch Henderson, Charlie Spivak, Elliot Lawrence, Xavier Cugat, and dozens more. The biggest name bandleader involved in this put-a-band-together-then-dump-'em routine was Benny Goodman, and I worked for him for a couple of years, on and off. Benny probably wouldn't be on anybody's list of Great Human Beings I Have Known, but he was a brilliant player, and the musicianship of the band was always of the highest caliber. He went on two trips that I really wanted to be part of, and I didn't end up on either one of them: a South American tour and a State Department-authorized trip to Russia. As soon as he returned from Russia, he fired almost everybody and formed a new band, which included me.

We played a giant amusement park called Freedomland, New York's unsuccessful answer to Disneyland, and while there I was talking to one of the oldest Benny Goodman vets (who was now back in favor) and told him of my disappointments, especially missing out on the Russia trip. He wanted to know what I asked for in the way of a salary and I said, "Union scale. I just wanted to go!" Big mistake. "Benny doesn't respect you if you just ask for scale. Ask for the moon. He won't pay it, but at least he'll be interested and try to get you down to his price." I thanked him and said to myself, "lesson learned."

Jay Feingold, Benny's business manager at the time, came up to me one day as we were playing a matinee at Freedomland and talked about the next tour Benny was planning. It would involve flying to the West Coast and playing Disneyland for a couple of weeks, recording an album, and working back toward New York playing college dates along the way. About a month's work. Would I be interested? Would I! I loved the Coast, loved the idea of the album, and I'd get to see Red for the first time in years. Hiding my enthusiasm for his proposal, I started hemming and hawing about how expensive it would be to get me out of New York that particular month. I'd have to hire a lot of highly paid subs and I'd probably miss a Broadway show and a gang of record dates, but I'd go home and look at my book, and if they came up with enough money, maybe I could get out of a few things and make it work. But, it would cost them. In reality, the month in question was not all that busy yet, but I was curious to see if my new stance would work. I sure wasn't going to repeat mistakes of the past and I really wanted this gig.

That night the phone rang, and when I picked it up I could hear the King of Swing practicing on his clarinet in the background, so I knew it was Jay. He asked the dreaded question how much salary would I be asking for, and when I mentioned the unheard-of (for a bass player) salary of $500 a week, he just laughed maniacally and hung up the phone. I thought to myself: this is interesting, but did I go too far? And, before I could answer myself, the phone rang again, and once again I heard the inevitable tooting in the background, and Jay dangled the offer of $300 a week. Not bad! But let's see just how far this can go. I explained what a financial sacrifice I'd have to make, as well as the lost connections that had taken me years to build up and that even if I wasn't worth it, I'd have to have the $500. Several unsatisfactory phone calls later, the salary had escalated all the way to $325 and I still said "no," really enjoying this. Then he said, okay, no more games. What do you really want per week? I said it's not a game, I still need the $500 a week to get me out of town and that maybe Benny should look for a bass player he can hire cheaper. But if I'm going, I'll need the $500. Jay said just a minute, put the phone down and in a few seconds, the incessant practicing stopped, and I heard the sound of mumble-mumble-mumble, then Jay returned to the phone, saying, "The old man will pay you $490," and I said, "I'll take it!" It was the only time in my entire life when I was even close to being a businessman.

So we went to the West Coast, played Disneyland, recorded an album and I got to hang out with my brother. He came to the gig to see me, and we played a little trick on Benny. Before the last set, we went behind a fence where they were building the Haunted House and switched clothes. Red was now wearing my powder-blue Benny Goodman uniform and I was wearing his California casual earth tones slacks and jacket. Then, when the break was over, Red went up on the bandstand and pretended to be me. I can't tell you why we did this, but it seemed like a funny idea at the time. Under those stage lights, with Red and I being of similar size and physique and bone structure, it really looked pretty close, But Benny knew something was wrong, and kept whispering to the saxophone players nearby, "Is

The King of Swing arrives at Anaheim, CA for our Disneyland date, 1963.

that Whitey up there?" Yeah, Benny, that's Whitey. And no matter how many times he'd ask he always got the same answer. It rattled him a little bit, and his performance the rest of the set was not his best.

After the gig, I headed for the band room to put away the bass, still wearing Red's earth tones. He was right next to me in my powder-blue outfit and we had to pass Benny's dressing room. A confused Benny stopped us, wanted to know what was going on and refused to believe that Red was Red or that I was me, until at last it dawned on him that we'd put him on. He managed a weak fake laugh: "heh-heh-heh," and we went on our way. Decades later I learned from the drummer, Frank De Vito, that the next

Benny Goodman's bass player is the last to leave the plane.

day, while I was visiting one of my friends and heroes, Steve Allen, and having a good time at his local television show, Benny called a rehearsal for saxophone players only, the guys who had lied to him, and for three hours, the length of the rehearsal, they had to play the same difficult arrangement over and over and over again. Don't mess with Benny!

Had I known about it I would have apologized for our college prank and, if it's not too late now: Sorry, guys! But I loved that trip and visiting with Red, and I basked in the sun and in the knowledge that I was one of the highest paid bass players Benny Goodman ever had. But Benny had the last word . . . he never paid us for the album we recorded.

My $490 was certainly more than Red got the one time he worked with Benny. It was in the fall of 1958 and Benny wanted to record with Andre Previn and his trio (which included Red) and Helen Ward, his singer and girlfriend many decades before. The place was Benny's studio, a former carriage house/pool house adjacent to his Connecticut mansion. The guys were setting up and Benny was doing his usual incessant practicing and paying attention to no one, including Helen Ward, by this time a middle-aged lady, who was making all the body language of a woman freezing to death. It was Connecticut, it was late fall, it was cold. Giving up on subtlety, she finally grabbed his arm, stopped him from playing and called his name: "Benny!" A puzzled Benny replied, "What is it, Pops?" (Benny had trouble remembering people's names.) "It's cold in here!" Benny quickly put down the clarinet and left the room. When he came back five minutes later, he was wearing a sweater. Red told me the session went about as well as that particular communication, and when Benny later sent Andre a check for scale ($50 per man), Andre returned it.

Do you remember Carole King? She unwittingly made a big contribution to my growing dissatisfaction with the music business, or at least what I got to see of it. I was hired, along with a roomful of other studio players, to record with her on a session. She was probably about twenty at the time and I'd never heard of her. When I looked around the studio, it was a veritable Who's Who of prominent musicians, including the brothers Ernie and Marshall Royal, alumnae of the Basie Band, and Ed Shaughnessy, of *The Tonight Show*. The curious thing: there was no music in evidence, which is pretty strange, considering the size of the orchestra. Then Carole King came in and passed out the "music," which was not the usual hand-copied, beautiful arrangement we'd all come to expect. Her music was not an arrangement or orchestration, or much of anything. It was a few crude chords copied onto three-holed, lined schoolbook composition paper. Then she found the piano and began pounding out the song we'd be pursuing for the next three hours. It was her latest composition and we apparently were supposed to look at that primitive chord sheet and generate a rich background that made sense, had harmony, and would end up being an arrangement by Carole King.

Her significant other, who was all of about eighteen, was the executive producer, or some such title, of this strange recording. Carole pounded and sang and sang and pounded and, little by little, because of all the creativity in the room, it almost sounded like something after a while. During a break I went into the booth to hear a playback (God knows why) and while there, I overheard the young genius complaining about Ed Shaughnessy, one of the great drummers of the world. "Jesus Christ! Can't that drummer play more like Ringo Starr?," which is a little like asking an Olympic sprinter if he can't run more like Quasimodo. This set off a big alarm bell in my brain, and the thought occurred: This eighteen-year-old know-nothing snot-nosed kid is the future. I'll be working for him and people like him from now on. What a disturbing thought!

In 1965 a wonderful gig came along. It was a new Comden & Green Broadway musical starring Carol Burnett called *Fade Out, Fade In*. It was a very funny lampoon of Hollywood and the film business, and right on target, as I would discover in my next career. Julie Styne wrote the music, Marvin Hamlisch was the rehearsal pianist, and I was happy to be there. It had "hit" written all over it. At a point near the end of Act One, Carol would come swooping around the stage singing "The Usher from the Mezzanine," and come perilously close to the orchestra pit and look down and wink at the bass player. It made my day, eight performances per week. But, as with any show, after a few months of deadly repetition, I was doing Acrostic puzzles in the pit instead of bothering to get out the music, which I hadn't needed for a long time.

One day I looked around the pit and had an epiphany. The pit was full of mostly old, excellent musicians at the top of their field, some of them in their eighties. And they were all making the same check I was. This was the top of the line. All I could ever expect. Then I remembered Lenny Bruce's letter from a couple of years ago in which he called me a genius. Nobody in this pit was calling me a genius. Then I recalled the Carole King recording session . . . my future. It was a Rock 'n' Roll world and I was an outmoded be-bop musician. I might as well have been a Zeppelin pilot. I remembered solving the Gomer Pyle singing dilemma in one sentence, and the thought crossed my mind: If you don't want to work for Carole King's boyfriend, or be in this pit when you're eighty, you're going to have to get into another business. Hmmmm . . . why not writing?

When I got back home to New Jersey, I called Red in Hollywood and asked him a simple yes or no question: "Can I make a living out there as a bass player while I learn to be a screenwriter?" His answer, without a nano-second's delay was a loud "Yes!" and based on the speed of that "yes," Lenny's letter to *Down Beat*, and some encouragement from Andre Previn, who was still chuckling over the Julius Martinet piece, I sold the house and moved my wife, three kids, two dogs and basses to Los Angeles.

Chapter Fourteen
Welcome to LA ... Sort of

We had a couple of rude awakenings when we got to L.A. and moved into our rented house in Sherman Oaks that Red had scouted out for us. The first was that the movers demanded a thousand dollars more than the price we'd agreed to back in New Jersey. Too bad, but if I wanted my furniture I'd have to cough up. Or sue, and wait maybe seven years for a court date. I coughed up. The next rude awakening was a few days later when the 1965 L.A. riots occurred. I'd barely gotten the television to work and turned it on when I heard "Kill Whitey!" and I yelled "But I just got here!" As buildings burned in the background, I saw some guys trying to end it for an unlucky truck driver who happened to be passing by. I said to myself, "This is not a good omen."

Fortunately, I remembered that I don't believe in omens, and went about the business of finding bass-playing work, while pursuing my writing dream. Red's quick answer was right. I found work immediately and, as in New York, the opportunities expanded in direct proportion to the amount of time I was in town, and I wasn't going anywhere. Red had done another great thing for me besides finding that geographically - and financially -perfect house and that was he'd put together a list of ten names and phone numbers. It was a group of very successful writers who had some connection to music and that list would be my starting point. Out of Red's Top Ten List three were very helpful: Bill Richmond, Jerry Lewis' screenwriting partner and former drummer with Les Brown, Sheldon Keller, king of sitcoms/pilots and a wannabe jazz bass player, and Bill Larkin, a gifted joke writer on Bob Hope's staff and a former band boy (roadie) with Claude Thornhill's orchestra. They all took me to heart (and some even took me to lunch), listened to my story, showed me scripts, and gave me some valuable advice, and were very supportive and encouraging. Bill Larkin even gave me a place to start.

He and his partner, Mort Lachman, told me about a struggling young comic and part-time waiter named John Barbour who was funny, but who sometimes had questionable material and needed someone grounded (and funny) to bounce things off of. John was always hanging around Bill and Mort's *Bob Hope Show* office begging for jokes or maybe just scraps of food. About the time I came along John got a limited gig at The Playboy Club on the Sunset Strip and Bill suggested that I contact him, catch his act, and see what I could do to help punch it up. So . . . my first assignment as a writer would be for no money, no credit, no pension & welfare, no medical, and never a residual. Perfect!

I went to The Playboy Club, saw John's act and thought he had a lot going for himself. I also thought he shouldn't laugh so loudly at his own jokes, and shouldn't assume that the audience knew him and liked him. It takes decades to be a Jack Benny and just walk onstage to instant applause and love. I also thought he needed someone to bounce things around with, but more importantly to edit some glaring lapses in good taste, even considering it's Sunset Boulevard. I'm telling you these things, but I didn't heap them all on John at the time when we met for coffee after the show. I was just positive about the funny stuff in his act and opined that we could work together to improve it. Which is exactly what we did. We had a lot of laughs along the way and found that we worked together well.

Then John suggested that we write a spec script together. "What's a spec script?" thought I, but even though I hadn't heard the term before I was enthusiastic about the idea of actually writing a script. We picked the funniest new show of the season to tackle, *Get Smart*, and in stolen moments when John wasn't waiting tables or going to auditions and I wasn't playing in saloons on Ventura Boulevard with guys like Bobby Troup, we managed to write a pretty funny episode of *Get Smart*. I'm not sure a copy of that script still exists and if it does, it's probably in a landfill in the Santa Monica Mountains foothills under a golf course slowly creating methane gas. But I remember that it was funny and probably unproduceable, with dirigible crashes, the parting of The Red Sea and other hilarities like that.

We spent endless and useless hours trying to get that script into the hands of Buck Henry, the Story Editor and Co-Creator of *Get Smart*, but it never happened. And, by the way, the last place you'd want a spec script to go is to the staff of the series you decided to write for. And that's because no one knows a show like the people who actually work on it. They would spot a million little flaws that would turn them off instantly. Give your spec script to people who don't know anything at all about the characters or the premise. But John and I, though discouraged and temporarily short of Xerox money, were not about to quit because we both had what it takes to succeed in Hollywood: stubbornness and insensitivity.

John landed a small comedy role in a television pilot that was to be shot at Four Star Productions called *Manley and the Mob*, starring Paul Lynde and produced by Fred De Cordova, legendary producer/director of *Bedtime for Bonzo* and Johnny Carson's *The Tonight Show*. It was a nice, harmless confection that didn't sell, but wasn't harmless to De Cordova, who happened to be on the set during a violent shoot-out sequence and a blank that wasn't quite blank enough sent a wad of cardboard through his cheek that left a scar he lived with for the rest of his distinguished life. But the importance of *Manley and the Mob* to Barbour & Mitchell was that John didn't have to sneak onto the lot (which he was good at) and actually had a pass for each day of employment. Since his role was small, he had lots of free time and managed to look up a couple of producers he knew and talked them into reading our *Get Smart* script. They were Chris Hayward and Allan Burns, two bright writers who came out of the Jay Ward studio (*Rocky & Bullwinkle* ... plenty more about Jay Ward to follow) and were now on their own, writing a pilot for Four Star Productions. Hayward and Burns had created a show called *My Mother The Car*, starring Jerry Van

Dyke, which is widely considered the worst television show ever. Wrong! I happen to have been involved in the worst television show ever, which I co-wrote, a movie for TV, which I'll talk about when we get there. Hint: the name "Gilligan" is in the title.

But Hayward and Burns were now on their way and together, as well as separately, they both had great careers. John's timing was pretty good. He dropped off our *Get Smart* on the way to the set and Hayward and Burns, either undergoing temporary writer's block or just goofing off (I'll vote for goofing off), read it and thought it was funny. Then about ten seconds later their phone rang and it was Rod Amateau, Executive Producer of *My Mother The Car* wanting to know if Hayward and Burns could find the time to write a quick script for the show. NBC had just ordered four more episodes and his staff was far too busy fixing the material that was next in line. Chris and Allan had never written for the show they created, and weren't about to start now, because they had a nice development deal at Four Star. "Well, who can I get?" asked the desperate Mr. Amateau, adding that all he could pay was Writers' Guild minimum scale. Did Hayward and Burns know of any young and hungry writers that would work for scale? And, there, right in front of them, were the names, neatly typed, of two of the youngest and hungriest. So they recommended Barbour and Mitchell, probably so they could get Rod off the phone and get back to goofing off.

We called the *My Mother The Car* show and arranged a pitch meeting about a week away, which would give us a chance to see the show, think up some story ideas and try to sell one of them to Rod Amateau. We saw the show (it was really pretty funny) and came up with two and a half solid notions, and were all set for the pitch meeting ... until John announced he'd accepted a one week stand-up comedy gig at a nightclub in Dubuque, Iowa, and that he'd be on the plane the day of the meeting. That meant I'd have to go in on my own. Well, I told myself, we're born alone and we die alone. So what could be so bad about meeting Rod Amateau alone?

It wasn't so bad at all. I was familiar with and an admirer of Rod's work on *Dobie Gillis*, and was happy to be there. He bought the first idea I pitched, which was a story about someone polishing the title role car while wishing for something and, by coincidence, the wish comes true. Pretty soon the car (voice-over by Ann Sothern) is suspected of having magical properties, *a la* Aladdin and his lamp. The episode was called "When You Wish Upon a Car," and that's absolutely all I can remember about it (lucky for you). But the sale of that silly story was huge.

On the strength of our script sale John and I were now entitled to join The Writers' Guild of America. Once we did that, it was no problem finding representation, the Peter Fleming Agency, and making the rounds of the shows and a whole new world of rejection. To pass the time while waiting for meetings, John and I would play miniature golf, which escalated to pitch-and-putt golf, which escalated to real eighteen-hole golf to which I'm still addicted and, last I heard, so is John.

With Peter Fleming we achieved a measure of acceptance as a team and managed to get on the committee to write that year's Writers Guild Awards Show and meet with Groucho Marx and Hal Kanter and other biggies. Peter was able to get us double scale (which a lot of preferred teams were now getting, including Hayward and Burns) for our next assignment, which was an episode on a one-season show called *The Tammy Grimes Show*. It was on the Twentieth Century-Fox back lot, and it was fun to go to work along with Batman and Robin, The Green Hornet and Darren McGavin with his riverboat gambler show, whatever that was called. And all of this happened within five months of hearing "Kill Whitey!"

John and I continued our partnership and our occasional golf for about a year, working either at his small apartment or my half-a-garage office, and we bumbled along with the help of Peter Fleming and landed a couple of *Gomer Pyle* episodes, but the pace of our writing partnership wasn't keeping up with John's expanding stand-up comic opportunities and my exploding West Coast music career. John made a pile of money many years later co-creating one of the first reality shows to get aired. It was called *Real People*, and I was amused by all the hype and press releases and print media stories about John, which mentioned his year of birth, reportedly eight years after mine. What's amusing is that when we first met we were about the same age.

About this time my parents came to L.A. for a visit to see their long-lost sons and grandchildren and, being from New Jersey, they noticed the wonderful climate right away. Dad had just reached the chronologically correct (according to AT&T) age of retirement and was given his golden parachute (actually a watch and a camera) and told to go away. Now he was an organist and choir director full time. A dream come true. Mom was poking around a real estate office one afternoon asking about home prices, and when asked what hobbies or interests she and her husband had, mentioned that Dad was an organist. Four alarm bells went off in that realty office and Mom soon became the center of attention. Seems Bing Crosby's musical director, organist Buddy Cole, had passed away six months ago and nobody wanted to buy his lovely house in the Valley Village section of North Hollywood because it came with a 40' X 60' soundproofed organ studio complete with a full theatre organ.

That was one pipe organ too many for my dad, but I recommended that they make an offer on the house and studio alone, and let Mrs. Cole sell Buddy's pipe organ separately. That's what eventually happened and my dad, at age sixty-five, sold the Ridgewood, New Jersey house, dismantled and packed his entire classical pipe organ (one of the largest home installations in the world) into three moving vans, and moved his pipe organ to North Hollywood. It would be easier moving the city of Cleveland. Now he had to spend the next three years of his life working intensively getting it together and playable again. The good news: he enjoyed playing it for the rest of his life, which turned out to be another twenty-two years.

One day in 1966 epitomized my exploding music career and turned out to be a life-changing event. It started in the morning with a picture call (movie scoring) at MGM with a huge orchestra that included six or seven classical bassists (a lot of pressure . . . thank God for Homer Mensch) from 8:00 a.m. until noon, then a musical jingle recording session from 1:00 p.m. until 2:00 p.m., followed by a record date with Patty Duke from 3:00 p.m. until 6:00 p.m., followed by a shower and dinner at home, then an evening of jazz music at Ye Little Club in Beverly Hills with great jazz pianist (and former Ella Fitzgerald accompanist) Don Abney, who I'd met on Jazz at the Philharmonic. As good as the music was that was a long evening at the end of a ridiculously long day. When I staggered into bed around 3:00 a.m., having consumed maybe five packs of cigarettes during that marathon, I began having trouble breathing and was soon having pains in my chest and gasping for air. I'd inadvertently given myself a big dose of aversion therapy, although I'd never heard of it at the time. Here I was, choking, gasping and worried that I'd stop breathing altogether, and for the first time in my life I confronted my addiction. There was plenty of evidence in 1966 that smoking was linked to cardiovascular problems, lung cancer and other life-shortening catastrophes, and I decided with what seemed like my last breath that this would be a great time to quit a disgusting habit I'd had since age fourteen and my first gig as a musician.

So, between gasps, I said aloud words I'd never before spoken or even thought about: "I'm going to quit smoking!" and the voice at the other side of the bed said the perfect thing: "I've heard <u>that</u> before," thus assuring that I had more than enough motivation to quit cold turkey. Haven't had a cigarette since.

John began to get better and better gigs and so did I. More picture calls, more television scoring sessions, more jingles, recording sessions and classier work, including playing with the great Les Brown band, doing colleges and all the Bob Hope Specials on NBC. I didn't know at the time that a few years later I'd be working on the same show, but as a Hope writer. And the more gigs that came along for me, the more out-of-town comedy club offers came along for John. It became a struggle for us to find the time to work together or even communicate regularly as our two careers expanded in opposite directions. So we ended our partnership amicably, about the same time that my marriage ended not quite so amicably. The who, what, where, and why of that divorce will have to wait for my next book, which I'm never going to write. All I know is I was blindsided and suddenly single, broke, and unable to live with my three adorable children, and it left a huge hole in my life and in my heart. But nature abhors a vacuum, and what poured into my life helped fill the void: my writing career took off like a Space Shuttle…after several delays on the launch pad.

Chapter Fifteen
New Career . . . Bye-Bye-Bassist

When I left my house in Sherman Oaks more or less suddenly with my bass, my typewriter, my golf clubs and little else, I realized I had to have someplace to go and a tent in Griffith Park probably wouldn't have looked good on my resume. I remembered that my parents' housekeeper had recently left and her room adjoining the kitchen with its own bathroom and entrance might be available temporarily until my finances improved and I found my own apartment. And when I got there, just as it had happened on the worst/best day of my life, my mother was actually expecting me. I've always had two viable theories about Mom. Either she had outrageous extrasensory perception . . . or she was just nuts.

So the good news was, I was made to feel welcome, I had a roof over my head that included a built-in support group. But I was thirty-five years old and unexpectedly had myself and another household to support, a new car to pay off, family counseling people to pay off, charge accounts, legal fees, child support and alimony, and really needed to generate some steady income. *The Bob Hope Show* had ended for the season, and Les Brown was only doing two or three gigs per month. Not enough to live on.

Allen Goodman to the rescue! He was a drummer I knew who was working with a very gifted pianist/entertainer/arranger/composer named Stan Worth, who was a workaholic and the busiest guy in his category in L.A. I'd subbed with the group before and now there was an opening. Besides having a steady gig in a popular Ventura Boulevard restaurant called The Ruddy Duck, Stan was about to start a local music/variety television show and do some jingles and other recordings. Allen asked if I'd be interested in joining the group. You bet!

Allen Goodman now lives in Palm Springs and we see each other regularly, sometimes on the same bandstand, and if he spent the rest of his life doing terrible things to me (which he wouldn't) he'd still be my hero and I'd still be grateful, because that gig with Stan Worth saved my life. I had a decent income and could stay with my parents until I was on my feet again. Their house had a big pool and was perfect for hosting and entertaining my kids on weekends and that's where they all learned to swim. I'm grateful for that and I have wonderful memories of how helpful my folks were to my kids and me.

The local television show happened as promised, and that was extra bucks and a chance to keep my writing chops alive, because I regularly wrote jokes for the show. The only thing missing was a way to restart my prime-time writing career. Chris Hayward to the rescue! Again!

But first we have to talk about Jay Ward.

Jay Ward, a fifty-something potato dumpling of a man with the brain of an uninhibited eight-year-old child, had created wonderful sophisticated hip cartoons which people are still talking about today. *Rocky & Bullwinkle, Crusader Rabbit, George of the Jungle,* and *Super-Chicken* are a few that come to mind. He had a stable of wonderfully funny not-quite-mature writers working for him in the late sixties at his studio on the Sunset Strip, right next to the giant rotating Bullwinkle statue. The studio boasted a building full of clever funny cartoonists as well as a snow cone machine, a giant fresh-buttered popcorn cart, a steam calliope, many large stuffed cartoon animals, and a roomful of Kit-Kats, Mars Bars, and cokes. Jay was not exactly a health nut. He didn't pay his writers very well and his rationale was "Why do you need money? You live like a millionaire!" And he was almost right. He'd take them to Pebble Beach for golf, Del Mar for the races, or a quick trip to Mexico for fishing. Jay usually dressed in a rumpled sweater, cheap unpressed slacks, and sneakers and looked about as tidy as an unmade cot at the Rescue Mission.

He had a thing for sugar, never drank alcoholic beverages (although it was okay for other people) and never cursed or swore or used offensive language. The worst thing I ever heard him say, when describing the CEOs of a cut-throat company that had just cheated him out of perhaps millions, was "Oh! Those are dirty guys!"

And out of this collection of near-loonies came my new writing partner, Chris Hayward's friend and former Jay Ward co-worker, Lloyd Turner. Lloyd, eight years my senior, was looking to break into prime-time television writing like his buddies Chris Hayward and Allan Burns had, and I was looking for more than the four or five scripts I'd sold so far. So we were both motivated.

One of the unexpected benefits of working with Lloyd was that I quickly became an unofficial Jay Ward loony and was invited to lots of golf games at Riviera and other exclusive clubs, plenty of lunches at L.A.'s trendiest restaurants, parties at the office and occasional trips to the racetrack to cheer on Jay's (mostly losing) string of expensive thoroughbred horses of the famed Bullwinkle Stables. I actually got to stand in the Winner's Circle once with Jay and the other guys and in those encounters with Jay actually was living like a millionaire. The only work I had to do for this largesse was help Lloyd think of a funny, worthless Christmas present for Jay every holiday season. Jay hated a real present, and once had been given a clam steamer by a new writer who didn't know the rules. No reaction from Jay and no talk ever about the clam steamer. Years later when another new recruit gave Jay a nice sweater and never saw him wear it, he asked about the sweater. Jay responded, "I keep it in the clam steamer." But Lloyd's presents were the worst and the best and I was proud to become part of that tradition. Once on a golf course he and I gathered up as many little green rabbit droppings as we could find, carefully packaged them, and they became a part of Jay's next gift, a huge box which was labeled: "Caution! CONTAINS GENUINE LIVE EASTER BUNNY!" Inside was a silly-looking nest with no bunny, but lots of droppings and a small note: "Well, he was here a minute ago…" The smile on Jay's face told Lloyd he'd struck gold again, which was reinforced by Jay's next statement: "Ol' Lloyd-boy's a bum!"

A New Career... Bye-Bye-Bassist 115

Picketing Jay Ward who then took us to some expensive place for lunch.

And where was my older brother Red during all this? Very remote. He lived in a charming old Mediterranean-style house in the Los Feliz section of the Hollywood Hills, miles from my digs in the San Fernando Valley. My dream of moving to the West Coast and getting closer to my brother didn't work out. You couldn't just drop in on Red if you were in the neighborhood or if you might just be nearby in half an hour. The gate was locked and there was no response if you tried to use the intercom. You had to have an invitation, and they just weren't being issued. Looking back, there were probably a couple of things contributing to that self-imposed isolation that I wasn't aware of at the time. The first was that he seemed to want to spend every waking moment (and there weren't many of those during daytime) playing music, practicing, working on sound equipment, whatever. He was obsessed with playing jazz and, little by little, let his studio playing go by the wayside, as well as his marriage.

The other thing was drugs. Red was for them and used many kinds over the years, including alcohol, and he knew I wasn't ever a big fan of getting high. It's been my observation that people who include drugs in their lifestyle are uncomfortable hanging out with those who plainly don't and, in their paranoia, they might think that the non-users are violently anti-drug and are probably snitches for the DEA. If that's what Red thought of me, he couldn't have been more wrong. I'm not anti-drugs. I'm anti-drugs *for me*. But if other people want to do drugs or stick pins in their eyes or beans up their nose it's none of my business, as long as they don't hurt their neighbors or get behind the wheel of a car while stoned. I happen to think our current War on Drugs was lost years ago for all the same reasons as our previous War on Drugs, which was called Prohibition. But that's another book.

All I know is Red's withdrawal from the family was especially hurtful to me, and it culminated in his plan to change his life. He declared America a right-wing fascist police state and moved to Sweden for the rest of his life. He left his current wife and his current debts and went to the country that had treated him like a visiting rock star years earlier when he'd performed there with people like Gerry Mulligan, Red Norvo, and Billie Holiday. In my relationship with my brother I was a slow learner, but that exodus to Sweden convinced me it was time to stop pursuing Red and get on with my own life, which seemed to be better in focus from then on.

Lloyd and I really hit it off. He had a wonderful cartoon-like way of looking at things which I hope I've absorbed by osmosis, and we both had brother issues. As unsatisfactory as my dealings with Red had become, they weren't as bad as Lloyd's relationship with his younger brother, who he considered a ne'er-do-well as well as a constant pain in the ass. So we became sort of surrogate brothers as well as writing partners and both of us were grateful that Chris Hayward had thought to team us up. We worked together at odd moments coming up with concepts, comparing notes about where we could go to pitch ideas. These working hours were usually after Lloyd got home from the Jay Ward place and before I had to go play with Stan Worth at The Ruddy Duck. Finally, there was some light at the end of the tunnel.

We were invited to pitch ideas to the new producers of *Get Smart*, then in its fourth season. We rang the bell with a show about temporary invisibility called, not too surprisingly, "One Nation Invisible," and the episode turned out to be very funny, with lots of comedy shtick for the star, always a winning formula. Asked to come up with something else right away, we responded with a spoof of *Ironside*, a popular detective show of the day. Of course we called it "Leadside," and once again there was lots of physical comedy for Don Adams to get his teeth into. The producers were delighted and promised us a lot of work if the show got picked up for a fifth year. But NBC, in its infinite wisdom, took *Get Smart* off the schedule and we thought we were headed back to square one.

CBS to the rescue! CBS picked up *Get Smart* and the show moved to their Radford Avenue studio in Studio City, an old-fashioned movie lot, formerly the home of Republic Pictures as well as Monogram. The producers, as promised, gave us lots of work. They hired us as Story Editors and our contract included writing eight original episodes, as well as working on everybody else's scripts, at least the ones that came in the front door. What they neglected to tell us, which we found out at the end of the season, was that we also had to completely rewrite a script that came in the back door from a Don Adams family member that was totally unusable. Not a word, not a joke could be salvaged. In other words, write a script for free. Note to The Writers' Guild of America: the statute of limitations has long since passed.

But we were thrilled to have a staff job on such a prestigious show. It meant that Lloyd had to say bye-bye to Jay Ward and the cartoon asylum, and that he'd still continue to live like a millionaire (and so would I) but he would no longer be writing *Super-Chicken* or Kellogg's Cap'n Crunch ads, and could go to the bank each week with a check he wasn't ashamed of.

I had to give up working with Stan Worth, which turned out to be much easier than anyone could have imagined. Stan, with all his good attributes, most of them musical, was a very controlling kind of guy who wanted to be in charge of everything, including the lives of his sidemen. When Lloyd and I were working on that first *Get Smart* assignment, I happened to mention it to Stan and I could tell he hated the news. All of a sudden there were lots of daytime rehearsals, after-the-gig rehearsals, and auditions for non-existent gigs. I learned my lesson and never mentioned another script assignment again. While working as a Story Editor on the CBS lot, I still continued to work for Stan doing the *Lohman & Barkley Show* every Sunday on KNBC, an early version of *Laugh-In*. Stan was busy all week long preparing music and had no way of knowing I was writing television scripts Monday through Friday. I'd just waltz into NBC Sunday morning with my hated electric bass, rehearse all day long with Stan's nine-piece band, do the show live on Sunday night, go home and prepare for another week of *Get Smart*. This double-dipping went on for a few months until Stan called me and said that we had a recording session the following Wednesday at eleven and I had to tell him I couldn't make it.

"Why not?"

"Because I'm a staff writer on *Get Smart*."

"I'll call you back!"

About two minutes later the phone rang. "I got a bass player. You're off the band!"

Click!

See how easy that was? I lost a couple of other nice gigs too, when I switched careers, including an upcoming album with Lena Horne, but life isn't perfect. I was still Whitey Mitchell in those days and Lloyd thought that didn't look right on the screen, like Buddy or Stumpy or Porky, and would I consider using my real name? And I thought since I'm now giving up music, for who-knows-how-long, why not separate the two careers by becoming Gordon again? Everyone new I'd meet would call me by that name, and I'd retrain my old friends to start calling me Gordon. In golf, it became a two-stroke penalty to say Whitey. So I expanded into my new occupation as Gordon, and if the phone rang and someone asked for Whitey, I'd know it was a bar mitzvah or something else I no longer wanted to be involved in, and hang up. I sold or gave away all my basses and amps and didn't do music except at parties for maybe twenty-five years, and re-invented myself as screenwriter Gordon Mitchell. And Gordon Mitchell was able to move into a nice apartment in Sherman Oaks.

I loved that season on *Get Smart*. We delivered all eight scripts, plus the illegal one we won't talk about again, worked on every other script that came down the pike from outside writers and received a Writers' Guild nomination for Best Comedy Script for an episode called "The Apes of Rath." At the time I remember thinking, "What's so tough about becoming an award-winning screenwriter?" Not so fast, Mitchell!

One other fun thing from that year involved Executive Producer Leonard Stern's buddy Charlton Heston, who happened to have an office on the top floor of our building. Charlton was then in the middle of a long run as President of the Screen Actor's Guild, and every year Leonard (a great comedy writer) would "punch up" Charlton's State of the Guild speech at their annual Awards Dinner. But this year Leonard was going to be in New York, and the assignment to help make Charlton Heston funny trickled all the way down to the Story Editors. So we were given a copy of his speech and spent an afternoon on the project, added quite a few jokes and a funny attitude here and there, sent the altered script upstairs and forgot about it. About two weeks later we were invited upstairs to Heston's office and had a delightful meeting with him, which included coffee and a check for a hundred dollars apiece. Charlton was extremely amused at Lloyd's story about how his toupee had caught fire in his apartment kitchen that morning (I wonder why) and had to hear it over and over again. When our jovial visit was over, he asked what we were doing that weekend. I mentioned that I was planning to take my girlfriend with me to Palm Springs for a brainless fun-in-the-sun getaway. He asked where we'd be staying and I said I didn't know, but that we'd make it up as we went along. I was amazed at his response, which was: "I'm so jealous. I can't ever do that." I don't know if he was referring to his celebrity which would prevent an impromptu trip to the desert, or the fact that he was a married man, and we left before I found out.

Early on I realized that coming up with interesting stories was by far the hardest part of writing, and there are just so many stories from your personal life that you could use, or would even want to use. So I'd collect odd stories from the newspapers that might lead to episode ideas, including those little "space fillers" that get into newspapers for no other reason than to fill an otherwise uneven column of print. Apparently, newspapers abhor a vacuum too. I'd clip these tidbits out and drop them into a big manila envelope to scrounge through whenever sitcom story-pitching time came along. One little item was about a nine-year-old kid who got his draft notice because the local Selective Service Office misplaced a decimal point and thought he was nineteen. When *Get Smart* folded up shop for good, Lloyd and I got a chance to pitch to the brand-new *Doris Day Show*. The premise that first year (it changed every season and they never got it right) involved Doris' nine-year-old son named Toby, and without much effort we came up with "Toby Gets Drafted," about a nine-year-old kid who gets drafted by mistake. But we pitched it to the seemingly deaf ears of an unimaginative Story Editor who quickly shot it down with "They take one look at him and you got no Act Two." We put "Toby Gets Drafted" back into the large manila envelope and came up with another space filler for *The Doris Day Show*.

Not too much later we were invited to see the pilot of a new sitcom about a contemporary musical family on the road, and there was a nine-year-old kid in that show too. Rather than waste an entire morning working, we went golfing, and on the way to the golf course changed "Toby Gets Drafted" into "Danny Gets Drafted." That's how great minds work. We went in and pitched, they loved it, and it became the first of an eventual eleven episodes of *The Partridge Family* that we'd write. And, by the way, there *was* an Act Two. A very funny Act Two. Danny showed up for induction and made it all the way to the final swearing in before anybody noticed his little pink legs and high squeaky voice.

Chapter Sixteen
Mary Tyler Moore, Bob Hope and Beyond

The closest I ever got to actually working for Jay Ward was back in my Stan Worth years when I was part of the studio orchestra that recorded "It's So Nice to Be a Moose" (or something like that). But if that didn't entitle me to be a part of the Bullwinkle Entourage, being Lloyd's partner did, even though I was the guy who took away Jay's favorite writer. But to know Jay was to love Jay and hang around him as much as you could, and all of his writers/performers/cartoonists kept coming back to the womb, I mean the studio, long after they were employed there.

Through Jay Ward alumnus Allan Burns, we learned of a pilot he'd created with his new partner writer/director James L. Brooks called *The Mary Tyler Moore Show*, and Lloyd and I were invited to the taping. The pilot, of course, was brilliant, and a series was soon ordered, in spite of the demographics people who claimed it was the worst pilot ever tested. So much for demographics people. When the show got into production, Turner and Mitchell were invited to pitch episode ideas and the first idea we came up with interested them. On the set of *Get Smart* we'd watched with amusement as Barbara Feldon, Agent 99, stood around on her ankles or in a trench trying to look shorter or at least of similar height when next to Maxwell Smart, series star Don Adams, who was altitude challenged.

We thought this might give Mary a little physical comedy to work on if she were in a like situation, so we devised a story about her filling in for her station's regular talk show guy and interviewing Eric Matthews, an author on a book tour. The two of them are seated on the panel and, during breaks a little flirting goes on, with the good-looking author inviting Mary on a date, which she eagerly accepts. When the show is over and they both stand up, Eric is a full head shorter than Mary, who immediately slumps downward, and her embarrassment begins as she refuses to think of herself as a height bigot. She spends the rest of the episode falling all over herself trying not to make references to shortness while trying to make herself appear physically smaller, and make herself believe that height doesn't count. As an example of my theory that there are really only eight or nine jokes, and that every joke you ever hear is a relative of one of those prototypes, I'll mention our big joke at the Act Break and trace its ancestry.

One of my dad's favorite jokes was about a British couple who had aspirations of moving upward in high society, and one of their moves was to invite Lord Huffington to tea. His Lordship had an outrageously large nose and the woman became fearful that her young children might point at it, or say something honest and cruel about the huge proboscis so she arranged for them to be all ready for their nap by the time His Lordship arrived. Then a quick "bye-bye" and they'd be whisked away. When Lord Huffington arrived, his nose was even bigger and rosier than they'd remembered, and the children just stared at it, but managed a quick hello-goodbye before being taken away by the Nanny. The immensely relieved woman said, "And now, Lord Huffington, do you take lemon or cream with your nose?"

When we were looking for the obligatory Big Joke at the end of Act One, Lord Huffington (or a close relative) made another appearance. Mary was anxiously trying to get rid of her yenta neighbor Rhoda before her short escort showed up, and Rhoda protested, saying, "You think I'd do something stupid like calling him a shrimp?" and Mary tried to push her out saying something like "that's exactly what I was thinking." Just then the short guy enters and Mary is forced to introduce him to Rhoda, saying, "Eric, this is my neighbor, Rhoda. Rhoda, I'd like you to meet Eric Shrimp." The joke worked just as well in the seventies as it had in the forties. That episode was entitled "Toulouse Lautrec Was One of My Favorite

Artists," and it won an Emmy, not for us, but for Director Jay Sandrich, whose acceptance speech went something like: "I'd like to thank Mary and a great cast, our producers, all the folks at MTM and CBS, the wardrobe lady, the set decorator, the caterer, the teamsters, and . . . well, I guess that's about it."

With the acceptance we got from Burns and Brooks for that script, we could have done more MTM shows and possibly gotten a staff job, but we were being wooed by Mort Lachman, now Head Writer/Producer of *The Bob Hope Show*, to join his writing staff at a very good salary. We thought, in our vanity, that it was not just because they needed two more guys to write jokes. They already had plenty of joke writers. But because the sketches on the *Hope Show* were so notoriously poor, we hoped that that would be the place where we could really make a difference. Besides, Mort promised we'd have security for a year, and it would be like being at a country club. He was right, but he forgot to finish the sentence. "It would be like being at a country club . . . in the kitchen, washing potatoes and peeling onions." They actually wanted us because Hope was to do eight specials for NBC that season and they just wanted the insurance of two more bodies grinding out jokes every day.

In addition to the NBC Specials, which were scattered through the season and were only a few days work, the real job, disappointing to us, was to write jokes for the dais at whatever dinner venue in whatever part of the world Mr. Hope would be appearing. In other words, writing jokes for people, you'd never heard of that you would never hear performed. Kind of like playing golf in total fog. There weren't cell phones in 1970 or pagers or even answering machines, so the Hope office needed the phone numbers of the writers' home, golf course, girlfriend, favorite bar, restaurant, or bookie joint, whatever applied, and most of those did in my case.

Lloyd and I would work one week at his apartment in Studio City and one week at mine in Sherman Oaks. A call would come from Mort or his secretary around eleven o'clock or so (no time to sneak in nine holes of golf or a movie before then) with the topics of the day. There were usually about eight or more, but seldom less than eight. Some of the topics repeated day after day, and some were new, and for each topic each team (working independently and scattered all over L.A.) was supposed to come up with ten jokes. That's a minimum of eighty jokes! As I've theorized, there are really only eight or nine jokes, so if you've ever wondered why *The Bob Hope Show* seemed to rely on formula jokes that you think you've heard before, you're right ... you *have* heard them before. Coming up with that many jokes every day was like working on a chain gang smashing rocks, only tougher. At the end of the day we'd take the jokes (one joke per page in large capital letters) either to "the office," meaning Mort's office, or "over the wall," meaning to Hope's house on Moorpark Street in Toluca Lake, where a butler would emerge, pick up the jokes wordlessly, then disappear back into the mansion, and the gate would slam shut electronically.

Sometimes, Hope wanted to work at home for the next special, and one particularly hot night in Toluca Lake he gathered Mort and the staff into his backyard, seated around a big table. After a while, Hope, noticeably sweating, complained, "Boy, it's hot. I mean, *really* hot. Isn't it, fellas?" Some mumbling, "Yeah, Bob, it's hot." After a beat Hope had a thought: "Ice cream! Ice cream, fellas?" More mumbling, this time with a little more enthusiasm. "Yeah, Bob ... ice cream." Hope stroked his chin, deep in thought: "Hmmmm. Peach! Peach ice cream, fellas?" Now there was definite interest and even enthusiasm: "Yeah, Bob ... peach!" Hope whispered something into an intercom and work resumed. A few minutes later his butler emerged from the mansion and walked over, carrying silver service, which included a large bowl of peach ice cream ... for Bob. "Now, where were we?" And work resumed, as Bob consumed.

There were a few other code words that we needed to know besides "over the wall" and "in the office." One was NAFT (need a few things), which was an S.O.S. from Bob, somewhere in the world, for emergency jokes about breaking news like whales beaching themselves and dying on San Clemente Island or a killer tsunami in Asia, and there aren't any jokes for either category. But when an NAFT came in you were expected to stop doing what you were doing, even if it was just sleeping in your own bed at night, and go to work and come up with jokes.

Another code phrase was "Crumbs for the Bear," which came from the older writers and dated back to *The Ed Sullivan Show* and the famous skating bears. Breaking news: bears hate to skate. But once the skates are on and they're pushed out onto the ice, what else can they do? So the trick is to get the skates on your bear, by distracting him with handfuls of cookie crumbs, and while he's enjoying these, you can easily slap on those skates. How does this relate to Bob Hope? On an especially weak show in which none of the sketches are working, and a major page one rewrite is obviously needed, you can always distract Hope with an extra flood of cookie crumbs, I mean monologue jokes, and while he's lapping these up, there will be no mention of an all-night rewrite. It worked every time.

Bill Larkin, Mort Lachman's former partner, couldn't understand why Mort and Bob got along so well. Part of the explanation has to be golf. Mort loves golf beyond reason and with Bob, he got to play with Presidents, Kings, Emperors, and even Arnold Palmer, who represented golf royalty. In fact, part of his job was to play golf with Bob every afternoon they were in town. About three o'clock the phone would ring, Mort would answer and there'd be a one word command: "Now!" which meant close up the office and go to nearby Lakeside Country Club and suit up. They'd play for two dollars per hole, unless they were only playing nine, in which case it'd be four dollars per hole. Bob was by far the better golfer and would win just about every day. But Mort wasn't allowed to pay off on the eighteenth green. Oh, no, it had to be in the clubhouse bar in front of witnesses. To this day, Mort has nothing but good feelings for the guy. But Bill couldn't warm up to him, figuring that Hope just wanted more. More money, more monologue jokes, more women, more golf, more acreage in the San Fernando Valley, more of everything. Bill openly referred to him as "Piggy" and actively sought out ways to get his goat.

Hope and the writers would hold a "golf meeting," a working session in Hope's huge den which took place as Bob pitched golf balls from a giant pile on one side of the room into a large waste basket on the other, which he was pretty good at it. The stack of golf balls, perhaps a thousand or so, all donated to Hope by Titleist golf balls, the number one golf ball in the world, was seemingly inexhaustible and the work continued until Bob was tired of pitching golf balls and declared the meeting over. At the meeting in question, Bill Larkin started juggling a single golf ball absent-mindedly, just by throwing it straight up in the air and then catching it and when the meeting was over, he casually tossed the ball one more time, then slipped it into the side pocket of his coat and Bob noticed. As everyone filed out, Bob whispered to him:

"You mind putting the ball back, Bill?"

"What ball?"

"My ball!"

"I don't have your ball, Bob."

"Goddammit, it's not the ball, it's the principle of the thing, Bill. You took my ball."

"I didn't."

"Did!"

"Didn't!"...

And with that, Hope reached into Bill's pocket and pulled out a golf ball ... clearly marked PROPERTY OF BILL LARKIN. Bill was an amazing joke writer, mechanically gifted, did a wonderful impression of Art Carney, and was an interesting human being. One of his little-known accomplishments was his ability to make that disgusting knuckle-cracking sound some people make by stretching their fingers until they pop. But Bill was able to make that sound just by manipulating his big toe within his shoe so that no one could ever tell where that scrunchy sound was coming from. One day as Hope was taking the writers through his solarium and bragging about his new parquet floor with wood imported from Italy, which was installed by a local artisan, Bill walked around approvingly, stepped on a couple of squares and made that scrunchy sound. Bob asked, "What was that?"

"What was what?"

"That sound!"

"I didn't hear anything, Bob."

Then he scrunched again, this time in a different place.

Hope became livid. "That sonofabitch! He promised me he knew how to install Italian parquet!"

And Bill threw a little gasoline on the fire. "I think he fucked you, Bob."

A nearly apoplectic Hope followed Bill around making chalk marks on each offending square.

Weeks later at another meeting in the solarium Bob said, "I made that sonofabitch do the floor again!"

And Bill walked around noiselessly, nodded and said, "And he did a good job, too. It's perfect!" And then he scrunched again.

But when he wasn't being upset by one of Bill Larkin's cruel jokes, Bob was really in his element delivering monologue jokes, especially when overseas entertaining the troops at remote locations near the front lines. The formula was always the same. Before coming to a particular venue for a show, Mort would send in a team of writers who would scout out the local topics: who was the C.O.? Who was the equivalent of the village idiot? What was the absolute worst thing about that location? What rules needed to be made fun of? When unmilitary Hope would saunter onstage with his three wood rakishly riding on one shoulder and deliver his standard proven jokes they would be salted with as many of these topical references as the guys could dig up and the G.I.s would go wild. Mort told me about one show in Vietnam where everything just clicked, the guys were laughing so hard they peed in their pants and as Hope was winding up, they gave him a standing ovation. With the laughter and the applause still echoing through the jungle, Hope came offstage beaming. Mort was nearby and Bob came right up to him and said, "I bet you think it's you!" and Mort replied, "I bet you're afraid to find out." And, for about thirty years he was.

When NBC cancelled the last four of Hope's projected specials for the season, we were off the hook, and quietly worked out the rest of our contract, anxious to get back to actual writing again. Which we quickly did, but it was as if we'd been in a Tibetan monastery for about a year.

Chapter Seventeen
Love & Marriage . . . This Time for Real

After Bob Hope there was barely a letdown for Turner & Mitchell and we no longer needed any miracle help from Chris Hayward, and it's a good thing. At one time he was Lloyd's best friend, partner, drinking buddy, golfing buddy, and womanizing buddy, but their relationship at first cooled, then went completely south. Chris had always been very friendly to me and a fan of my musicianship, and was instrumental in pointing the way to my first script assignment. Not only that he was the guy who put Lloyd and me together and we succeeded beyond our dreams. Apparently, a little beyond Chris' dreams, too, and his enthusiasm for us dampened noticeably. And then there was some fight between him and Lloyd that ended their relationship and either I can't remember what that was or I never knew, but something tells me that alcohol was involved. Whatever. I'm eternally grateful to Chris Hayward, a very bright and funny man, for his help and guidance and I was sad to read that he'd passed away several months ago.

Lloyd and I were invited to pitch to a new show called *Love, American Style*, an anthology show with no regular cast or repeating characters, just contemporary love stories of varied lengths. It was an idea whose time had come and writing for it was like making your own little short film, so we were attracted to the idea. Out from the manila envelope of saved clippings and snippets came a space filler about a guy who kept marrying women that he met. He wasn't a con man after their money, he was just a guy who loved women and couldn't bear to say "no" when the subject of marriage came up. He didn't look like a Hollywood gigolo and, on the contrary, was short and ordinary looking. But apparently very attractive to women who couldn't resist him and fell in love with him. When his multiple trips down the aisle came to light none of his wives wanted to press charges. We thought it would make a perfect *Love, American Style*, and we had an actor in mind to play the anti-hero and it was Henry Gibson, who'd played a similar character named Simon the Likeable on a *Get Smart* episode. It's easier to write a character if you have a definite image of him in your mind.

The pitch meeting was one of the worst in my entire career. Both alleged producers were constantly answering the phone and shushing us, had their feet on their desks, and one of them was eating sunflower seeds and spitting the shells in the general direction of the wastebasket, while pretending to be listening. I've recreated this scene in a play I've written and am trying to get off the ground, and I can't wait to see it on its feet. Somehow, although the producers couldn't have cared less or listened less, they got the gist of the story and we went to script. The script just sat there after it was turned in, and they never got around to producing that episode that entire season. A year later, the new producer discovered it, filmed it, and even cast Henry Gibson as the lovable bigamist, and it turned out just the way we pictured it would.

Meanwhile, on the personal home front, my three kids seemed to me to be in a good place. Fifteen-year-old Lesley was beginning to get the acting bug, which was her passion for many years. Thirteen-year-old Brian was beginning to toot a clarinet, a first step toward what became his career as a brilliant saxophonist who toured with Ray Charles, Mel Torme and other bands, starting at age eighteen. Ten-year-old Karen was growing up beautifully and, like her siblings, showed signs of musical ability. They'd all moved with their Mom and step-dad about forty miles northwest of Sherman Oaks to Camarillo. My only knowledge of Camarillo was that it was once the site of a well-known mental institution and a place where hopeless junkies would find themselves incarcerated, including the famous

Charlie "Yardbird" Parker. But now Camarillo had a golf course and lots of new homes and I'd drive out there to pick up the kids for weekend visits. As my career went onward and upward I'd arrive in better and better cars and we'd go to better and better places, such as Sea World, Magic Mountain, Disneyland, a helicopter ride, a goldmine, Knott's Berry Farm, Calico Ghost Town and other Southern California destinations. At the end of the visit during the forty-five-minute ride from Sherman Oaks to Camarillo, we'd play a sadistic version of *Name That Tune,* in which you had to figure out what tune was being sung by whoever was "it" by hearing one note at a time, totally out of meter. (I'd had more experience at this, having worked with Eddie Fisher.) I remember this era fondly because I really enjoyed being able to treat the kids to nice things, and also I wasn't so mature that I didn't enjoy driving up to their house in a brand-new sports sedan once in a while and watching the reaction from the ex.

For a team of comedy writers it's a sign that you've arrived when producers start calling up with offers of involvement in some sure-fire pilot or movie. And it's an even better sign if they bring an actual check instead of a lot of talk about a very generous back-end deal, but we weren't quite there yet. So when veteran producer Lew Gallo approached us with his project, we decided to get involved. Former actor and fun golfer, Lew was one of the most popular guys around and he had an interesting idea for a series, but it needed to be fleshed out and he had no pretensions of being a writer. We had some nice working sessions with him because:

1. He was so much fun to be around.
2. We thought his idea had comedy potential.
3. He promised that he and Frank Barton, Mr. CBS at the time, were very close and that he could get a series commitment out of Frank if only we'd go through the formality of a pitch meeting.

Not bad! So we had some nice lunches with Lew that didn't interfere with whatever else we were doing at the time, kicked his idea into a funnier direction, and said we'd be happy to go to CBS with him whenever he could arrange it. The meeting was set up quickly, which we thought was a good sign, and we all met at CBS.

After keeping us waiting far too long, we were ushered into the inner sanctum, Frank Barton's office, with a very nervous, sweating, and suddenly choking and coughing Lew Gallo. What seemed like about a dozen gnome-like un-introduced people appeared and entered the room with us, most of them armed with pad and pencil. The room was unlit except that the north wall facing Beverly Boulevard, which was all glass, allowed the bright sunlight to stream through. Frank's desk, on a raised platform, *a la* Mussolini, was right up against the glass wall, which means that he was backlit and we would have no eye contact with him. And as if to make sure of that, he was wearing dark shades. He was also smoking and affected a foot-long cigarette holder. When we settled down in our pecking order, Lew, Gordon, and Lloyd on one side of the room and gnome-like people on the other, Frank opened the meeting not by saying hello, or chit-chatting with his "close friend" Lew, or by meeting the writers who would be involved in this sure-fire series. He simply growled, "What've you got, Lew?" and Lew started out "We have this idea" … followed by a paroxysm of coughing, hacking, and throat-clearing. He started again. "We think it would be funny…" Another loud coughing fit and hacking noises, then, "Tell him, Gordon …" So the not-so-long-ago bass player had to pitch to Mr. CBS.

My voice was a little squeaky and nervous too but, without coughing, I was able to come up with: "We have a small-town couple with kids. The wife, upset with City Hall, runs for Mayor and unexpectedly gets elected. This means the dad…" Frank cut me off right there: "If I hear another fucking role-reversal idea I'm going to puke!" Lew quickly said, "Thank you, Frank," and we all filed out. Total length of meeting: two minutes forty-two seconds.

If you live in Los Angeles for any length of time you're going to experience an earthquake or two and there was a biggie on February 9, 1971 called The Sylmar Quake, which affected the northern San Fernando Valley. It's easy for me to remember the date because it happened on Lesley's fifteenth birthday. It was a serious quake with many fatalities and significant destruction, and the epicenter was not that far from my Sherman Oaks apartment building, which sustained no damage. It was a typical Valley apartment building, two stories built around a quadrangle, which had the usual swimming pool and community recreation room. My apartment was on the second floor, and when the quake hit, the building seemed to be made of Jell-o. It wobbled, it rolled, it moaned and groaned, and did some snap, crackle and pop, but nothing ruptured, which is a tribute to green wood and cheap dry wall construction in favor these days. Nothing fell in my pad and I couldn't see any damage, but I knew that somewhere the story would be different. That's what's great about earthquakes . . . by the time you know what's going on, you've already survived. I heard a lot of yelling and screaming and commotion outside, so I went out onto the balcony overlooking the quadrangle and I could see a lot of scared people huddling together near the pool, which now had tidal waves lapping over the edges. I remembered a line from a movie called *The Twelve Chairs* that was spoken by a thoroughly corrupt defrocked priest who had just been busted for some act of degradation and I thought it would work great right then and there and "borrowed" it. Looking heavenward I called out plaintively, "Oh, God, you're so strict!" The huddled people laughed and some of them pointed in my direction and said, "He's a comedy writer, you know" and, thirty-six years later, I'd like to belatedly give credit for that joke to its author . . . Mel Brooks.

My divorce was now four years old, my kids seemed to have accepted their changed circumstances pretty well, and I was having a certain amount of financial independence. I was enjoying being a thirty-nine-year-old bachelor and I wanted to find out just how young I could go, dating wise. I found out quick by taking a ravishing twenty-one-year-old starlet to the Aware Inn in Sherman Oaks, a sexy restaurant if there ever was one. The candle lit ambience was really conducive to intimacy and I think they were putting some stuff in the homemade bran muffins. Over a glass of wine Miss Lovely and I were getting to flirt and know each other better and somehow the subject of my previous career in music came up.

"So . . . what did you do in the music business?"

"Musician. Studio player, and before that I played with bands." I thought I saw a cloud of misunderstanding come over her.

"Bands? Like who?"

"Well, like Gene Krupa, for instance."

"Who's Gene Krupa?"

The evening was over. I summoned the waiter. "Check, please!"

I also dated lots of nice ladies who were at least thirty that I was never going to marry. Maybe it's time for another blanket apology.

I don't remember what we were working on in the spring of 1971, but we got a call from one of my favorite agents, Rick Ray, of Adams, Ray & Rosenberg, who said a new NBC/Lorimar series called *The Good Life* was staffing up at Screen Gems (Columbia Pictures Television) and would we be interested? Should he pitch us? We said okay, not knowing anything about the show and trusting his judgment that it would be something we'd enjoy working on.

When Rick Ray pitched Turner & Mitchell to Executive Producer Claudio Guzman for the job of Story Editors, he flipped. Turns out he was the director of that *Partridge* episode "Danny Gets Drafted," loved that script and whoever wrote it, and the search for writers was over. He was pleased, we were pleased, and Rick Ray was thrilled. Agents love to put writers into series. They know there'll be no annoying phone calls from them for at least a season or longer, not to mention a steady ten-percent commission and they'll have yet another friendly place to go to pitch some of their freelance writers.

For me the deal was a life-changing event. Not because of the show, or Lorimar, or NBC, or Claudio Guzman, but because of Claudio's choice of a Production Assistant, the gorgeous Marilyn.

Once I met her, I knew my single life was over. Marilyn had been through a devastating marriage, had been deserted by her husband and was left on her own with their two-year-old daughter, Michele, eleven dollars in the bank, and the car he said she might as well have, which turned out to be stolen! I was impressed with the way she'd reorganized her life, found meaningful re-employment in show business, arranged for good and affordable child care for Michele and a comfortable apartment in North Hollywood. She was already a jazz fan since high school, knew the music and the players and I think she was impressed with me after I told her I was Red Mitchell's brother, and I was impressed with her for a lot of reasons, but mainly because she knew all about Gene Krupa. We started dating and Sundays I'd want to go to open houses or new home developments and check out what was available (and I still do). Marilyn always wanted to know why and we always ended up doing something else. After I asked her to marry me, I said, "Now can we go look at houses?" We were married within six weeks and are still happily married thirty-six years later, and all without the help of Dr. Phil.

She came into my life and brought her adorable daughter, Michele, along and I became a ready, willing and able new dad once again. We found a newer home in what is now Tarzana in the San Fernando Valley. Two years later when the timing seemed right for me to adopt Michele, we needed a couple of things signed by Marilyn's ex, who had never sent as much as a dime for financial support. He was magically available and was hoping that some funds would be transferred from us to him as an "incentive" to sign. The word "bribery" never came up, nor child-selling, but what came up was Marilyn's offer to him: if he'd sign the document she would

Wedding Day, June 10, 1971.

Adoption Day, 1973.

see to it that the warrant for his arrest would be quashed. Done deal. All it cost us was dinner, and we didn't see him again for about sixteen years.

The Good Life was a cute show with a thin premise, even for those days, and a very good cast: Larry Hagman, Donna Mills, David Wayne, Hermione Baddley, and Danny Goldman. Marilyn and I were able to work out four clear days over a weekend to be safely away from production and get away without causing any ripples. Well, maybe one ripple. Larry Hagman was throwing a big party (on the day we were to be married and start our brief honeymoon) at his pad in Malibu. Seems his living room was actually a huge hot tub and the party protocol was: everybody get high, get naked, get into the tub and do who-knows-what to who-knows-who. Look at all the fun we missed driving to Carmel for our honeymoon! That was thirty-six years ago and Hagman (who has long since cleaned up his act) is probably not pissed with us anymore. Of course, Marilyn is still feeling a little bruised because I brought my golf clubs along and managed to play Pebble Beach twice. Never since then, of course.

I don't want to gush on too much longer about marriage and my wife and soul mate Marilyn and have this chapter turn into a sweet rerun of an eHarmony.com commercial and put everybody into insulin shock, but I want to say it took both of us a while to find the right person, and it was well worth the wait as far as I'm concerned. Marilyn, with all her other attributes too numerous to mention, is a very good critic of everything I write and I have learned to pay close attention to her suggestions, which tend to fall into two categories: marvelous or mediocre, and I have to have the wisdom to know the difference. For example, she suggested I leave out the part about bringing the golf clubs along on the honeymoon.

Chapter Eighteen
Movin' on Up

The Good Life was fun to write and Donna Mills was a delight to work with, as was David Wayne. Donna had a huge dog which was her personal security system and she kept the animal close by because she was worried about an ex-boyfriend who might be trouble. I remember thinking at the time what kind of jerk would allow himself to reach the category of "Donna Mills' ex-boyfriend"?

David Wayne, with a long and distinguished movie career behind him was cheerfully doing television and loved hanging around with writers. And we loved hearing his mostly unprintable stories of Hollywood in the glamour days. One that comes to mind includes David and two of his drinking buddies, Broderick Crawford and Sonny Tufts, who were tying one on at the classic bar of the Beverly Wilshire Hotel. Late in the evening, after an unimaginable amount of alcohol had been consumed by the trio, Brod Crawford fell off the barstool and announced that it was time to go home, and that he couldn't get up. So little David Wayne and big Sonny Tufts said Ten-Four and somehow managed to haul the huge and inert Broderick Crawford out of there and into a cab. The hero of *Highway Patrol* was able to give the cab driver an address just before he passed out. They reached the location and it took all the strength David, Sonny, and the cab driver had to half-carry, half-drag Mr. Crawford to the front door of an elegant and completely darkened house in Beverly Hills. They rang the bell and nothing happened. Rang again and nothing happened. Then they pounded on the door and began to shout, and a light went on upstairs. Pretty soon they heard a slippered person heading toward the door, which then opened, and a middle-aged lady in elegant nightwear peered out at them, saw Brod and reacted. "Him again? He hasn't lived here for twenty years!"

The summer of fun was soon over and the fall and the new television season arrived and NBC was in big trouble. CBS had a radical and very funny new show, *All In The Family*, and *The Good Life* was up against its lead-in show, and we got clobbered. But instead of realizing the true situation, that *All In The Family* was unique, profound, and would change television comedy forever, the network Suits decided that there was something wrong with *The Good Life* scripts, the same ones they'd loved all summer long. In reality the show was no better and no worse than the competition and no show could have bucked the excitement over *All In The Family* and its lead-in, but somebody had to suffer for the ratings and it became us. With the network Suits running around like recently beheaded chickens, we got two completely contradictory memos on one of our scripts within minutes of each other. One was from Leonard Goldberg, President of Screen Gems, and the other from the NBC Vice-President of programming who was in charge of our show:

From Len Goldberg: "This is embarrassing!"

From the NBC Guy: "This is exactly what we want to see!"

From Turner & Mitchell: "Let's not lose any sleep over this show!"

The best way to find out if your show has been cancelled overnight is to drive to the studio in the morning and notice that your name has been painted out on your parking space and that there are two guys in your office playing darts with your dart set and all the rest of your stuff is out in the hallway in cardboard boxes from Ralph's Market. A quick call to Rick Ray revealed that, yes, the show had been cancelled and, come to think of it, there haven't been any checks lately. Even though we had a contract that guaranteed us a year's work, which was signed by us, by Screen Gems, Lorimar, NBC, and approved by the Writers' Guild of America, Screen Gems had decided not to honor their commitment, and when Rick Ray confronted them with the signed contract, their corporate response was "Sue us." That was thirty-six years ago, and had we sued, we'd still be waiting for money.

Then Screen Gems offered a carrot. We could work out the checks by writing some *Partridge Family* episodes. So we ate carrots garnished with humble pie and the checks kept coming. Extremely helpful since I'd just bought Marilyn a new house in Tarzana.

Rick Ray found what he felt was the perfect show for us at Paramount and went in and pitched us. He heard nothing from the producer and after a few weeks called up to find out what happened to Turner & Mitchell.

"They're not right for the show."

"Well, what kind of writer are you looking for?"

"Writers who write like me. And, besides, they don't come from New York and they're the wrong religion."

It's the first time I'd ever heard articulated the widespread myth that you have to Jewish to be funny. And, if you're not Jewish, you'd better be Irish. Bigotry very similar to what I was exposed to in the music business: that if you're in the rhythm section, you'd better be African American. Fortunately for me and my two careers, the vast majority of potential employers believe what they hear with their ears, and what they read with their eyes.

But even though we weren't geographically or ethnically correct in the eyes of one producer, other work came along, including a nice television movie for actor/producer Sheldon Leonard, of *Make Room for Daddy*, *Andy Griffith*, *I Spy*, and *Gomer Pyle* fame. Sheldon was a delightful gentleman, great to work for, who appreciated good writing, and he involved us in the producing end with casting and post-production, two things I've always enjoyed. Our story and screenplay were based on a very funny British movie about a likeable, inept guy who was trying to lose his virginity by talking his girlfriend into having sex with him (now there's a brand-new idea) and she and circumstances kept getting in the way. We called our version of this story *Not Now, Norman*, and our problem was the British version was much too racy for American taste, in the opinion of the Suits.

For example, we couldn't even use the word "virgin," and so our nice little movie, though cute and funny, was pretty tame.

On three occasions in my writing career I've been part of classic projects created in another era by famous writers. One such involvement was with *The Odd Couple*, based on Neil Simon's hit play and movie. And it was such a good feeling putting words into the mouths of characters I'd loved for maybe decades. Another was *You Can't Take It With You*, a one-season syndicated series based on the hysterically funny Broadway show written by George S. Kaufman and Moss Hart. Who knew I'd ever be creating dialogue for Felix and Oscar or breathe life into a hit Kaufman & Hart show and movie from fifty years earlier and be a small part of a literary continuum? Not me. More about the other revival, *Twilight Zone*, later.

The producer of *The Odd Couple* was Jerry Davis, a former screenwriter and holdover from Hollywood's Golden Age. Jerry was a witty, self-effacing man who really took to Turner & Mitchell much as we really took to him. He was funny and had a million anecdotes from the old days and listening to him was much more fun than working. He described his can't-miss formula for success in Tinseltown, which was: dress British and think Yiddish. I must admit Jerry looked great on the set. But he was much more than that. He knew how to tell a story and had a good ear for dialogue. He also had two faults that come to mind: gambling and marrying movie stars. Jerry had had lots of ups and downs in his long and checkered career, and he had many three-martini lunches with fellow writer/producer and buddy Bernard Slade over a period of time, and he'd talk about his life, his relationships, his failures, and his triumphs. Bernie, of *The Flying Nun* and *The Partridge Family* fame, was a great listener, and Jerry felt he never had to go to a shrink as long as he could have lunch with Bernie. But the lunches stopped when Bernie, who by now had become a playwright (*Same Time, Next Year*) came out with his newest play called *Tribute*, which also became a movie. *Tribute*, in essence, was Jerry Davis' life, complete with all the issues he had with his son, his ex-wives, and everything else he'd spilled his guts about. Jerry was astounded. "How the hell could you do that to me? If I'd wanted all this stuff to come out, I would've written it myself!" Bernie, to his credit, gave Jerry thirty percent of *Tribute*.

We wrote three episodes of *The Odd Couple* and Jerry was a lot of fun to be around. He told us how his short marriage to gorgeous movie star Marilyn Maxwell ended. As a pre-condition to marriage, he'd foolishly agreed to give up gambling completely. The fact that he did that was either a testimony to her gorgeousness or to his plain blind lust. They were married and presumably things were going along okay, except: no more weekly poker games with the guys, no more phone calls to bookies to bet on baseball, football, basketball, but most hurtful, no more trips to the racetrack and delightful afternoons making or losing fortunes. It was grim, but he was surviving. Then one day Marilyn said, "Let's go to the track!" and Jerry didn't want to go. If you're not betting, what could possibly be the reason to go? But she got her way as usual and off they went to Hollywood Park and Jerry's luxury trackside box, which he'd never given up. Marilyn looked over the racing program, closed her eyes and blindly put her finger down on a horse named Gumlegs. Jerry winced. Gumlegs was the worst horse in the history of the sport of kings, with a mediocre pedigree and no record of ever having crossed the finish line first. Marilyn said, "Here, put two dollars on Gumlegs" and Jerry headed sadly to the betting window. On the way there he noticed that Excelsior was running in the same race of undistinguished nags and was the only one with any real chance of winning. So he bet $500 on Excelsior and $2 on Gumlegs and went back to his box. And they're off! It's Excelsior by two lengths as they reach the first pole. Jerry has to hide his grin, as Marilyn begins to pout. And as they make the turn it's Excelsior, followed by Gumlegs, one length behind. Wait a minute! Gumlegs is picking up speed and is now only half a length behind. Jerry bites his lip as Marilyn jumps up and down in excitement: "Come on, Gumlegs! Come on, Gumlegs!" And as they head to the wire it's Excelsior by a neck, but Gumlegs won't give up. It's going to be close! No, it's not! It's Gumlegs by a nose! Marilyn screamed and jumped up in total excitement, "We won! We won!" And Jerry hauled off and decked her. End of marriage.

I can only remember one joke we wrote out of all our *Odd Couple* scripts that we turned in and it had to do with Oscar trying to hide something small from Felix. Someone suggested he unscrew the cardboard back of the TV set and hide the object in there. Oscar shakes his head "no" . . . "It's the first place he dusts."

The revolutionary sitcom *All In The Family* made it to the air on its third try. Based on a British TV hit called *Til Death Do Us Part*, Norman Lear had done two pilots at ABC and ABC passed. Then, using the same script, he painstakingly recast the show with Sally Struthers and Rob Reiner and it became magic. CBS liked it and used it as a mid-season replacement, and it had fair-to-poor ratings. But then they ran the thirteen episodes Norman had produced during the summer months, and by fall had a big hit on their hands. Now that it was a hit, the critics courageously jumped aboard and *All In The Family* changed television forever. It was all that anybody was talking about around the water coolers of America.

Turner and Mitchell were invited to pitch to *All In The Family* and we came in several times, but we could never get an idea past the Story Editors, one of whom appeared haughty and the other appeared goofy. So we never broke through and figured either the show wasn't for us or we weren't for the show. But we got busy doing other things, including surviving a devastating major strike, which, of course, the Writers' Guild won. As a matter of fact, we won every strike and will continue to win every strike. They occur semi-regularly every few years when new management teams are installed at networks or in production companies and then have to be taught the same lesson we'd taught their predecessors: that they can't get their scripts written in Indonesia or Taiwan by children at fifteen cents an hour, or even in English-speaking countries because the writers there don't speak American. And so we always win, but sometimes it's a Pyrrhic victory, as in 1988, when the strike lasted six months. Writers lost their homes, small literary agencies went belly up (including my agency) and networks lost viewers who have never returned.

After the 1973 strike was over our new agent, Silvia Hirsch of the William Morris Agency, said she'd had a call from *All In The Family* asking about our availability. Did we want to come in and pitch? We told her of our previous unsuccessful trips and she said, "Never mind! They really

Hitting the bricks during one of our strikes.

like you and want to work with you." So it was a little like offering a man who's just crawled out of the Mojave Desert a glass of ice water and we said yes to the invitation. Out came the bulging manila envelope and from there we found a clipping about a man in Texas who, through a simple typographical error, had been listed as a deceased person. One computer talked to another, passing along this erroneous information and the local, state, and Federal governments were now completely alerted to the fact of the man's death, and to all intents and purposes he was dead. He couldn't deal with his bank or conduct his life until he went to court to prove that he was alive. We thought Archie Bunker would be great as the frustrated not-so-dead man, but we never got to find out.

In our pitch meeting, which now included the talented English Writer-Producer, Don Nicholl, we gave them the story of the Texas guy and Don said that we'd inadvertently stumbled onto the "B" story about computers running amok that would blend well with an incomplete "A" story about

Edith sending away for prunes that they'd had for three seasons. Our Texas guy story now went in a completely different direction, but, meanwhile, we'd broken through and gotten our first *All In The Family* assignment. Which eventually led to four other episodes and, for me, a seven-year career with Norman Lear.

Chapter Nineteen
What's so Great About Norman Lear? I'll Tell You . . .

When we were writing our first *All In The Family*, the Story Editors warned us: you'd better have a big joke on page one. I'm glad we did, because it was one of the few things we wrote that survived the final rewrite, or so it seemed. What was our big joke? I'm glad you asked. The Bunkers were having a Sunday brunch and Edith offered Archie some cold sliced tongue, and Archie turned her down saying, "Edith, I don't eat nothin' that comes out of a cow's mouth. Pass the eggs." Well, it was a big joke at the time and, apparently, for outsiders like us, we contributed enough to that script to be invited back and that was fine with us.

Norman wanted to expand the role of neighbor Louise Jefferson, portrayed by Emmy-winning actress Isabel Sanford, and in order to do that he felt that the audience should meet the husband George she only talked about. After a couple of try-out Georges, Norman discovered part-time postal worker and funny actor Sherman Hemsley, who was appearing in a road company production of *Purlie Victorious*, and once Sherman showed up, Norman knew he had his George. Turner & Mitchell came along right about then and when Louise and George had their first fight it was in an episode of *All In The Family* we'd written. Norman loved that script and that battling couple scene and suddenly it seemed we might have a future with Tandem Productions, Norman's company in partnership with Bud Yorkin.

During this time an important family development cropped up, and

I'll have to go back a couple of years. Remember when I was describing my army days and that weekend pass to New York to do Arlene Francis' *Talent Patrol*? I spent the whole weekend I wasn't in the studio trying to catch up with Red and find out where he was working. But due to one coincidence after another and a lot of missed phone calls, it didn't happen. I was upset, but chalked it all up to a failure to communicate and soon forgot about it. But the fact that we didn't get together that weekend was no coincidence. Red and his then-wife Doe just plain didn't want to meet me because in the fall of 1953, she was eight months pregnant and they were planning to give the baby to an adoption agency and get a divorce and didn't want the family to know or get involved. My guess is they knew they weren't going to be together anymore and neither of them felt capable of raising a child on his own. Doe, of Russian extraction, had one stipulation, which was that the child would be adopted by suitable parents of her ethnicity.

Eighteen years later my parents had retired and moved to a lovely home in the Valley Village section of North Hollywood. They invited Nonnie, the mother of Rosie, the wife Red left behind when he went to Sweden, over to tea. They were chatting pleasantly about the old days when they were related by marriage and got on the subject of Red and the time he contracted tuberculosis on the road. My mother mentioned the theory that the vulnerability to TB might be genetically inherited, and it's just as well that Red never had children. Nonnie agreed, and then added, "Except for Allan…" and my mother spit out her tea. And that's how my parents learned that they had a grandson somewhere out there and I learned that I had a nephew. My parents immediately wanted to find Allan and welcome him to the family. They contacted the adoption agency and were told only that Allan would be eighteen years old, had red hair, was musical, played the guitar and attended a junior college somewhere in Los Angeles. And the agency would not help put them together and would give them no more information. But I thought that was plenty of information.

My advice was to hire a private investigator for two or three days who could probably check out all the junior colleges in L.A. in that amount of time and leave some kind of message on student bulletin boards to the ef-

With Red and Allan at Donte's nightclub in North Hollywood, where Red was appearing.

fect: "If your name is Allan and you were born in October 1953 and you have red hair…," etc., and mention a potential inheritance and that his biological grandparents were looking for him. But, just as I've ignored much of their advice over my lifetime, they completely ignored mine and went about finding Allan by going to séances and prayer meetings, neither of which produced their missing grandchild and my nephew. But they did do one more thing. They wrote to some nice lady in Utah who solicits letters from people who want to trace lost family members and somehow cross-indexes them, keeps track of them and occasionally is able to make a match.

In the mid-'70s, a few years after the Nonnie tea, the doorbell rang at my parents' house, Dad answered and opened the door and looked out at an exact replica of himself as a young man and Red in his twenties. The exact replica said, "My name is Allan and I think I'm your grandson." My dad nearly fainted. And that's how Allan Zolnekoff, who had written to the same nice lady in Utah when his wife became pregnant and they wanted some information about his birth parents, came into the Mitchell family.

He was thrilled to hear about his father and the rest of us and went out and bought all the Red Mitchell LPs he could find, contacted Red, and they had a close if geographically distant relationship for the rest of Red's life. Allan had been raised by the Zolnekoffs, a solid Russian-American family in Whittier, California, has children of his own, is active in local government, and is a former Mayor of Whittier.

Now back to that other family with interesting inter-generational relationships, the Bunker family. By this time, *All In The Family* is in its third season, is a solid gold hit and two of the principal cast members are starting to chafe. Sally Struthers was thinking the show was ruining her career and wasted a lot of money on adventuresome lawyers who, of course, could not get her out of her contract if she wanted to continue her acting career. So she'd show up year after year, and Norman would send her an obscenely large flower arrangement and back to work they'd go. But it was different with Carroll O'Connor, starting with his testosterone level. You really couldn't do *All In The Family* without Archie and he knew it. Now he was holding out for a better deal than the one he was offered and a new production season was upon Norman with no assurance there'd be an Archie Bunker, and Norman and CBS were standing firm: no more.

So Turner & Mitchell were busy writing our fifth *All In The Family* and were meeting in Norman's office at CBS Television City to get his notes on our first draft of "Archie's Funeral," which was to kick off the season, with other Archie-less stories in the works. Someone came in and whispered something to Norman and he excused himself from the meeting. We continued working with producers Don Nicholl, Mickey Ross, and Bernie West and pretty soon Norman came back in with a big grin on his face and said, "I don't think we'll be needing this script." To this day I don't know who caved but I like to think that a script called "Archie's Funeral" had something to do with Carroll's new attitude, and he continued in the show for another seven or eight years.

One thing that happened during our *All In The Family* days should be mentioned because it taps into a widely shared myth among American people, one they're passionate about, which is that their beloved comedians write their own material. You probably have no idea how pervasive this disinformation is and a lot of America's beloved comedians (not beloved by their writing staffs) foster and nurture this false belief wherever and whenever possible. Bob Hope, who lived to be a hundred years old, never mentioned the word "writer" publicly, and Red Skelton was constantly fighting the Writers' Guild and trying to remove writing credits from the crawl at the end of his show. Most people think that Johnny Carson thought up all that funny stuff for thirty years on his *Tonight Show*. Carson performed, edited, and contributed to the stuff and gave his writing staff credit all the time, as did Jack Benny, but people just don't want to hear that and like to believe that today's heroes, like Leno and Letterman, just make it up as they go along.

Elroy Schwartz is the younger brother of Sherwood Schwartz, who has had two really good ideas in his entire lifetime: *Gilligan's Island* and *The Brady Bunch*. Elroy tells the story of a dinner at his father's house. All the boys were there, including himself, Sherwood, older brother and master joke writer Al, and a fourth son who was an attorney. During dinner the senior Schwartz asked all his sons to recap what they were doing, and they gave their reports. The attorney was lawyering, Al was busy writing for Bob Hope, Sherwood was working on a comedy pilot about castaways, and Elroy said he was writing the Groucho Marx show *You Bet Your Life*. The old man exploded. Groucho doesn't have writers! He doesn't need writers! He ad-libs that show. Elroy begged to differ. The interviews were scripted after the guests met with the writers and were given very carefully prepared set-up lines which lead to Groucho's punch lines, plus a few "ad-libs," which were part of every script. "Not true! You're lying to me!" Elroy excused himself, went to his car and came back with a script, which he showed the old man. On the cover was printed YOU BET YOUR LIFE, starring GROUCHO MARX, Show #137, Written by Elroy Schwartz. The old man turned seven shades of red, picked up the script and flung it against the wall. "Never bring that script into this house again!"

Lloyd's dad didn't understand about writing either, and could never figure out what Lloyd did for a living. Lloyd had come to Hollywood as a young man and a terrific artist with dreams of working for Walt Disney but never got there. He got as close as working at Warner Brothers Cartoons as an In-Betweener, which is not very close at all. It's a boring job of grinding out intermediate animation, cel by cel, which is now done by computer, and later moved up as a writer of cartoons for Jay Ward and then primetime comedy with me. But his father didn't seem to comprehend these changes. He was due to visit Lloyd at a time when our next *All In The Family* would be taped at CBS Television City, so Lloyd decided to bring him to the taping and clear up Dad's misunderstanding.

Taping day arrived and I saw Lloyd's dad (the one with the straw still sticking out of his ears) being herded in with the rest of the tourists and free-ticket fans and he looked like a country bumpkin in New York City for the first time, gawking at the skyscrapers. Dad settled down in time for Norman Lear to come out, do a little warm-up and introduce the writers of tonight's episode, Turner and Mitchell, and we took a bow. Applause. Applause. Dad noticed. Then a tiny piano was rolled out, Jean Stapleton sat down and rattled off an arpeggio and was joined by Carroll O'Connor in a rousing chorus of "Those Were the Days," which tickled the audience. Then the play began (and every episode of *All In The Family* was a twenty-three-minute play with no special effects or trick photography) and was well received. At the act break Edith stood up to Archie for the first time in the history of the series and said something like "Up yours, Archie!," or whatever we were allowed to say back then, and the audience cheered wildly. After the curtain and the applause and a few retakes the audience filed out and there was Dad, still sitting in his seat in the bleachers, still staring at the lights and the equipment. Lloyd said, as we went toward him, "Now he knows what I do for a living" and we reached the old man and Lloyd asked him what he thought of the show. His father answered, "That Carroll O'Connor! How does he <u>think</u> of that funny stuff week after week after week?"

When CBS ordered the *All In The Family* spin-off series called *The Jeffersons* they just saw more dollar signs. No one was hotter than Norman Lear and they gave the new show a protected time slot, right next to *All*

In The Family. Nicholl, Ross, and West, who now called themselves NRW, left *All In The Family* to produce *The Jeffersons* and the first thing they did was hire Turner & Mitchell as Story Editors. Just the two of us. That was the staff. We wrote episode #1 and wrote or rewrote about sixty-six other scripts during the three seasons we were aboard, and we ended up as Executive Script Consultants and Showrunners, although the term "Showrunner" hadn't been coined yet.

We moved into a nice office at CBS Television City on a Monday morning and the first thing we noticed as we left the building to go to our first lunch at nearby Canter's Delicatessen was that today and every day, every time we'd enter or leave the building we'd have to pass right by Frank Barton's car, which was parked with the other biggies very close to the door. (As you may recall reading, Mr. Barton, in this same building, was responsible for the most demeaning, horrible meeting Lloyd and I ever experienced.) Lloyd had a talent I hadn't noticed before, which was the ability to spit with great accuracy. He could place a saliva oyster within a six-inch circle from a distance of twenty-five feet ten times out of ten. How did I learn this? On our first pass of the Barton vehicle Lloyd casually planted a spittle spitball in the middle of Frank's windshield and, when we returned from lunch did an encore. Frank now had two disgusting globs side by side, and by Friday his front windshield was so covered with dried saliva, I don't know how he could see to drive home. Monday his car was always clean and shiny and the revenge of SUPERSPITTER would begin anew. Apparently, Frank never connected his windshield desecration with Turner & Mitchell, because about ten years later he offered me a job as Vice-President of Development at Warner Brothers Television, where he was President. I turned it down because it would have meant no more Writers' Guild writing, something I wasn't prepared to give up.

CBS Television City is on Fairfax Avenue in the heart of a Jewish neighborhood, so getting good food nearby was never a problem. Canter's Deli was a favorite lunch destination and one day I spotted Mel Brooks having a bite with his then writing partner, Rudy De Luca. I knew Rudy slightly but had never met Mel and couldn't resist playing a little joke on him. I wrote something on a piece of paper and folded it over so that what I wrote was obscured, leaving plenty of space at the bottom. I went over to their table, said I was a big fan of Mel's (which is true) and could I have his autograph? He said "sure," didn't seem to be annoyed and wrote his name at the bottom of the paper. Then I said, "Schmuck! Don't you ever read what you sign?" and showed him the opened-up page, which read, "I promise to write six episodes of *The Jeffersons* for scale," followed by his signature. He laughed a lot, we introduced ourselves, and he took the paper back and added to his name "Mel Brooks the Pharmacist." Later, we exchanged a couple of humorous letters.

Carol Burnett's wonderful variety show originated at CBS Television City and I would walk past her in the hallways several times a week. One day she was heading toward me intently reading a script and the hallway was particularly crowded. Just as she went past me in the opposite direction I mentioned the character name of her leading man in *Fade Out, Fade In*, by saying, "What do you hear from Byron Prong?" Her head snapped around, she looked amazed and a little puzzled and had no idea who had said that. I was able to repeat my harmless joke a couple of times more and that lovely woman never knew who her tormentor was.

Norman soon had another show on the air, *One Day at a Time*, and between that show and *Maude* and *All In The Family* and another spin-off, *Good Times*, Tandem Productions became too big for CBS Television City and Norman's Associate, Al Burton, moved us all east a few miles and the company took over Metromedia Square, where other shows cropped up like mushrooms. *Mary Hartman, Mary Hartman, Fernwood 2Nite*, and *Hot l Baltimore*, to name a few. Marilyn and I were movin' on up too ... into a bigger house on the West Course of Braemar Country Club in the hills of Tarzana, overlooking the billion lights of the San Fernando Valley.

Lloyd and I got so busy with *The Jeffersons* that finding time for family and normal activities was tough, but we both managed. I joined a fun golfing group exclusively for showbiz people called the Hollywood Hackers who would hold tournaments once a month someplace in Southern California, give out prizes, eat, drink, and be very, very merry. It was started by

What's So Great About Norman Lear? I'll Tell You... 153

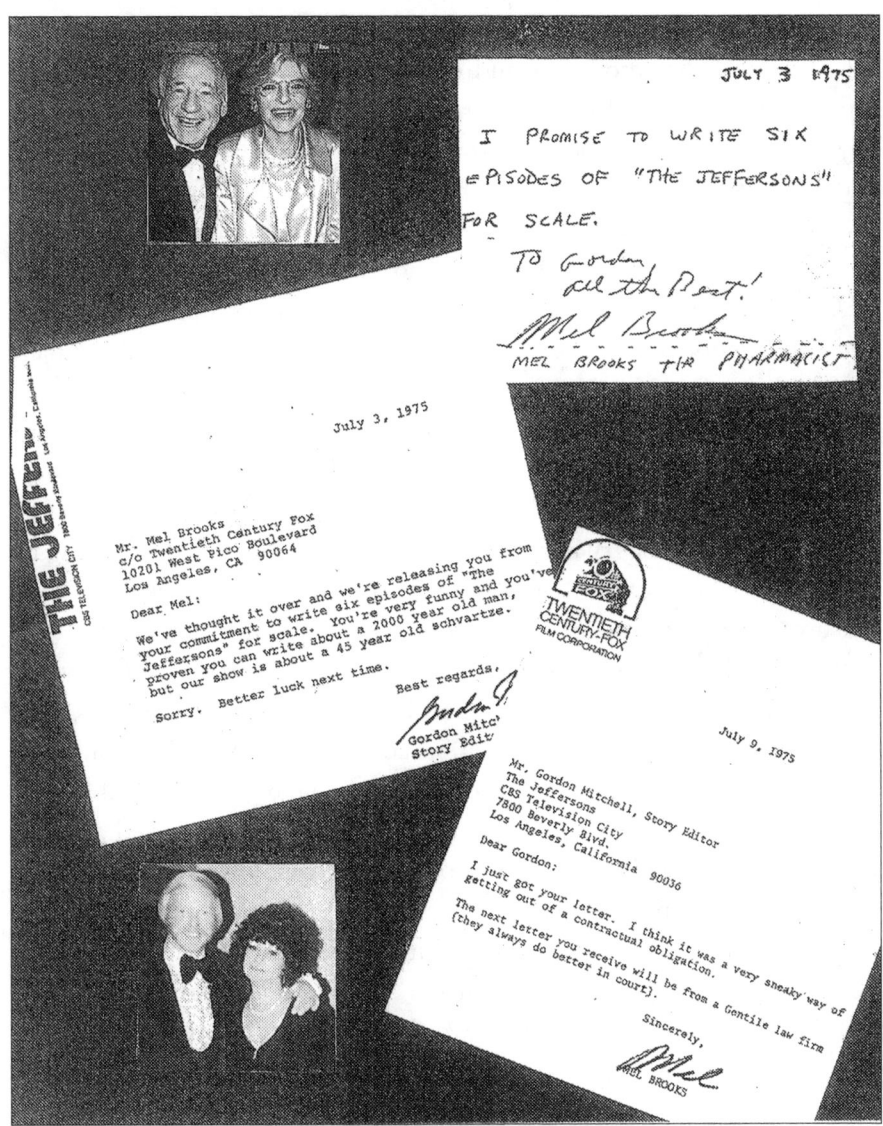

Fun with Mel Brooks.

actors and was restricted to that category until the President, a character actor, realized that producers and directors actually hire actors, so those types were suddenly allowed to join. Then he realized that writers eventually become producers, and so I was allowed to join. And with me, they also had a bass player who could join the combo that played the charity shows they'd put on, in exchange for a weekend of mindless golf and a great family getaway. Not a bad deal. And they had a piano player, too, in the person of Irwin (Irv) Kostal, an Academy Award-winning composer/conductor and orchestrator (he orchestrated the film *West Side Story*) and a wannabe golfer. He loved golf and took it very seriously.

Once, he and his partner were playing golf with Lloyd and me at Rancho Park, an excellent but very busy public course in Los Angeles. We were playing for something huge like a two-dollar Nassau, where the most you can lose is six dollars. Irwin and his partner should have been mopping up the floor with us because they were the better golfers, but we were holding our own. On the eighteenth green it was up to me. If I sank a forty-two-foot downhill putt we could eke out an even score and no money would change hands. Irwin was gloating and itching to collect a few bucks. No one could make that putt, because it broke three ways. So I closed my eyes, stroked the ball in the general direction of the hole and it snaked its way down-hill, picking up speed as it went. Irwin grinned. It looked as if the ball would pass the hole and end up off the green, but it hit a pebble at exactly the right moment, which slowed it up and deflected it and sent it right into the hole. Lloyd and I did our version of a high five, which had not yet come into existence, and Irwin stormed off the green without a word. I followed because I wanted words. I said, "Irv, how come when you were a big-time conductor in New York and I was a big-time bass player, you never hired me?" And he replied, "Fuck you then and fuck you now!"

Lloyd's passion was fishing, but he added another passion in the person of Darlene, and he and his bride moved to Marina Del Rey to be near their twin-diesel forty-foot yacht. Darlene was named First Mate and the boat was named *Aw Frigate*. Marilyn and I were invited for a day out on the Pacific Ocean and it was totally enjoyable. But I learned enough about boats just from hearing Lloyd's side of a thousand maritime-related phone calls per week to keep me on land. There were dock fees, fuel costs, divers, Radio Ron (to spin the compass, whatever that means), guys to paint, repair, mechanics to overhaul the engines after so many hours at sea . . . an endless parade of people wanting money, and Lloyd cheerfully doling it out. When compared to having a boat, golf is almost free.

We heard about a forthcoming Sunday when the studio would be closed. Christmas? Easter? Yom Kippur? St. Swithins Day? I don't remember, but it was going to be a day off and Lloyd made plans to go to Catalina Island, about twenty-six miles from the mainland, while trying out his new radar. Radio Ron had sold and installed the equipment and gave Lloyd his mantra for the next several weeks, which was: TRUST YOUR RADAR, and he believed Radio Ron. The big day arrived and the Marina was totally fogged in. No matter. This was a day off and LLOYD WAS GOING TO CATALINA! He started the engines, eased out of the dock, assisted by the First Mate, who was on the bow with a marine lantern and a long stick as Lloyd headed toward the rock-bordered channels. With Darlene on the bow, Lloyd successfully made it through the twisting and turning channels and out to sea, thinking the fog would lift. But it didn't. So Lloyd had to TRUST HIS RADAR all the way to Catalina at such a slow pace, that by the time they got there it was time to turn around and head back, also completely in the fog and by radar, inching his forty-foot vessel between the rocks, entering the Marina in a reversal of the grueling outward-bound trip. Did I ever mention that Lloyd had no left arm, due to a childhood accident?

Monday morning Lloyd came in exhausted but happy and told me the story of his harrowing day off. I believe my harrowing day consisted of taking Marilyn and Michele to brunch. Then he called Radio Ron to report on the radar. From across our two desks I could hear Radio Ron screaming into Lloyd's phone:

"You went yesterday? To Catalina and back . . . through the fog . . . and you're still alive?"

"Well, sure. You told me to trust my radar."

"It's a fuckin' miracle!"

And Lloyd asked the rhetorical question, "I <u>shouldn't</u> have trusted my radar?"

I mentioned that Sundays off were rare during those early *Jeffersons* days and that's true. Until we got a bigger staff it was all Lloyd and Gordon, and every time we thought we were busy, we'd take a look at Norman. He kept track of and participated in every draft of every script for every episode of every show which, of course, is impossible. But Norman was human and would occasionally misremember his remarks on a given script and we would nail him by playing back a portion of tape from a previous meeting in which he expressed an opposite view of what had to be done, and he'd smile and offer some cop-out like "I never claimed to be consistent."

Then he'd lecture on "Joyful Stress," a concept he heard about on talk radio on the way to work one morning. The guest shrink said that if you're involved in work you love and it's stressful, that's okay because it's "joyful stress" and that's actually good for you. One Sunday morning at about 9:20 a.m., as Lloyd and I were heading to our office because Monday morning's script was in dire need of jokes, we heard Mickey Ross' voice coming from the NRW office comment on the approaching footsteps: "Here come the laggards." And at 3:00 p.m., having taken care of the humor drought, we went home. Enough joyful stress for one day.

One of the great things about being part of Norman Lear's company in its heyday was the interesting high-profile people we'd meet through Norman like Jessie Jackson, Carl Reiner, Henry Fonda, as well as the best comedy writers alive; people like Hal Kanter, Mort Lachman, Milt Josefsberg, Larry Gelbart, Mel Tolkin, and Larry Rhine. Larry Rhine was a lot of fun and believed that life was wonderful now that he no longer worked for Red Skelton. He used to introduce his actress wife (who fortunately had a good sense of humor about it) with "I'm sorry . . . this is my wife Hazel."

We loved Milt Josefsberg and when he joined *All In The Family* as a producer, his office was right next to our *Jeffersons'* office, and we'd hang out often. Milt had written for Jack Benny both in radio and television and had an endless supply of Jack Benny anecdotes and, over time, we heard

What's So Great About Norman Lear? I'll Tell You . . .

Lloyd and me in our *Jeffersons'* office. This photo was our Christmas gift to NRW, with the caption: "Thinking of you during this Holiday Season."

every one of them. And when his affectionate book, *The Jack Benny Show*, came out we each bought one. We couldn't find one story he hadn't told us, but it was great to see them all there in print. One day when Milt was talking about the good old days on the *Jack Benny Show*, something he said triggered a memory I had of being the bass player at The Ziegfeld Theatre in New York when Jack Benny was booked there for about eight weeks. At the Ziegfeld, an immense theatre on Avenue of the Americas, there was an enormous orchestra pit and the bass player and drummer were usually located in the center. So when Jack would come out to center stage to do his monologue, I would be right below him about eight feet down. I marveled at his ability to do the same monologue, word for word, for eight different audiences per week, and time it perfectly to get the maximum laugh for every joke every time. That was about forty-four years ago as I'm writing this and, under hypnosis, I could probably remember the entire monologue.

That day in the office I recalled one joke and told it to Milt. Jack was

Lloyd on left and me, with *The Jefferson's* cast.

talking about how expensive hospitals had become: "A dollar-seventy-five for an enema." And when the audience heard their icon say the word "enema" they screamed, and when the laughter finally subsided, Jack followed it up with "And who do you tip . . . in a case like that?" More laughter, more screams, and I noticed that Milt had tears in his eyes. "I wrote those jokes!" Then he recalled writing that monologue for Jack's trip back East, which he had never heard performed. What perfect karma that the orchestra pit bass player could let him know, thirteen years later, how certain jokes had worked.

Another of Milt's jokes from that show: Jack would come to center stage for a special announcement and say that it wasn't part of the show, but that he had friends in the audience who had asked him to play a short classical piece that was one of his favorites that he often played while raising money for symphony orchestras. He mentioned that although he jokes around with the violin as part of his act, he's actually a good player. Would the audience like to hear this piece? Applause, whistles and screams. Then he'd turn to the wings of this huge theatre and say politely, "May I have my violin, please?" and out from the wings, forty-something feet away, a stagehand would throw a violin, which would come crashing down at his feet and shatter. And then there was Jack's wounded expression, which would keep them laughing for another three minutes. I rescued one of the damaged fiddles, which had come from a giant box of perhaps a hundred really cheap student violins made in China by the Long March Violin Company, brought it home, glued it together and hung it on the wall of my home office where it stayed for years.

One other Milt joke, from the radio days, had Jack walking to his neighbor's house in Beverly Hills and being stopped by a holdup man. His demand, "Your money or your life!" is followed by some hemming and hawing and no other response from Jack. The holdup man (if you can believe Mel Blanc as a holdup man) repeats his demand. "Come on, Mister! Your money or your life…," after which Jack says, "I'm thinking it over." This caused the longest laugh in the history of radio network comedy, and Milt told us how the joke was created. He and his partner Hugh Wedlock took the "your-money-or-your-life" speech as a straight line from some gangster movie and knew that it would be a huge laugh if they could find the proper punch line. But they couldn't come up with it and they were on a deadline to finish the sketch. The harder they tried the worse the punch lines. Hugh began to pace nervously as Milt went to the sofa, head in his hands, undergoing a big headache. Hugh yelled at him, "For Chrissakes, Milt, we have to come up with something!" And Milt shot back, "I'm thinking it over!" and they both raced to the typewriter.

When you're on a show for a long period of time and you work with cast and crew every day it really becomes your extended family, as we hear over and over again at every awards show. But, like most clichés…it's really true. *The Jeffersons* cast was the nicest group of people I've ever met. Isabel and Sherman as Louise and George were like good buddies you were always glad to see. And Franklin Cover and Roxie Roker, as television's first interracial couple, were totally professional and good team players. Marla Gibbs, who played Florence the maid, had one line in the first episode of *The Jeffersons*, and got such a big, well-timed laugh with it she was invited back time after time. A few seasons later, when Zara Culley, as Mother Jefferson, became too fragile to continue working, Lloyd and I suggested moving Florence into the apartment as a continuing source of annoyance and aggravation to George and comedy to the show, and we were able to make that happen. It was a nice reward for us to receive from the NAACP an Image Award nomination for our work on *The Jeffersons*.

Roxie and her husband Sy Kravitz, a news producer, became Marilyn and my friends and I remember once at a dinner in their home that their ten-year-old son, Leonard, was going through the painful experience of learning guitar. I mean it was painful to everyone else but Leonard, and he would practice his garage band rock 'n' roll way too loud and, to my taste, way too obnoxiously. He's still doing that today, while he counts his mil-

Nominees at the Image Awards.

lions and breaks eardrums everywhere as the internationally famous Lenny Kravitz.

As I mentioned, Norman managed to keep abreast of all the scripts of all the shows all the time, plus find time to found People for the American Way and support the ACLU, National Organization for Women, the Equal Rights Amendment, and other liberal causes, and articulate the reasons why to the news media. Norman is Rush Limbaugh's nightmare, and for that reason alone he is one of my heroes. But one story I like to tell hints that at some point he was stretched a little too thin.

In our third season of *The Jeffersons*, producers Don Nicholl, Mickey Ross, and Bernie West turned more and more of the show over to us, but would not give us the title of "Producer," which rankled a little. We were planning the season, organizing the stories, meeting with staff and outside writers, doing all the meetings with Norman and functioning as Showrunners. NRW were busy forming their own production company and getting ready to launch their new series, *Three's Company*.

One particular *Jeffersons* script had to do with George getting the idea that collegiate son Lionel is ashamed of him because he doesn't have a formal education. George believes there are all kinds of intelligence besides scholastic ability, including "street smarts," which he has in abundance. At the denouement George teaches Lionel a lesson and demonstrates "street smarts" by outwitting him in a bar bet. Only the outwitting scene in the script wasn't very good, especially the bar bet, and Turner & Mitchell went to Norman's house on a weekend so that he could bail us out with his wisdom and a good street smarts bar bet.

We showed up at his beautiful house in Brentwood and were led to the tennis court where Norman and his pro partner were playing doubles against Bud Yorkin and his partner. We sat on the bench next to Norman's then-wife Frances Lear, who later founded *Lear Magazine*, and was said to be the inspiration for *Maude*. The match was nearly over and Norman's team was behind. The ball came to Norman and he flubbed the shot and the match was over. Frances was really upset and said under her breath (but loud enough for me to hear), "Oh . . . I hate being married to a loser!"

Norman really enjoyed that story when I told it to him at a meeting about ten years later.

After tennis we went to Norman's home office overlooking the Olympic-sized pool, recapped the story and explained our need: a really good bar bet or street con of some kind. Norman thought for a moment, and then said he had one. He took an over-loaded pencil-and-pen box and took out all the writing implements except seven pencils and pushed it toward me:

"How many pencils in the box, Gordon?"

"I think there are seven."

"I say there are three. Look again."

"Still looks like seven."

"Three!"

"Seven!"

"Three!"

"Seven!!"

"I say there are three! Will you give me ten bucks if I'm wrong?"

"Okay!"

"You're right, there are seven. So give me ten bucks because I was wrong!"

Norman smiled. That was our bar bet. Perfect! We thanked him for the drinks, the snacks, the bar bet, and the brief glimpse of Championship Tennis. We went back to the studio on Monday morning and started fixing the script. Don Nicholl wanted to know if the meeting with Norman was helpful, and we told him Norman saved the day. What example of street smarts did he come up with? I cleared out my pencil box except for a few pencils and asked him, "How many pencils in the box, Don?" and he laughed and said, "Not the pencils again! We used that twice in *All In The Family*, and they used it again on *Maude* and *Good Times*." Back to the drawing board!

One of the producers of *All In The Family* that year was Lou Derman, who was an amateur magician and a member of the Magic Castle, a fantastic restaurant, place of entertainment, the site of Michele's Sweet Sixteen party, and unofficial World Headquarters for magicians everywhere. Lou said that there's a guy who lives in the attic of the Magic Castle named Old Gus and he knows the secret to every magic trick ever performed as well as every bar bet or street smarts trick known to man and that he could bail us out. So he gets Old Gus on the phone, explains the situation, gets out paper and pencil, poised for some Old Gus knowledge, and begins to write: "How many pencils are in the box . . ."

But Old Gus came through on his next try and we used his bar bet in the script. George gets Lionel aside, tells him that he's proud of Lionel's college education, but that he's going to need more than the ability to take tests to make it in life. He's going to need common sense and a quick wit. Then he takes a deck of cards, spreads them out face up and tells Lionel to put ten bucks on the table. Lionel puts up the money, and George matches him and then tells Lionel to "pick up any pair on the table" and Lionel thinks for a minute then picks up two aces. George says, "Here's the pair I pick" - and takes both ten-dollar bills.

So what's so great about Norman Lear? I'll tell you. Before Norman, a typical sitcom premise was: Bud's got two dates to the prom. What to do? Or, Norman's favorite: The roast is burned, and the boss is coming to dinner! Norman changed that forever. Every show had to be about something, especially if it was something nobody had ever tackled before. He had a lady in the office who was wired to Washington, D.C. and who had reams of research on all the problems and issues of the day, so that if we involved our characters in controversy or dealing with sacred cows, we could handle the subject matter with sensitivity, understanding and facts. Sometimes we'd come to Norman, if he wanted to go in a particular direction, and say, "But, Norman, breast cancer isn't funny" and he'd say, "That's your problem." And the interesting thing is that the more serious issues helped the relief humor to work, and the humor helped the issues to be more accessible.

Chapter Twenty
Good Times . . . Keepin' Our Heads Above Water

Wednesday morning was new script day on *The Jeffersons* and we'd all sit around a big table with the actors as they read aloud the play they'd be learning that week. All writers have egos and some egos are way bigger than others and Lloyd and I learned early on that if the cast really loved a script we'd written and made a big deal about it, NRW, who were terrific writers with the aforementioned huge egos, would see to it that there was a lot of extra work for Turner and Mitchell that particular weekend. So we were always on the horns of a dilemma: we wanted the cast to love the script but if we'd written it, we wanted them to shut up about it. One week there was a reference to Roxie Roker's character Helen Willis going someplace and the damp rainy weather completely screwed up her hair. Roxie stopped the reading and said, "This had to be written by a black writer! None of you guys know what happens to black women's hair in damp rainy weather! Tell me it's a black writer!" I told her it was written by two of Hollywood's best black writers . . . and she screamed, "I knew it!" and then I finished my sentence . . . "Turner and Mitchell." It got a big laugh around the table and completely prevented any talk about whether the script was good or not (it was) and saved us some grief.

In Tinseltown if you're part of a writing team you have to be prepared to give up a little of your own identity and accept that you'll be permanently linked to your partner in the eye of the beholder. I came to work one morning and was passing the open door of NRW's office and Mickey Ross looked up at me and said, "Good morning, fellas."

The season was ending and it was time to talk about next year and we got no indication from NRW that we would ever be promoted beyond Executive Story Editors, so we went to Norman and said, basically, "They won't let us produce and we're not coming back as Story Editors. So it looks like we're outa here." He said, "Not so fast," and offered us the job of producing *Good Times* and we accepted. If that sounds a little arrogant of us, and maybe it was, it was supportable by the fact that we were a hot team then, with big agencies like Creative Artists Agency and others wanting to represent us.

About that time I'd determined that my weight had ballooned up enough for me to get professional help. Working six and seven days a week just sitting on your butt and eating everything in sight (nothing makes me hungrier than writing) isn't anybody's idea of a healthy regimen. And Tandem/TAT had a chef and a kitchen right on the premises so the writers could keep on writing and not take time off for annoying things like going out for an actual lunch. I told you they were smart! I went to The Schick Center for the Terminally Fat, endured the aversion therapy, which is too disgusting to delineate in these pages, followed all their rules, went to group sessions with a room filled with fellow breakfast-skippers, underwent private counseling, worked hard, walked on the golf course, and lost about fifty-five pounds which has stayed off all these years. That was thirty years ago and today the thought of biting into a glazed doughnut still makes me nauseous. Let's hear it for aversion therapy! My success with their program put me in line to do a Schick commercial and when they learned that Marilyn was a graduate too (she'd quit smoking at The Schick Center as a wedding present to me several years earlier), they decided that we should do a commercial together. It paid for a nice between-seasons cruise to Mexico.

Lloyd and I showed up to produce *Good Times* and it was great to be involved in casting and post-production, meet a new cast and get started with a new season. But, unlike *The Jeffersons*, *Good Times* was a troubled show from the git-go with "creative differences" (read: egomania) all over the place that never stopped plaguing the show. Esther Rolle, the star of the show, was upset because originally minor cast member Jimmie Walker, playing J.J., was getting all the laughs and all the attention. My guess: because he was funny, and fun to watch. John Amos, who played her husband, never really believed his character and would tell anyone who would listen that a man like him "wouldn't be married to no woman who looks like that."

When we got to the first script reading there was no Esther Rolle. Her brilliant manager had talked her into boycotting the show while he attempted to upgrade the contract she'd signed presumably after she'd reached age twenty-one. John Amos had already left the show, and I think they killed him off so there'd be no talk of his returning any time soon. We made the Esther-less story work by shifting the interest to Winona, the nice lady who lived next door and who would become a surrogate mom. I've never met a more talented or lovely actress than Jan'et Dubois, who played Winona, and she's a musician too. She wrote and performed "Movin' on Up," *The Jeffersons* theme song, and she bailed us out week after week as Esther Rolle's boycott continued. Esther's manager kept assuring us that he'd work things out and she'd be back soon. In the meantime we had to have two scripts prepared each week ... one with her and one without.

We managed to do some good writing that season, including an episode entitled "Fishbone the Wino," about a street person who's killed by a cab and has no known family to step up and make final arrangements. So the *Good Times* family, with Winona sitting in, sees to it that he has a proper funeral, and they do a little research on his life, based on the pathetic few belongings that he left behind. Seems he'd been a baseball star in the Negro League in the pre-Jackie Robinson era, and it was a chance to do a little social commentary in the one-page eulogy that Jimmie Walker, as J.J., would deliver. As an added comedy device, the audience, but not the Evans family, finds out that Fishbone the Wino was not killed by that cab. The deceased is another homeless dude who'd stolen all his stuff while

Fishbone slept off a bender in an alley. So Fishbone, played by the outstanding actor Robert Guillaume, got to go to his own funeral and hear wonderful things said about him that brought tears to his eyes. Wonderful things would have been said about Turner and Mitchell (we honestly thought maybe an Emmy) if Mr. Walker had only read the words of our one-page eulogy, which was the point of the whole show. But Mr. Walker, very busy staying up all night doing jokes at The Comedy Store, didn't memorize our page and merely shuffled around the stage delivering brilliant things like "Dy-no-mite" and other inspiring words not in the script, and an otherwise great show fell flatter than a Denny's omelet.

With the show's Executive Producers, Austin and Irma Kalish, we wrote and produced a four-parter on child abuse which turned out well, with Chip Fields playing the abusing mother and eleven-year-old Janet Jackson playing her child in an amazingly professional performance. Her support group included her mom, Katherine, dad, and all the brothers, and they all attended all four tapings, and I was left with the impression of a really nice family.

A rare thing happened that season. We got an unsolicited script through the mail that was actually very good. It came from some small town in the deep South not noted as a cultural center and the author's first name was the initial "M," so we had no idea of the age, gender, ethnic background or anything else about the writer…just that his or her script was funny. It's the first and only instance of anything coming in "over the transom" (that is, not through an agent) that was of professional quality. We told everybody about it, passed it around and eventually sent it to Norman, who immediately offered the writer an assignment on *Good Times*, which also turned out well. The next year the writer, Michael Moye, was added to the staff, spent some time with the company and eventually created his own show, *Married…With Children.*

We still saw all the friends we'd made at Tandem/TAT every day. It was like a big campus. Norman's annual Christmas party, which started in one booth of a Chinese restaurant, was now a black-tie affair at the Century Plaza Hotel with perhaps fifteen hundred guests drinking champagne and noshing on steak, lobster tail, hummingbirds' tongues or whatever they brought around. It was a chance for Lloyd and me, who lived totally different lifestyles, to get together socially with our wives. Tandem/TAT became a big extended family and we were working next to people like Mort Lachman, now Executive Producer of *All In The Family*, Milt Josefsberg, legendary comedy writers Bob Schiller and Bob Weiskopf (known simply as "the two Bobs") and kept abreast of all the happenings on all the shows. I was asked to be the bass player in the band of *Fernwood 2Nite*, which wouldn't have interfered with my *Good Times* duties at all, but that was vetoed from higher up.

The buzz around the campus was that Carroll O'Connor had brought in rubber stamps and an inkpad to a reading of *All In The Family*, which he passed around to fellow cast members. As the reading got under way, he'd react to a joke or a piece of business he didn't like by slamming his stamp down onto the offending script page which would now have the red letters NF, meaning NOT FUNNY, emblazoned on it. To her credit, Jean Stapleton, the undisputed World's Nicest Person, did not participate in the NF stamp orgy and as soon as the producers realized what was going on, they cancelled the reading, went to Norman's office and resigned en masse. I was never told exactly what happened next or who blinked first, but once Norman got involved, the NOT FUNNY magically became FUNNY, the producers returned, the cast returned and the show was taped. And I wonder if any living witnesses can even recall which episode that was.

At one meeting we'd scheduled at Norman's office about some long-forgotten *Good Times* crisis we got there just as Jessie Jackson was leaving and Norman felt obliged to introduce us and momentarily drew a blank about our names. The closest he got was "Lloyd and George," but he knew that was wrong and finally said, "Oh, to hell with it . . . these are the two Bobs."

Somewhere toward the end of our *Good Times* season Norman left the company and founded Act III Communications in Century City, and installed a bright young executive named Alan Horn as President of TAT Communications, which was the company that succeeded Tandem Productions about the time *The Jeffersons* spun off. TAT stands for "Touchas Aufen Tisch," which, roughly translated, is Yiddish for "YOUR ASS IS

ON THE LINE," but Norman, for reasons unknown to me, has always denied that TAT has that meaning.

As Norman was leaving his company he named another guy, an attorney by background, as the guy we on *Good Times* would now report to. I don't mind that there are "Suits" in showbiz as long as they're involved in suit-type activities, but this guy got caught up in the wonderfulness of his new gig and suddenly became creative and a humor maven. This was the same guy who negotiated my contract with my agent when I first got to Tandem/TAT. At script readings he'd be there still wearing a suit, but with tie removed, kind of like Nixon at the beach, and he'd be pontificating on why such-and-such wouldn't work and why thus-and-so would. I started a tradition of betting him a quarter on every disputed joke or piece of physical comedy, and this tradition ended very quickly when he realized that, for some unknown reason, he was wrong about ten out of ten. He later put his name on some scripts he allegedly wrote and on the strength of that joined The Writers' Guild. It's guys like him that inspire all those lawyer jokes.

I wasn't anxious to re-up with a Norman-less company and Lloyd wasn't anxious to work as hard as we'd worked that year ever again. The magic of Tandem/TAT was gone, our contract was up and we said bye-bye for now. As for Esther Rolle, CBS, not anxious for another year of so-so ratings, completely caved and met her every demand, including that the white producers (whom she'd never met) would be gone. And CBS was rewarded for this wisdom with a final year of so-so ratings for *Good Times*.

Writer/Producer Garry Marshall should be in *The Guinness Book of Records* for the shortest pitch to a network that resulted in a series. He had a firm commitment from ABC to produce thirteen episodes of a sitcom whose basic premise was well-to-do yuppie marries girl who comes from blue-collar trailer trash family (or something like that) and he got a call from ABC saying basically that his show didn't really fit into their needs for the upcoming season and did he have any other ideas? Thinking fast he remembered a guest star in a *Happy Days* episode called Mork, an alien from the planet Ork, who'd been played by a hysterically funny unknown comic genius, Robin Williams. Garry ad-libbed that Mork comes back to earth and meets Mindy . . . *Mork & Mindy*. The whole conversation probably took twenty-five seconds and ABC said, "You're on the air!"

So Garry hired veteran line producer Bruce Johnson and teamed him up with a Co-Producer, far-out and funny writer Dale McRaven. Dale remembered Turner and Mitchell (he'd worked for us on *Get Smart* and we'd worked for him on *The Partridge Family*), called us in and we agreed to write *Mork & Mindy*. There was no pilot, no staff, and no premise other than Garry's effective pitch on the phone. So we showed up at Paramount, met Robin Williams and saw some videotape of Pam Dawber in a failed pilot about a nun. I remember thinking at the time . . . sure, lots of nuns look like Pam Dawber. Bruce Johnson put his expensive shoes on his desk and made important phone calls to the Pope and other close friends while Dale and Lloyd and Gordon kicked around how the show would work, and then Lloyd and I wrote episode #1 . . . "Mork Moves In." Later on, Dale wrote a pilot, which filmed several weeks after production had started, but was on the air first, so that the show could be considered created by Dale, Garry Marshall, and the guy who wrote the *Happy Days* episode in which Mork first appeared, but who never had anything to do with *Mork & Mindy*. Am I complaining? No. I was well paid and it was a real ego boost and a thrill to be on such a monster hit and to know that we wrote it.

It's now the fall of 1978. *Mork & Mindy* went from zero to number one in the ratings within five weeks. It was all anyone could talk about in America at the time and it was our episode entitled "Mork Goes Erk" that got to be number one. It was about a cynical cult leader well-played by up-and-coming comedian David Letterman. That same week when we reached that rare ratings number, Turner and Mitchell had to go to ABC to get our whipping for what the demographers said were elements missing from the show. Talk about insecure network executives! Fix the show . . . it's only number one. These same executives, who were smart enough to green-light Garry's idea, never understood that *Mork & Mindy* was a show about America as seen by an outer space weirdo, not a space show, and when Lloyd and I were no longer there, they turned it into a space show, and the series disappeared much too soon.

Robin Williams was a delight, a brilliant but hyper-kinetic stream-of-consciousness comedian and well-trained actor who, when he wasn't running up and down walls and ceilings could be found asleep in some unlikely nook. Audiences loved him so much he could do or say anything and it wouldn't offend. One time during an afternoon filming (the one kids were allowed to go to) he dropped his pants as he scampered bare-ass naked up his little ladder leading to Mindy's attic. Grandchildren and grandmothers and everyone in between all screamed their approval.

Pam Dawber, much too nice a person to be in show business in the first place, seemed tiny and mousy in person, but as soon as the lights went on and the cameras captured her gorgeous bone structure she was stunning, and her flashing eyes lit up the screen. She was going with Christopher Reeve, one of Robin's fellow Julliard students, and he would come to see the shows filmed. He had no problem with paparazzi in those days because, although the first *Superman* was already in the can, it hadn't been released yet.

The working conditions weren't really great that first season on *Mork & Mindy*. (And I suspect they never improved.) Dale McRaven was, in my opinion, a wonderful writer and yet a disorganized producer. He didn't use his writing staff well at all. When the staff was just Turner and Mitchell it was okay and we were able to write four out of the first twelve episodes. You'd think that with additional writers the workload would be eased, but not the way Dale worked. Rather than assign reasonable work reasonably he liked all-night writing sessions with everyone in attendance yelling and screaming and working on this week's script, which was already great, and he didn't seem to care that next week's episode was a shambles and the one for the week after that didn't even exist. All ten of us (mostly Garry's friends, funny guys without a lot of experience) would assemble in Dale's office. He'd show up and we'd begin work, which consisted mostly of jumping up on the coffee table and yelling, "Listen to this!" This was tough to take when the producer in me kept reminding me that the next three episodes were not a lot more than memos at that point. This would go on until the smokers in the room ran out of cigarettes and the script was pro-

We reached #1 in the ratings by our fifth week on the air with *Mork & Mindy*.

nounced funny, which events normally occurred simultaneously, about one or two in the morning. Then we'd take the rest of the day off. Marilyn, the greatest career wife of all time, was very understanding. A showbiz veteran herself, she knew that was my fate for this particular gig.

Something that really bugged me was the rumor that was rampant that Robin Williams was ad-libbing the show. Normal television viewers bought into this immediately, because they already believe that their favorite comedians come up with their own stuff, as I've mentioned. But the main TV critic of *The Los Angeles Times* wrote a story in which he blatantly claimed that "the writers just hand Robin blank pages and tell him to ad-lib here." How ridiculous! Doesn't the man whose job it is to know these things know that television cameras and crews operate on specific word cues, which are taped to the floor when the show is blocked?

What would happen on a typical weekly schedule was that Robin and Pam and the cast would read the script Monday morning and everyone would laugh hysterically and we'd get the feeling that this week would be different and that nothing could possibly go wrong with this show. Wrong! By the third day when everyone knew all the jokes and the laughter from the crew had almost evaporated, Robin would get "comedian flop sweat" and start throwing in pieces of his act, sophisticated Sunset Strip drug jokes and references totally out of character for Mork, the space innocent. Then we'd have to tell him, no, Mork wouldn't say that and the ensuing brouhaha would lead to another all-nighter in Dale's office. So, yes, he ad-libbed when he thought things weren't going well, but those ad-libs were edited out and never became part of the show unless they were in character and once the show was blocked, there could be no more changes.

I was on the first tee playing golf on a Saturday with my friend, attorney Sam Perlmutter (who had handled my adoption of Michele even though he was a showbiz lawyer), and some of his totally non-show business buddies at Montebello Country Club east of Los Angeles. As I was waggling my driver and getting ready to tee off I was still getting questions about screenwriting and my career. Yes, I admitted, my partner and I are the head writers of *Mork & Mindy*. I drew back the club slowly for the terrific drive that was to come and reached the top of my backswing. Then I heard, "Oh, he's the guy who ad-libs the whole show!" SWOOSH! CRACK! And the ball hooks out of bounds and I've already lost the first hole.

Lloyd's problems with the show were worse. He really suffered from the working conditions and it made his life miserable. When he began to look beet red and then, finally, almost purple he went to the doctor and discovered that his blood pressure was elevated above the numbers that human beings can survive and he was approaching the deceased category. The doctor asked what he was doing. He said, "Writing *Mork & Mindy*," and the doctor said, "Don't do that!"

So he started coming in to the studio around 10:00 a.m., no matter how far behind we were in our work, and going home at 5:00 p.m., until he slowly returned to his normal pink color. It probably saved his life on the one hand, but it definitely cooked our goose on the other. By this time Turner and Mitchell were becoming unpopular with Paramount and neither of us would ever work there again, in spite of the fact that I continued to stay up all night with the troops and never left the lot until the work was done. This, too, put a strain on the partnership, and I began to realize that Lloyd's point of view was that he was terminally tired of the business, tired of being raped by Hollywood, and, by this time, tired of yours truly.

I began to look around for something I could write on my own, sensing that Paramount and Lloyd would soon be history. Through golf I got a little gig writing a short film starring Lee Trevino. And it was a nice boost to know I could write without a partner. After the *Mork & Mindy* season was over Lloyd and I still owed Paramount and ABC a pilot that they weren't thrilled about and neither were we. We soldiered through, wrote it and turned it in, but we were pretty sure that it would never see the light of day, and we were right.

We cleaned out our Paramount office, deciding important questions like who gets the stapler, who gets the thesaurus, who gets Bartletts and the dictionary, and can we remove the pencil sharpener and the three-hole punch without guilt? Then we went to lunch and, as expected, Lloyd announced he wanted to retire. He'd been in Hollywood much longer than me and he'd had enough. That was okay with me. I think by this time we both had a little cabin fever. I was eight years younger, in perfect health and wanted to do more, not less. I wanted to write for the big screen and produce more television. I felt as if I was just getting started. So we agreed to end the partnership. We split the check and we split.

Chapter Twenty-One
Me, Myself & I Versus Hollywood

During the *Mork & Mindy* days on the Paramount lot when I was looking around for something I could write on my own, I ran into a very bright young writer/producer guy named Lloyd Schwartz, son of Sherwood Schwartz, and we had a mutual admiration society going. Lloyd Schwartz always had about seventeen irons in the fire and I liked that about him. I got myself involved in one of the irons, which was a pilot for NBC, the latest landing pad for network president Fred Silverman, who had already blessed CBS and ABC with his presence. I use the word "bless" in the same sense that tourists in St. Mark's Square in Venice are blessed by the pigeons. If I remember correctly the project never got as far as a pilot script assignment, but NBC was very interested and had us do a step outline which is sometimes called a scene-by-scene and basically tells the story by dividing it into scenes and describing each scene briefly and usually without any dialogue. I don't remember much about the story except that I liked it and was able to push it into productive comedy areas that would serve the actors well. The big block comedy scene at the denouement took place in a fish factory and was on the level of Lucy and Ethel trying to sort out the chocolates which were coming along on a conveyor belt much too fast. But it in no way relied on a fish factory and would have worked in a hundred other factory venues.

Sometimes it's good news if you don't hear from a network right away.

It might mean they're considering the project and want everyone to read it and get behind it. But usually it means they've passed and nobody wants to make the necessary phone call to let you know. Somebody from the network finally did make the call (or at least return Lloyd Schwartz's call) and let him know the project was rejected because, in the words of Fred Silverman, "fish aren't funny," which was the least thought out idea I'd ever heard up 'til then, but that was before "If it don't fit you must acquit" and, more recently, "If we don't fight them there we'll be fighting them here." But Lloyd Schwartz and I had fun working together, if only briefly, and we both hoped we'd work together some time in the future. This happened sooner than I'd expected.

The aforementioned Mr. Silverman, who was a brilliant programmer (in other words he could take a good show and put it in the perfect slot) when he was at CBS, kept getting promoted until CBS wouldn't promote him any higher, and then he went to ABC as President and inherited some very good shows ABC had been developing, including the excellent series *Roots*, based on the novel by Alex Haley. I was told by a Vice-President of CBS who I knew socially that Silverman called him complaining about the show and said, "Who wants to watch a show about those people?" and then when on to say, "I know what I'll do . . . I'll run it every night until it's over. People will forget." By the third night *Roots* was a mega-hit and Fred Silverman was a genius.

Each time Fred Silverman arrived at a new network his public pronouncement would always be "We're not looking for ratings, we're looking for quality television entertainment" and it seemed to me every action from that point on was a feverish scramble for ratings. Case in point: he noticed in the trade papers that a made-for-TV movie called *Rescue from Gilligan's Island* had gotten huge numbers, and that same week a documentary about the highly entertaining Harlem Globetrotters basketball team had done well also and that got his creative juices going. What about *The Harlem Globetrotters on Gilligan's Island*? He called in the creator of *Gilligan's Island*, Sherwood Schwartz, and asked him what he thought of the idea. "That's a terrible idea" was Sherwood's first reaction, so Silverman offered him an unconscionable amount of money and Sherwood said, "That's a great idea!"

Sherwood called me and his older brother Al and the three of us came up with some kind of story of less-than-cartoon believability, divided it up, and went our separate ways to write possibly the worst movie in the history of cinema. But it got on the air, got big numbers, I was well paid, and believe it or don't, twenty-seven years later, the residuals are still coming in, so somebody somewhere must be watching Fred Silverman's "quality television entertainment."

Finding work as a single writer wasn't as difficult as I'd imagined. Before the *Gilligan* experience, I was offered a job as head writer of *Joe's World*, a new Norman Lear show, and I took it, not knowing what it would be like facing the terror of the empty page in an empty room after thirteen years of having somebody to bounce ideas off of. Except the room wasn't empty. Lloyd Turner was still there whether he knew it or not. If I came to a joke or a situation that needed a decision, I didn't ask, "What Would Jesus Do?" I just pictured what Lloyd's response might be. By the end of our partnership we were finishing each other's sentences anyway. Nobody ever sets out to write or produce a bad show, but *Joe's World* just didn't catch on with viewers, and it was a one-season show. But that one season established me as a single writer and I sailed right on with other shows, pilots and movies.

Meanwhile, it was vacation time, and Marilyn, Michele and I went back East to New York and Washington, D.C. and behaved like tourists, having lunch at the restaurant at the top of the World Trade Center, visiting the Statue of Liberty, taking the boat ride around Manhattan, and other fun things. On our last day in New York, before moving on to Washington, D.C., I decided, since it was a Wednesday and therefore a union day, to visit the Musicians' Union (then at Roseland Ballroom on 52nd Street) and see if anybody remembered me after an absence of fourteen years. The same street vender was in place on Eighth Avenue just outside the door selling those incomparable New York hotdogs, and the same tough-looking guys were guarding the front door (what musical instrument could they possibly play?) and inside, on a giant stretched tarpaulin covering the immense ballroom floor, were a couple of thousand musicians milling around, schmoozing, hanging out, and booking weekend casual work. I quickly found dozens of friends and former bandmates and was holding court, telling them about screenwriting, my new career as Gordon, my new wife and kid, and how I'd reinvented myself as a former musician. I noticed a man with a familiar face holding an opened notebook, and he was looking at me. He came over and said, "Hey, Whitey, are you open Saturday or what?" and before I could answer, the guy next to me (who later became President of the local) said, "Don't go with him! I got a better gig for you in Jersey!" So, Gordon thanked them both on behalf of Whitey, and headed for Washington, D.C.

After we got home from that trip, a really good gig came along. An independent movie producer, Tony Unger, who I knew socially and through golf, bought the rights to "Big Bad John," Jimmy Dean's hugely successful record about a mythical coal miner who sacrifices his life to save his fellow miners. Big Bad John, according to the song, never spoke much, but when it was time for courage and action he was right there. Tony, who'd produced *The Madwoman of Chaillot* and *Force 10 From Navarone*, among other movies, had interested Arnold Schwarzenegger in the idea of portraying Big Bad John for the film version of the heroic ballad. Up until then Arnold's only film work was playing himself in a semi-serious documentary about bodybuilding called *Pumping Iron*. Tony and I talked about the project and he hired me to write the screenplay for what would be my first theatrical feature.

Tony is a very creative guy with good story instincts. I enjoyed working with him and coming up with a wrap-around period piece story for *Big Bad John*, which included the device that it starts in a coal mine in Austria where we meet our hero and, therefore, for the rest of the picture, never have to explain "Vy he tahks diss vay." We also had a Hollywood ending (surprise!) in which Big Bad John survives the pivotal mine disaster so that he'll be available for sequels. I put a lot of time and research (if talking to your parents about a particular era is research) and wrote a first draft I was proud of which had a ton of action, a love interest, a young kid, many opportunities for Arnold to take off his shirt, and lots of humor of the *Butch Cassidy & The Sundance Kid* variety. Tony loved my script and gave me some very good notes. I did a second draft and a polish and turned it in. Tony took it to Arnold and scheduled a meeting so that we could get his thoughts, which turned into my all-time favorite meeting in show business. It was at Arnold's beautiful home in Santa Monica and Tony and I and a director who wanted to be aboard listened as Arnold went through the script page by page and gave his notes while his wife Maria Shriver served drinks and goodies. Arnold raved about every single page of the script, laughing where appropriate, crying where appropriate, and enjoying himself thoroughly. I said to myself, "So . . . this is what's it's like to write for the big screen," and that's as wrong as I've ever been. It took months, but Tony and Arnold and my script were laughed out of every major studio in town because, as everyone knew, Arnold would never be a movie star. The picture never got made.

A few years later one picture that did get made (that shouldn't have gotten made) was for an Israeli producer who, in my opinion, was a genius at making deals but not, unfortunately, at making movies. He thought he knew the formula for young-people flicks, but in my opinion he is without the talent for storytelling, which he has proved with every picture he made. And mine turned out no different. I reported to his studio (no fair writing at home where you can actually think) and wrote the picture in ten weeks under garish fluorescent lights, and the minute I turned in the script and went out the door for the last time, he put the names of his Israeli director and the director's buddy on the title page. I guess he was hoping to avoid paying me the second half of my agreed salary, which was contingent on my name still being on the script. But what he didn't know was that the minute the Writers' Guild sees a script with a picture executive's name in place of the original writer's, it's an automatic arbitration. That meant about a year of my life waiting for memos written in Hebrew to be transliterated into English and countless trips downtown to Guild headquarters for depositions, interrogatories, and suppositories.

In the original deal, I was hired to write the screenplay only, because the producer said he already had the story. When I showed up to write the screenplay I asked to see the story and it didn't exist. There were some

Arnold Schwarzenegger

321 Hampton Drive • Suite 203 • Venice, California 90291 • (213) 396-5917

December 13, 1982

Mr. Gordon Mitchell
Har D Har Productions, Inc.
19525 Braewood Drive
Tarzana, California 91356

Dear Gordon,

Thank you so much for your letter of November 22nd regarding the BIG BAD JOHN project. I really appreciate your effort to make me feel comfortable about avoiding a typical, big, dumb guy character in the movie. But I have total confidence in you and Tony, and I'm looking foward to seeing the re-write and then the script. I think we should now go out, sell it and do it.

I'm looking foward to another meeting, and in the meantime have a Happy Holiday and a Good New Year.

Sincerely,

ARNOLD SCHWARZENEGGER

AS/al

A letter from the man they said would never be a movie star.

funny scenes in the minds of the director and his buddy, but nothing written down and not even a vague storyline. They wanted me to start right in on those alleged comedy scenes, but I refused, saying that it would be like asking me to construct the wall of a building hoping that the steelwork would fit later. The Israelis screamed but I insisted on writing down a story that everyone would sign off on. Billy Wilder once said the three most important elements of a picture are story, story, and story, and that's something I also learned from Norman Lear. So when a story outline was reluctantly agreed upon, I started on page one and began to grind out a script. It wasn't anything heroic on my part, there's just no other way to write a screenplay. At the end of the day I would turn in my pages and Mr. Producer would get out his crayon and proceed to take out every shred of good writing, nuance, or humor, replacing it with words I wouldn't want to use in this book.

A year later, when the arbitration was concluded, I not only won full screenplay credit, but also shared story credit, something I hadn't even asked for, because I was the only one who had bothered to create a step outline and write it down on paper. Of course the Israeli producer objected but he was forced to pay me the second half of what my contract called for. When I got the check, I had to restrain myself from donating the whole thing to the PLO.

That picture, too, demonstrates Mitchell's Motion Picture Law: that the worse the picture, the better the chance it has to get produced and once produced, the better the chance it'll make a fortune in television rerun land. That particular film was bought and distributed by a major movie company who took it out of theatres quickly and put it on late-night television, where it scored big time, and from whence many residuals droppeth. Years later, The Writers' Guild of America, (the smartest group of people ever assembled) found that the major movie company was cheating and had been cheating regularly on twenty different films, including mine, by under-reporting television revenues, so the Guild sued them, as is their custom. The day before the case came to trial, the company decided to pay off the Guild's demands at the rate of ninety cents on the dollar. My end,

My favorite photo of Lesley, Karen and Brian.

which conveniently reached me at the end of a bitter and devastating strike in 1988 that lasted six months and put a lot of writers and small agencies on poverty row, came to a high five-figure sum. God Bless the Writers' Guild of America.

The era this chapter deals with . . . me, myself and I, working alone as a producer/writer was a very satisfactory one. I'd really come into my own, and would never again be walking alone in a hallway and hear "Good morning, fellas." I was still in close touch with my nearly grown-up kids, Lesley, Brian and Karen, and had my lovely second family with Marilyn and Michele and a nice house in Tarzana overlooking the San Fernando Valley, as well as a small Bischon Frise that Michele had named Schroeder. They all got along great and we have lots of wonderful memories of our holiday dinners, swimming and barbeque parties with our blended family. There were also occasional visits from older brother Red, who had to learn to call me "Gordon" and never got very good at it. He'd come from Sweden with or without his latest wife and would stay with us or at our parents' house in North Hollywood in the pipe organ studio, where a day bed was always at the ready. Our relationship, as the people who subscribe to Transactional Analysis might say, was a plus-plus relationship, simplified as, I'm Okay ... You're Okay. That is, one between two adults who are not trying to outdo each other or be better than each other and who are both comfortable in their own skin. The visits were fun and sometimes included the long-lost Allan Zolnekoff, who fit into the Mitchell family beautifully.

Back to showbiz and a true story. Some names and circumstances have been changed so that I won't hurt the feelings of the main participant ... or his attorney. I was one of four writer/producers working on a hit sitcom. Part of our job (in addition to casting, interviewing outside writers, and going to endless meetings at the network) was to "polish" each script as it moved closer to production. This means that the four of us would sit around and go over the script line by line and try to make it funnier, better written, tighter, so that there'd be a chance that an audience would enjoy the show and laugh a lot. Usually, a polishing session was a pleasant exchange of good ideas and fixes, new jokes, and all four of us were suckers for a good new joke. Most rewrite-polishes were a pleasant way to spend the afternoon.

Not this one. The head producer, who I'll call Sheldon, came in with an attitude. Maybe trouble at home, maybe illness, maybe world news ... who knows? But it soon looked like a day not to mess with Sheldon, which turned out to be the case. He grumped around, not liking anything the rest of us were contributing, then condescended to offer a joke, which we all hated. Possibly because it was out of character, against the premise of the show and hurt a joke that was a few pages away, but mostly because it wasn't funny. Three out of four writers really loathed the joke, but Sheldon, especially on this day, had to have his way and insisted that it go into the script, and in it went. I didn't mind too badly because I knew that lame joke would never survive a week's worth of rewrites once the script was put into production. I've long since forgotten (or maybe blocked out) the actual pukey joke of Sheldon's, but let's assign a fictional punch line: "How do you think I rang the doorbell?" Three of us were waiting for the first reading and the removal of that alleged joke.

With the cast assembled around the table the reading of that week's script began, and when the actor read his line, "How do you think I rang the doorbell?," it was followed by silence, except maybe a polite groan or two. And Sheldon quickly came to the rescue of his unsuccessful line by saying, "We'll have to work on your reading of that line" and moving on without removing the offensive "doorbell." Normally during a week of production lots of script changes are made based on how the material plays and as the director works with the cast and puts the play "on its feet." The producers look in whenever they can, and suggest cuts or fixes where needed or instant rewrites, and that's why writers become producers. But, somehow, Sheldon's precious awful joke stayed in, in spite of the fact that everyone (well, nearly everyone) hated it.

Tape day. Two shows, both with studio audiences, are performed, one in the afternoon called "dress" and one at night called "air." With two complete shows (including audience reaction) on tape, we could then look at both, pick the better performance, make that the base show, mix and match various scenes from both shows and come up with a composite better than either. And this composite is what you see on the air. That's how it works in theory anyhow.

As we went through the "dress" afternoon show the actor read his line, "How do you think I rang the doorbell?," and there was absolute silence from the audience. There's an old saying, and a good one, that the audience is never wrong. "Hooray," I said to myself, now we have proof Sheldon's atrocity isn't funny and we can get rid of it during the final rewrite at dinner between shows. Wrong again. In spite of the fact that all writers, cast and crew now wanted that joke out, Sheldon insisted that, if properly read, it would get a big laugh, and proceeded to give the actor yet another way to read his line as the rest of us rolled our eyes heavenward. So it stayed in to the bitter end, the joke that had more lives then Wile E. Coyote. And when we did the "air" show once again the joke bombed big time. It was so quiet you could hear the plumbing from the restrooms in the next studio. Very symbolic.

As I mentioned earlier, one of the producers' functions was post-production, which is taking the rough cut of each show, timing it perfectly, making strategic cuts that don't hurt the story if necessary, or adding audience reaction or actor reaction if the show's a little short, but most shows come in long and then look good with a little trim that puts them right on the money. Once again the four of us were together in the same room, this time in the editing bay doing the post-production. When we reached that part of the show with the dreaded line, "How do you think I rang the doorbell?," there was the usual complete silence that followed every time these words were spoken. Sheldon said to the studio engineer, "Put a laugh in there. That's funny!" and a fake electronic laugh was added.

So Sheldon was right all along. It's more than two decades later now and if I were to look at some of the shows from that series today it would be hard for me to remember which jokes evoked real laughter and which got a laugh track, and I've forgotten the actual hated words of Sheldon's "joke" that wasn't. But if I saw the show ten more years from now and that joke line came up, I insist I could pick it out in a second. Trouble is I don't remember which episode it's in. And, what's worse . . . which series. (Possibly an exaggeration.)

I got a call out of the blue from TAT Communications. They needed a head writer for *Diff'rent Strokes* and would I be interested? Sure. The seven-days-a-week era seemed to be over and although Norman had left the company, the show had a good producer I'd worked with before and it was a typical Norman show. That is . . . it had a good social message built into the premise and there was lots of room for humor, especially from little Gary Coleman, whose personal life, I learned later, was far from humorous.

So I showed up for my seventh season with the company and went right to work on scripts, including a couple of originals. It was nice being back at Metromedia Square and Tandem/TAT again and I dusted off my tuxedo and Marilyn and I went to lots of charity shows and events and sat at the Tandem/TAT table courtesy of Norman Lear, who supported every decent cause that ever existed. It was the beginning of the production season and the actors hadn't arrived yet, but I was familiar enough with the show ("Whatchou talkin' 'bout, Willis?") to write it. An actors' strike was being talked about in the trades but so was global warming, and in those days no one believed either one was real.

Actors are usually fairly insecure people and rarely do they strike, but that year, apparently, they felt they had their backs to the wall and they struck. I wish I could tell you what the burning issue was, but I can't. This is just a wild stab in the dark, but I'll bet it had something to do with money. So . . . no actors, no show. *Diff'rent Strokes* shut down and I was sent home. The lawyer guy who was now in charge of Tandem/TAT told me there'd be no more checks and my contract was null and void. Force Majeure is the applicable legal term and he should know.

So I went home, played golf, played with Schroeder and played with Marilyn and life was okay. And then the phone rang. It was Sherwood Schwartz and he had sold a series to Fred Silverman at NBC based on the hit record of a few years back called "Harper Valley PTA." Sherwood asked if I'd like to write and produce the series with him at Universal and I said yes. There were no scripts so they were starting up now, not waiting for the actors' strike to end. The story is about a free-spirited good-looking lady who is the object of persecution and the subject of lies and rumors about her and her daughter which originate somewhere within the coven of uptight, jealous, ultra-conservative ladies who make up the Harper Valley PTA. Barbara Eden was all set to star in the series, which resulted from a successful television movie that got big numbers and Mr. Silverman's attention.

In the ninety-minute movie the first eighty-five minutes were devoted to these PTA ladies and the whole town putting down our poor heroine and doing horrible things to her and her daughter, and the last five minutes were devoted to her revenge, which included arson, explosions, and the dumping of wet cement into someone's brand-new convertible, all of which was justifiable and satisfactory. Revenge pictures always do well. I remember looking at the film in the screening room and thinking: this could have legs as a series as long as revenge is not the centerpiece. What worked very well in the movie would not work every single week. A vengeful person is not an attractive person and no one would want to see beautiful Barbara Eden getting revenge week after week after week.

I've guessed wrong lots of times in my writing career and I guessed wrong then. What they wanted was revenge week after week after week. I kept saying, as each new revenge show was being plotted, "not attractive!" but I was largely ignored.

As soon as I checked into Universal Studios and had an actual office, I called "The Tower," a tall, gray-and-black monolithic metal-and-glass building which is home to the Suits that run the giant studio. I explained that I was a new producer on the lot and that I had a pretty good-looking tuxedo and a gorgeous wife and that we would be happy to sit at the Universal table at any charity or awards function they supported, just as I had all those years with Norman Lear. They said they'd get back to me. A few days later somebody's male secretary called and delivered The Tower's chilly message: we don't support many charities or awards shows and if we're forced to buy a table at one of them we give the seats to permanent personnel on a seniority basis, not to producers of shows on the lot whom we regard as "transients." Off to a great start at Universal!

We developed a formula for *Harper Valley PTA* scripts. Each show started with a "teaser," that is a cold opening scene at the top of the show (before any title or credits), which forecast the trouble that was brewing that week, and the perfect teaser ended with a good joke. Then the main title would come on, then a commercial break, and then the show would unspool.

In my first original script for the show I somehow remember the title of the episode, "Moonlighting Becomes You," and not much else, but I suspect from the title that it had something to do with Barbara Eden's character making a few bucks moonlighting at some gig that shocked the ladies of the PTA, and I remember that I wrote a cute teaser that forecast the story and ended with a big joke. Then, as we were about to film that episode, Sherwood said, "By the way, we'll need a new teaser. Have it ready for tomorrow's shoot," and I asked what was wrong with the original teaser. His answer: nothing. But Fred Silverman read that script on the plane on his way to Hawaii and loved the teaser so much that he wants us to build a new show around it. So go write a new teaser! The remarkably long arm of Fred Silverman had struck again. I've never met the guy, but he's dampened my day on at least three separate occasions, advocating changes that were lethal to one project, and then rejecting another because "fish aren't funny," and now The Great Teaser Theft. So I had to scramble around and come up with something that had to do with that week's show but in no way resembled the stolen teaser and what I came up with was mediocre at best.

By the way, the original teaser never did get developed as an episode.

As many problems as that show had, it was still a lot of fun to produce and I enjoyed meeting Jed Allan, a soap opera heartthrob who we were considering adding to the show as Barbara Eden's love interest. Jed did a great job in his guest appearance, and the only reason I was ever able to learn he wasn't added to the cast was that he was too good looking, which was a new one on me. A small recurring speaking part opened up and I was in a position to recommend an actress and contacted my daughter Lesley to see if she could do it, but she was on the road singing with a musical group led by her husband. Luckily, my friend Aubrey Tadman's wife, Henriette, was available and had her SAG card.

I was the designated dude to visit NBC each week and receive the whipping for what was wrong with the show. (Why is it always me?) Fred Silverman's days at NBC were rumored to be nearly over. His subordinates, the ones I met with, were by now openly referring to him as "The Ayatollah," referring to an Iranian lunatic very much in the news in those days.

A couple of other things were going on in real life in those days that deserve mention. Marilyn had joined a charity group called Girls Friday of Show Business, which was founded by the executive secretaries of people like Gregory Peck, Bob Hope, Johnny Carson, Frank Sinatra, and other high-profile biggies. At their monthly dinners they'd honor some celebrity and raise money for their charity, reconstructive surgery for mostly third-world poor children who were burn victims or who had facial abnormalities, and the plastic surgeons performed their work pro bono. A really good idea and a nice bunch of ladies, which began to change shape as more young professional film and television people began to join. Marilyn and some of the newer members winced a little at the group's name feeling that "Girl Friday" was a demeaning term and managed to push through a name change to "Women in Show Business" to better keep up with the times. Some of the older members never forgave her for spearheading that movement and she was never going to be President while they were around. But Marilyn was happy being Vice-President/Program, which meant she got the monthly guests, and got to produce the annual Celebrity Benefit Ball, their big fundraiser.

With Steve Allen, a guy I looked up to physically and mentally, at a Women in Show Business function.

Doing that show every year was fun and I had a new purpose for my decent tux. We had nice people like Gregory Peck, Carol Burnett, Steve Allen, and Harvey Korman who would lend their talents and their presence, usually at some great L.A. hotel, and we had emcees of every stripe, from terrible to wonderful, and guess who got to write the shows? The best ever emcee was Regis Philbin. I spent an afternoon with Regis and Joy at their Hancock Park home and he was delightful to work with. A naturally funny man, he enjoyed the material I brought, helped to improve it and did the best benefit ball ever. We have his picture on our brag wall in the office and it's inscribed: "Dear Marilyn, Please don't tell Gordon about us."

Back to my friend, drummer Allen Goodman. He and his wife Bobbi opened a storefront pizza parlor & Italian restaurant called Pizzamania in Studio City and we would go there whenever possible for lunch or dinner. Marilyn got the idea that Pizzamania should have live jazz Friday nights and my friend Tommy Newsom (of *The Tonight Show* fame) and I would play there, with a couple of other volunteers, for dinner. It started

My favorite host, Regis Philbin, at a Women in Show Business Benefit Ball.

small, but word spread through the grapevine and pretty soon the place was packed on Friday nights and more and more people knew about the restaurant. It was good for me to keep my bass-playing chops up, even with the dumb electric bass I bought when I'd do shows with The Hollywood Hackers. And playing with Tommy Newsom, one of the great jazzmen of the world, was always a treat.

Allen and Bobbi did so well with Pizzamania that they moved a few doors down the street and opened a bigger venue, which they called Mulberry Street, named after a famous street in Little Italy in New York City. The music got more serious and soon major players would show up and entertain the likes of Johnny Carson, George Segal, Steve Allen and San Fernando Valley jazz fans. Allen started a Dixieland group with George Segal, Conrad Janis, producer Paul Maslansky, writer Sheldon Keller, pianist Arnold Ross and others, called The Beverly Hills Unlisted Jazz Band, which attracted a lot of attention and eventually did concerts, including an appearance on *The Tonight Show*. Without mentioning any names, some of the players who had marquee value were not really great jazz players like Allen Goodman, Conrad Janis and Arnold Ross and my private name for the group was (sorry, Allen) *The Beverly Hills Ungifted Jazz Band*.

Meanwhile, *Harper Valley PTA* limped along to so-so ratings for a year doing nothing but revenge shows and when my commitment was up I didn't re-up and wasn't asked to, and that was fine with me. I wanted to write something better than Fred Silverman-type television and do more movies and, in short, be a contender. Once *Harper Valley PTA* was over I was quickly off the Universal lot, never having attended one black-tie dinner. The Tower kept its word. And because the lawyer guy was still in charge of Norman's company and would never forgive me for accepting a producing job at Universal rather than sit home without salary waiting for an endless (I think it lasted three months) actors' strike to end, I knew Marilyn and I wouldn't be going to any more Tandem/TAT charity dinners or Christmas parties.

What I didn't realize at the time was that during his reign at all three networks Fred Silverman and his protégé Brandon Tartikoff and like-thinking executives in the major networks, production companies and talent agencies had planted some seeds which were about ready to blossom. And over the next ten years of my career the illegal practice of ageism took root in Hollywood. You thought this book would only be about <u>good</u> news?

Chapter Twenty-Two
Logan's Run . . .
Hollywood Imitates a Movie

As a transient I didn't feel I had to call The Tower and say bye-bye when my gig at Universal was over. It was time to find an office because for the first time in many years I wasn't on staff or part of any production entity. In Studio City, an artsy-fartsy enclave of actors, writers, directors, producers, wannabes and old movie lots, on the main drag called Ventura Boulevard in the heart of town, stood The Andrews Building. It had been there since the 1930s and was a two-story structure with storefronts on the ground floor and a dozen offices upstairs, some with private bathrooms. It had always been a writers' building except for a brief time during World War II when it's whispered it was a bordello. I'd had my eye on The Andrews Building because it was full of writer friends, and I knew that Beverly, the widow of the late owner, Fred Andrews, was stuck in the 1930s. The rents were ridiculously cheap, so there was virtually no turnover. But Mr. Magoo just keeps stumbling ahead and there was a nice corner suite available when I came to look. Beverly Andrews approved me on the spot and I grabbed that suite. It would be my writing home for about twelve years.

    I learned that Niven Busch, novelist and screenwriter from the old days (*Duel in the Sun*, *The Postman Always Rings Twice*) had once occupied my office and, in fact, had written *Duel* there. Good vibes, I thought. I wanted to verify that and found out how to get in touch with him through the Writers' Guild, and we exchanged a few letters and phone calls. I had just missed his visit to Los Angeles and invited him to lunch and a tour of his old digs on his next trip, and we talked about The Andrews Building. I kept mentioning septuagenarian Beverly and he didn't seem to know who I was talking about until I described her: a tiny lady with red hair who'd been a dancer in the movies. "Aha! That's that little girl who was sniffin' around Fred Andrews!" Nice to know that the sniffing was apparently successful.

Beverly cared more about her writers than their paltry rent money and she was a great steward of the building and its tradition. We had some good writers with very good careers going such as Rick Mittleman, Aubrey Tadman, novelist Richard Setlowe, comedian/ writer Bruce Howard, John Herman Shaner (*Goin' South*). In the dozen years or so I was there Beverly only goofed once that I can recall. The building was in constant need of paint and repairs and she found some painter/derelict with whom she made a barter deal. He could have a little office in the front of the building if he'd paint the place and keep it ship-shape. I saw his car, which I think he was living in, and it was full of half-eaten fast food, crumpled wrappers, cigarette butts, and hundreds of losing lottery tickets. Based on that, I didn't predict the building would ever be ship-shape. He painted it all right, including a giant sign hanging in front facing Ventura Boulevard advertising his painting business. So now it was no longer The Writers' Building. It became The Writers' and Painter's Building . . . until the building started to look more and more like his car.

The building had a definite personality of its own and was the subject of many stories in the trade papers and the *Los Angeles Times*. It's within walking distance of a lot of great lunch places including Art's Delicatessen which, over the years with its overstuffed sandwiches and huge portions of fatty foods, is rumored to have killed more Jews than Hamas. The building is still there, but Beverly isn't, and the rents are no longer from a bygone era. Au contraire, they're from the next projected real-estate boom, whether it ever happens or not. I just hope nobody's in the building when "The Big One" hits . . . or even one of the little ordinary ones, because I remember how it shook when two of us used the stairs at the same time.

Screenwriters today don't have it easy. If they're in their thirties they

Hard at work in my Studio City office. The caption on the far left picture reads: "Leave Daddy alone, dear. If he can't think of something funny to write, we all starve to death"!

have to save their money, because unless they own a show or their own studio and can hire themselves, they'll be given a one-way ticket out of town when they're forty. If ever there were a profession where the appearance, race, age, gender, religion of the craftsman shouldn't count, it's writing. What's on the page should be the only thing that matters. If a script is full of clichés, past and irrelevant references, and is just plain no good ... don't use whoever wrote it. But don't discriminate in advance because of an artificial cut-off date related to chronological age. And the big networks, big studios, and big literary agencies have to stop what they're doing and be reminded that it's against the law. But they already know that.

Logan's Run, an interesting sci-fi flick from the late seventies, had as its premise that life was great in the futuristic society portrayed, but nobody seemed to be over thirty. That's because, to the horror of the protagonists, everyone is routinely killed when they reach age thirty . . . and that same mind set is alive and well today, where the movers and shakers are in league with each other and Madison Avenue (who think that old people never buy anything) and actually believe that veteran writers "don't have it anymore" and only fresh, new writers can come up with fresh, new ideas. The first time I ever heard that erroneous theory articulated publicly was in a speech by Brandon Tartikoff, who had succeeded Fred Silverman as President of NBC. In my instant knee-jerk angry letter to *The Times* I hoped that if Tartikoff ever went to the hospital for brain surgery, they would assign him a veteran surgeon with a proven record of successful surgeries, not some fresh new intern with fresh, new ideas.

In reality, having dealt with hundreds of writers over the years from veterans to students in my UCLA classes, I've noticed that it's a truism that the younger the writer, the more clichés and half-baked ideas show up, almost without exception. Writing involves thinking and I don't know too many people who think better at eighteen than at forty-eight. But in Hollywood perception is often the reality and so appearance counts heavily. I remember a network meeting at NBC where one of the up-and-coming young executives was wearing a light khaki short-sleeved shirt with one chevron on each arm, as if he were a private first class. At another meeting a month later everyone was wearing chevron shirts, but now it was mostly two stripes, signifying corporals. Then came epaulets. Whatever the show was that sent me there ended before I ever found out what was next. Network people, who are temporary people making permanent decisions that affect lives, all seem to be interested in what I call contemporariology . . . the study of what's happening right now, this minute.

When I first heard about and actually noticed ageism it affected some older, mediocre, and in my opinion, ungifted writers who were properly being weeded out from the work force. Those people only worked when employment was full and they never worked at the same place twice, so it was not an outrage if they were under-employed. But then more and more excellent writers with great track records began to complain they were having trouble getting an agent and getting meetings, let alone getting work. I wondered if this was a coming plague, and the answer came sooner than I expected. I kept right on working right up into my late fifties, maybe because I never looked my age, but I hated it when my latest agent asked me to take *Get Smart*, *All In The Family*, and *Mary Tyler Moore* off of my resume because to have worked on those shows I'd be too old to employ. I took that agent off my resume instead.

I loved that office in The Andrews Building. I wrote my first feature film, *Big Bad John*, there, and it was a great place to write, to think, to go to lunch, or to take an afternoon nap. From that office it was walking distance to my new agent, Mike Rosen, of the Dade/ Rosen Agency, and he came up with a very interesting gig. He had a relationship with an independent producer who wanted to shoot a movie in Yugoslavia. This was in the post-Tito days, but Yugoslavia was still considered behind the iron curtain and under the Soviet sphere of influence. What they had was a story outline from the director, an award-winning filmmaker from Croatia (which in those days was only an ethnic area of northern Yugoslavia), and did I think I could make a screenplay out of it? I read the outline and had to ask the question, "Who's the audience for this picture?" Americans. Well, Americans are not going to understand a World War I movie that takes place in Europe, does not involve Germans, and requires an extensive knowledge of The Austrian Empire as well as Balkan history. If we moved it up to World War II when the Nazis were around they'd know who the good guys and bad guys were without a lot of dull exposition and it would be accessible to a much wider audience.

They liked that idea and I soon found myself jetting to Frankfort, Germany, and from there to Zagreb, the capital of Croatia, a city of about one million, to meet their local-boy-made-good director Rajko Grylic, which is pronounced: Rye-Ko Grill-itch. The idea was to hammer out a story with him, which satisfied his original concept and yet make a comedy that Americans would want to see. Rajko was a wonderful host and my two weeks in Zagreb more than made up for the Benny Goodman trip behind the iron curtain that I'd missed two decades earlier.

He took me to the movie studio, Jadran Film (Jadran means Adriatic in Serbo-Croatian), where the picture would be shot, and set up sort of an office and sort of a phone and sort of a typewriter. I was staying at the Intercontinental Hotel, the best hotel in town, where everyone whoever made a film in Yugoslavia stayed. Yugoslavia was a communist country completely controlled by the Party hierarchy in Belgrade, but was nothing like the Orwellian Big-Brother-Is-Watching-You kind of country I expected. Even though there were police with automatic weapons everywhere, the government was not like a fierce totalitarian oppressive regime spouting communist slogans and suppressing rebellion in the public squares. There was no rebellion and the government was considered a vast, dull bureaucracy, which people laughed at and paid no attention to. It was like a society governed by the Department of Motor Vehicles. And, speaking of that, I noticed how well everyone was driving. Stopping for STOP signs, stopping for red lights, waiving the right-of-way, etc. I'd just come from L.A. where people only slow down for red lights, creep through STOP signs, and give you the finger if you happen to be in their way while they're breaking the law. Rajko smiled. "You know what you'd get in Zagreb for running a red light? Six months in prison." Sounds like something we should try back home.

The best part of my days was evenings. We'd stroll through Zagreb, a city with zero street crime, and find outdoor cafes everywhere, filled with people discussing world events, smoking very powerful cigarettes, drinking even more powerful European coffee, or sipping slivovitz, which is so powerful it's a good thing Lindsay Lohan hasn't heard about it yet. Rajko knew everyone and everyone knew Rajko and wanted to meet the American screenwriter. Even though nearly everybody spoke English, I was determined to learn at least a smattering of Serbo-Croatian and bought a little tourist book, and by the end of the two weeks I could order my breakfast in their language.

Rajko and I did actually work during my visit, and came up with a solid story with a lot of comedy potential about an all-girl band working for the USO entertaining American troops during World War II who get stuck behind German lines and have to do unusual things to regain their freedom. I called it *Horns Up!* So I said bye-bye to Zagreb and Rajko and went back to The Andrews Building and wrote the script. And what was the experience like returning to that lovely country to shoot that funny picture? I wish I knew. Rajko and his studio, Jadran, loved *Horns Up!*, as did my agent, Mike Rosen. But there was an ominous silence from the independent filmmaker, the guy with the rest of the money. He suddenly produced a daughter, a wannabe writer/director who attached herself to the project. A person with no writing or directing credits (but with great connections) was now going to go through the script, become an auteur, and make her debut at the Cannes Film Festival, I suppose. There was no further involvement for Gordon after being paid for script and story, and there was no word of the daughter ever completing anything. Jadran Film Studio backed off, and the independent filmmaker and his money just sort of dried up and blew away.

Something that did get made, a segment of *The Twilight Zone*, turned out well and I used that script as a writing sample from then on. The actor who played the leading role put it on his tape reel as did the director. How I got this gig is just another example of knowing the right people. And in this case I happened to know Marilyn, who worked in the studios as a Production Assistant. She'd done a couple of CBS Movies and when the network decided to revisit *The Twilight Zone* in color and make it a little darker than the original Rod Serling series, Marilyn took a job working with Executive Producer Phillip De Guerre. She'd come home at night and tell me amusing stories about the yelling and screaming that went on daily and how angry young man and sci-fi writer Harlan Ellison finally found a comfortable spot for him and his old-fashioned manual Smith-Corona typewriter to work, outside on the building's balcony. There were some impressive names, both actors and directors, who were waiting in line to do the show. People like Robert Klein, Danny Kaye and director Gus Trikonis.

Marilyn thought that I might like to write an episode even though I'd never done anything but comedy; however, I never really considered it. Then one day a *Twilight Zone* story popped into my head as I was cleaning the swimming pool and I couldn't get it out of there. So I asked Marilyn to find out if I'd be welcome to pitch my one idea to the Story Editor, a bright young man named Rockne O'Bannon. She brought him my credits and said that I had a story for them and could I come in a pitch it? He said, "Why not?"

I came in with a perfect premise for them. One of America's beloved comedians (who we will learn is really a rotten person) gets into a terrible auto accident and, while his life is hanging in the balance, finds himself in *The Twilight Zone* and has to go on stage immediately to perform. He's in a bizarre other-worldly comedy club (*a la* the *Star Wars* bar) and he goes out there and does his "A" material and impressions and nobody laughs at anything. As he's dealing with a heckler, he lets something slip about his personal life that's far from flattering, and a few patrons snicker. Then he fills in some of the deplorable details and he gets a huge laugh. What's this? He quickly learns that in the *Twilight Zone* comedy club they only laugh at reality, not material, and the dirtier and more lowdown the truth, the harder they guffaw. Soon he's torn between getting no laughs and telling the truth about himself (no matter how disgusting) in order to get laughter, love and acceptance from his weird audience. Rockne loved the idea and so did everyone else and I was sent to script.

When it came time to film the show, they found a drag queen nightclub on Ventura Boulevard in Studio City called The Queen Mary and the set decorator made the place even weirder than normal. Marilyn pulled some strings and was able to get Michele, by now a very pretty young woman, into the mix of extras. The day of the shoot and unknown to Marilyn or me, Michele walked right up to director Gus Trikonis and said, "My dad wrote this script." So Gus, not knowing if her dad was a biggie who might have an impact on his career, put her in a prominent place up front, and she's all throughout that comedy club sequence. Tim Thomerson, who played Billie Diamond the tormented comedian, did a great job, and it was a big thrill for me to see that audience of well-trained extras react in complete silence to jokes and then laugh hilariously at Billie Diamond's sordid and nasty life. Rockne and I became friends and later, when he needed an office, I got him into The Andrews Building.

I heard about a writers' club within the walls of Lompoc Maximum Security Federal Penitentiary. The Writers' Guild was looking for volunteers who would go in small groups to Lompoc, a few hours away by car, and conduct seminars, hold workshops, and generally help with their screenwriting program. I thought it would be an interesting experiment in terror management for me to be locked up for a few hours with those guys, and just might do them some good, even though most of them will never get out. There are two Lompoc facilities, one of which is light-heartedly called Club Fed, where there are no walls and plenty of soccer, volleyball, and basketball, and after they're tired of that, the happy hour, which lasts until 6:00 p.m. Where I went was the other place, with lots of walls, towers, razor-wire enclosures and guys with machine guns. I guess I wanted to know what it would feel like having seven doors slam behind me.

As you approach the mammoth structure you are under the watchful eyes of the guards in the tower that controls the main entrance, and as you park and head toward the entrance you start to get loudspeaker instructions: HALT! PREPARE TO SURRENDER YOUR I.D. And about the time you get there a bucket on a rope comes down about forty feet and further instructions: PUT YOUR I.D. AND EVERYTHING YOU'RE CARRYING INTO THE BUCKET. You do that and, through the miracle of thirteenth-century technology, the bucket is hauled up and while you wait you can read the notices posted all over the place about the rules and that if you're carrying drugs or weapons you will go directly to jail and be tortured and never seen again, or something like that. Then the bucket returns with your stuff and ENTER NOW! And the first of two razor-wire doors opens, you walk in, and it closes behind you, leaving you trapped between them. Then the second door opens and you head to the actual main door, which is nothing special. Every Scottish castle has one like that. Once inside that door there are pat-downs, metal detectors, more signs, more instructions, and four doors and a maze of locked corridors. Later, you're in a cafeteria, which has been converted to a room suitable for the seminar/ workshop. Now the inmates start to enter. They're clean as a whistle and dressed in freshly washed and pressed khaki jump suits and have themselves just been through a complete screening and search including body cavities, and they're real glad to see anybody, especially Hollywood writers. The workshops involved nothing heroic on our parts. We'd talk about our philosophies of writing, a bit about our careers and programs or movies they might have seen, and open things up to questions,

Marilyn talks to an inmate at Lompoc State Penitentiary during their thank-you dinner.

some of which were specific about a particular piece or story the individual was working on.

During a break the inmates would be allowed to mingle with the writers and buy us drinks . . . from a soft drink machine, which took quarters, and they were furnished with lots of coins. I learned a lot during these minglings and what I concluded was that these folks, most of whom would never see freedom again, were normal human beings in every respect . . . except one. They were all apparently missing that part of the human brain whose job it is to tell its owner, "Hold on! If you do that there will be a consequence!" Another interesting tidbit: every single con I talked to admitted that he was guilty as charged. But most of them said they shouldn't be there at all because it was a bad bust, with lots of police/prosecutor error. And they were all champion rationalizers . . . my crime was no big deal, but see that con over there? He's one bad dude.

I visited Lompoc four or five times and I hope the members of the writers' club got as much out of it as I did. The program eventually ended with a thank-you dinner, which included Marilyn who'd become curious about Lompoc. Then there was a change of wardens, and the new guy never restarted the project. I never heard of any successful writing or story or script sales coming out of those sessions, but I can assure you that absolutely no one was maimed or murdered during the hours that we met.

Another career move came along that I enjoyed, in spite of my feelings about classrooms and colleges. The head of UCLA Extension was looking for writers who wanted to teach screenwriting for their Adult Education series. No college degree necessary ... just actual experience writing for television and film. My kind of town! I applied, was accepted, and over a period of eight years or so taught many TV and Film writing classes for UCLA Extension. The classes were at night, on campus and full of students who were interested in learning. At least two of them had nice careers and eventually won Emmys for comedy writing. It was a kind of a rewarding way to spend some time as I got older and work got slimmer. Also, I was paid, and there's nothing like the dignity of being paid. I brought in some great guests like Bernard Slade *(Same Time, Next Year, Tribute)* and it was fun not hating going to college.

Ageism began taking root in the Los Angeles basin like billions of square yards of crabgrass. I noticed a lot of the older writers wearing girdles, having face lifts, and dyeing their hair ridiculously young colors I said to myself, "I'll have none of that." At the same time, Marilyn was beginning to bug me about my drooping eyelids and reminded me that my eyes were so saggy and my peripheral vision so poor our excellent WGA Health Plan would probably pay for an operation. Not interested! Really not interested! I won't be like those other dudes. I'm still working and many people think I look young for my age. But Marilyn continued her campaign to have me submit to eyelift surgery and I continued to ignore her pleas. One day I picked her up at her manicure place after a manicure/pedicure session, as we were on our way to dinner. She introduced me to the Vietnamese lady who'd just done her nails, and Ms. Ho Chi Minh took one look at me and said, "That you husband? He much older than you!" I made an appointment the next day to have my eyes done.

Chapter Twenty-Three
Big Changes . . . Ready or Not

The quantity and quality of phone calls as well as employment opportunities definitely descended in the mid-eighties and the number of unreturned phone calls was definitely on the rise. Ageism affecting writers was being discussed openly in the trade papers as well as *The Los Angeles Times*, and it was something the tenants of The Andrews Building knew all too well. In fairness, older writers should expect a certain amount of slowdown due to attrition . . . favorite producers getting older, getting out of the business, or dying. For instance, Sheldon Leonard, who obviously liked the way I wrote, was no longer in a position to hire me or anyone else . . . or even get a meeting. And other producers and movers and shakers a generation older than me were either already out of the business or deceased. But attrition couldn't explain 100% unemployment for a lot of guys my age and younger. The explanation can only be blatant, agreed-upon industry-wide ageism among networks and production companies and okayed by talent agencies.

When things were really slow, I wrote a few cartoons for Hanna-Barbera, which is the bottom of the barrel, writing-wise. Cartoon writers have some sort of union totally without clout and what they need is The Writers' Guild of America, but for reasons I don't fully understand, it'll never happen. Ray Parker, a friend of mine going back to the days of my incarceration on *The Bob Hope Show* when we were both on staff at the same time, had been a good and funny writer for a long time, putting funny words into the mouth of Art Linkletter, among other radio/TV guys. Ray ran out of WGA work, which was a shame because he's an articulate and amusing guy with the work ethic and a good attitude. He'd been hired by Hanna-Barbera, in a rare instance of good judgment, to produce their animated version of *The Dukes of Hazzard*, and if you must write cartoons to keep some kind of cash flow going, you can't do better than work for Ray Parker. He offered me as many as I could do and I wrote three episodes and, surprisingly, didn't mind it a bit. It was like writing little movies with short little scripts and short little paychecks. Fortunately, I only remember one joke from those three episodes. The Dukes were somehow involved with that week's villain, an old-fashioned pirate and his crew operating a pirate sailing ship proudly flying the Jolly Roger. The Captain was a stereotypical pirate with a patch over one eye, a peg leg, and a hook where his left hand should be. He was always saying things like "Har-har" and "Avast!" and "Belay that, matey!" and the joke was that after he and his crew sailed away from the pier where they were docked, a big blue HANDICAPPED DOCKING ONLY sign was revealed. Not a biggie, but it got a chuckle out of Ray.

A less fun experience was writing an episode of *The Jetsons* for a couple of other writer/producers at Hanna-Barbera I knew. These were the same two guys who moved out from the office next to Lloyd's and mine when we were on staff at *Get Smart* because there was "too much laughter coming from that room." Well, they absolutely took care of the "too much laughter" problem when I was working with them. As a small kid (or even as a grown-up) if I made some kind of corny joke, my mother, who would laugh at pretty much anything, would slap her thigh and while still giggling would say, "Oh, Gordy!" as if to say "stop punishing me with this great humorous material." Marilyn picked up on this through the years and if she ever heard me say anything she considered dumb or unfunny, she'd imitate Mom and say, "Oh, Gordy!" So, logically, the only pseudonym I could possibly use for those Hanna-Barbera scripts was O. Gordy.

A very good writer with great credits in both comedy and drama who enjoyed a lot of respect in our business really got everyone's attention when he took a full back page in both *Variety* and *The Hollywood Reporter* ranting on about how stupid ageism was. It got the industry's attention and, as far as I know, he never worked again in any kind of meaningful employment. His ad sounded a lot like whining and bitching and I hope that's not what I'm projecting here. But a lot of people my age were accurately assessing what was happening to us and rather than rant and rage about the illogic of it all, we wanted to do something about it. I've always been a fan of the Lloyd Schwartz operational system: have about seventeen irons in the fire at all times. One of my irons was participation in group discussions with a few of my peers about the problems of the day for older writers. This culminated in the formation of a company to create pilots, movies, and dramatic series and pitch them to the networks and production companies. We all put up a few bucks, got stationery, business cards, elected officers, met in my office, and actually got some buzz and excitement going. We called the company New Wrinkles Productions (either humor or a death wish) and stayed with it for quite a while. But the buzz was quickly gone, the excitement had been mostly on our part, and a bunch of us in a room pitching turned out to be more off-putting than just one of us. And as it happened, individually we were all working more than collectively, so New Wrinkles just kind of withered on the vine.

Two pilots came along around that time. One got produced and one didn't. Jerry Harrison, an independent producer I knew, came to me with a pilot script that was supposed to shoot in about a week. It was for direct syndication, not a network, and had been written by a sitcom writer whose work I knew. It was a nice idea, but poorly executed, with less than wonderful unmotivated jokes, sometimes out of character, and the script just lay there and said "Help me!" It was intended to boost the careers of the Landers sisters, two gorgeous gals who had everything going for them but their own series, and it needed a page one (from top to bottom) rewrite, in my opinion. Jerry agreed and asked me to do the rewrite. It meant I'd have to give up everything else and live in the office and just write for the next three days or so or they'd lose the tape facility where the pilot was to be shot. I accepted the gig on condition that I would produce the pilot with Jerry, largely to protect what I'd be working on for the next seventy-two hours or so. We made a deal, I got to work and three days later I'd become a hero to Jerry Harrison. There was no word from the original writer. Besides the Landers sisters, who did a great job, we cast Lyle Waggoner, Dick Van Patten, and David Lander (from *Laverne & Shirley*) and the shooting went well, the audience loved the show, and everyone knew that *Rock Candy* would be a hit series. Everyone was wrong, and it never got on the air.

But that's a more typical story than the next, which is about a pilot that never got made. It involved Aubrey Tadman, a Canadian-born writer/producer who had a musical background like me and worked as a jazz singer at some of the same clubs I'd worked. Aubrey had an office across the hall in The Andrews Building, was a golf buddy, and was the reason I'd heard about that magic building in the first place. We both happened to have the same agent and she pitched us to a development executive of a big production company who had a project that had series written all over it. We met her and made a deal to develop a charming little book into a sitcom about a compound of Russian immigrants stashed away by themselves in Santa Monica who'd been brainwashed by the Soviets for so long they were having difficulties adjusting to freedom, American culture, etc., and were paranoid and believed that they were constantly being watched by the KGB. In other words . . . a building full of fish-out-of-water characters. Perfect!

So we did a lot of work, taking from the book what would work best for American television, coming up with character names, relationships, consolidating a large bunch of people into a more usable group and created some episode stories (to prove that the series had legs) and got the show to the point where we were convinced . . . as long as there's a Soviet Union this series will be great.

The production company executive was thrilled with our work and off we went to CBS to pitch the idea. The pitch went well, not only because it was a slam-dunk idea, but also because we were well prepared and confident. We bowled over the CBS lady who not only loved us, she loved the show we described and asked if she could have a first draft by the end of September (about four weeks away) and as Aubrey and I said "Yes!" our partner, the production company executive, said, "No, it wouldn't be fair to the guys to work that fast and besides, I'm focusing on another project right now. Could we postpone the pilot until January?" Well ... okay, I guess. Aubrey and I were as amazed as we were crushed. Our alleged partner had just turned a big money script commitment into a let's-wait-until-next-year-and-then-see full-fledged maybe. I had trouble containing my displeasure and I don't remember holding the door for her as we left. Of course, the Berlin Wall came down about a month later, the Soviet Union collapsed and with it, our premise, and the accumulation of big bucks.

Jerry Harrison came through again, this time because he needed some writers to produce and write a roast "honoring," if that's the word, famous Yankee baseball coach Billy Martin. Mickey Mantle would be there and so would Yogi Berra, Whitey Ford, Howard Cosell and other sports biggies and it would be filmed at one of the casinos in Atlantic City. I don't know a better joke writer/roaster than Aubrey, so I got him aboard and we went to work. It was a lot of fun and we even went to Dodger Stadium where the Astros were playing the Dodgers and interviewed Yogi Berra (the Astros' Manager at the time) to see if we could get anything usable for the roast. We couldn't. Yogi has said many funny things over the years, like "when you come to the fork in the road ... take it" and, when asked by a waiter at a pizzeria if he wanted his pizza cut into six pieces or eight pieces, said, "You better make it six pieces. I can't eat eight pieces of pizza." But he didn't come up with anything memorable that day. Maybe because the Dodgers were beating up on his team. The roast turned out funny and was actually pretty good, but I don't know if the main participants knew that or anything else, judging from the amount of alcohol that was consumed on that dais.

Other deals with other production companies came and went, but I've talked enough about things that almost happened. I also wrote a lot of shows that did happen and got produced and were on the air that I don't clutter up my resume with, like *Small Wonder* and *Mama's Family*, a spin-off from a *Carol Burnett Show* sketch in which Vicki Lawrence plays her Mama, and from which I just got another residual, twenty years later.

Family-wise things were going great. We still lived in our beautiful home in the Hills and we put Michele through beauty school so she could become a hairdresser. I've been able to get her gigs, from time to time, as a hair/make-up person on some productions, and she always enjoys that. And I get haircuts for life ... except that pretty soon Marilyn and I would be living in the desert a hundred and forty miles away.

After that deadly Writers' Guild strike of 1988 I've talked about, my agent went out of business and I had to look around for a new one. I found a terrific lady, not exactly new, named Sylvia Hirsch, who I'd known since the days when she was one of my agents at the William Morris Agency. Sylvia was a nice person to have in your corner. Apparently, she hadn't gotten the industry-wide memo about not dealing with writers over fifty (which has since been revised to forty and is headed toward thirty). She took me on cheerfully, which is more than I can say for all the big agencies, like CAA, who in years past had begged me to sign with them.

I got a call from Sylvia ... had I ever been nice to a young Canadian writer? She gave me the name, but it didn't ring a bell. I try to be nice to everyone and I couldn't imagine what she was talking about. But it seems this young lady was now part of a show called *City* that was gearing up at CBS Studio Center, which would be produced by her brother, Paul Haggis, as a first-time producer. It was going to be an hour-long "dramady" starring Valerie Harper (of *Mary Tyler Moore* fame), and Haggis specifically asked for me because I was once "especially kind and helpful" to his sister during my Norman Lear days when everyone else was far too busy to give her the time of day, and would I be interested in being Head Writer? Sure! Kind of like *Androcles and the Lion*, or one good turn deserves another or karma, or something like that.

Anyhow, I got Aubrey involved and the two of us showed up at CBS, met Paul Haggis, a writer from *Thirtysomething* who was being given his first producing job, and I re-met the sister, whom I barely remembered, but to whom I'm grateful. We began developing the show. Paul Haggis is a brilliant writer who went on to a very nice career in film and he's had a great run, including *Crash*, which netted him an Academy Award. But in 1989, in my opinion, he was not the best television producer and spent a lot of time on gang-writing, which may be popular in some circles but is antithetical to the process of getting scripts ready when you need them. And it became a cause of dissention early on.

But there was bigger stuff going on that year. One day I got a call from Mom saying that she couldn't seem to get my dad to wake up that morning. He was breathing but his eyes were closed and he was not conscious. I rushed over to their house and found him just as she said, alive but not responding. I called 911 and tried to get him alert, but to no avail. The paramedics arrived amazingly soon, looked him over briefly, and immediately took him to a nearby hospital, where X-rays and CAT scans showed that he had a subdural hematoma, that is, a lump under his skull. Seems he'd had a fall during a nocturnal visit to the bathroom and it caused a broken blood vessel inside his head that turned, over the next few days, into a mass of broken blood vessels and bruised tissue that had expanded to the size of a small grapefruit, which had squashed his brain and caused the unconsciousness and, if not discovered in time, would have caused his death. They had to perform emergency surgery, drilling a hole into his skull to drain out the mass and relieve the pressure. Ronald Reagan underwent that exact same process a few weeks later when he fell off his horse, and the joke that went around then was what came out of his skull was Grecian Formula 16.

But there was nothing funny about my dad's situation. He eventually recovered to the extent that he could be moved to a convalescent hospital. His acuity gradually returned and he became sufficiently alert that he could once again read his acoustical and pipe organ magazines and comprehend them. Not bad for a guy almost ninety with a squeezed brain. But, sadly, it seemed obvious that he was never really going to recover from this event. Mom was affected just as much and was really not capable of running a big

This gives an idea of Dad's final home-installed pipe organ in his studio.

house alone, but she chose to stay there and Marilyn and I knew we'd have to keep close tabs on her.

Meanwhile, back at the studio, Valerie Harper, a lovely person, was there along with a talented cast and CBS immediately threw a big monkey wrench into *City*. Instead of the show being an hour-long dramady, it was now scheduled to be a half-hour comedy. That meant that the seven major players in the ensemble each had to have a storyline in each episode by contract. A more experienced producer would have said "no . . . that's not possible in a half-hour show," and it wasn't. The scripts started coming in at fifty-four pages, way too long for a half-hour show, and not every character had enough to do to justify a storyline. But we pressed on. And when the actual shooting was over and the post-production began, the film was always several minutes long and had to be cut mercilessly. The show, by the time it aired, looked jerky and too abbreviated and there were punch lines that had been cut for time, as well as set-up lines which no longer had punch lines. In addition to this, there were some artistic differences that developed. This always happens when a show is in trouble and there are conflicting views on how to fix the problem. So it became an unpleasant experience, combined with what was going on with my family health-wise, and it was an awful time in my life. But somehow we made it through all the episodes ordered and my dad made it through to January 1990, his ninetieth year, before passing on. It was heartbreaking to see what had become of this brilliant man who'd been such a good, loving father and now could not do anything for himself. And so when pneumonia took him, it was probably a good thing. No wonder they call pneumonia "The Old Man's Friend."

Meanwhile, Mom had proven that she was no longer able to live alone, leaving doors open, the stove on, eating passé food from the fridge, etc., and so Marilyn and I had to find her a retirement home where she could be comfortable, and put the house into shape to sell, because we were in a years-long real-estate boom, and no one knew when it was going to end. It wasn't too tough finding a nice place for Mom closer to where we lived, and we got her installed there. But selling the house was another matter. The first question was what to do with Dad's pipe organ . . . his real life's work. It was probably the largest home-installed pipe organ in the world, with pipes made by long-gone craftsmen from Europe, a complete baroque classical pipe organ. The idea was to donate it to a church, but it would have to be a wealthy church, because the removal, moving, repair, and installation might run as high as fifty thousand dollars, by some estimates. Marilyn found the perfect church: The First Congregational Church of Los Angeles on Wilshire Boulevard. They had deep pockets and were currently upgrading their own pipe organs, and when they saw what Dad had created it was done deal. With the addition of his sixty-three-rank four-manual organ, they would have the largest church pipe organ in the world.

Marilyn, who had gone into real estate in the last few years and had done really well, knew just what had to be done to the house in those last months of 1989. While the market was still hot, we had to make the house look as attractive as possible and went through the place room by room passing along or throwing out stuff my parents had kept since the 1920s. They had lived through The Great Depression and didn't throw anything out. The grandchildren came over and took what photos and mementos they could find, and we had to deal with the rest. So . . . three boxcar-sized dumpsters later we put the house on the market and it wasn't there long. A developer bought it knowing he'd have to sink at least a hundred-grand into new plumbing, new master bath, new roof, new heating/air conditioning, massive pool repair, and so forth. But the house had charm, curb appeal, and location, location, location, and he made a new home out of it. Unfortunately for him, the market crashed and burned about three weeks after we closed escrow. Are you beginning to understand the Gordon-Whitey-Mr. Magoo relationship that's evident throughout this book?

After *City* mercifully ended, I did some more work, wrote a movie with Aubrey that he got me on for Canadian television, and taught some more at UCLA, but by now, I was a little too long in the tooth to be pitching episodes or writing cartoons.

My attractive daughters, lovely and sweet as they were, had all been through some relationships and marriages, hadn't found Mr. Right yet. My son Brian was on a disastrous flight plan and was about to be inducted into the Alcoholic's Hall of Fame. He became a brilliant musician while still in his teens, and had come a long way from the few exploratory toots and squeaks on his clarinet when he first got it in grade school. I was knocked out of my socks when I walked into Donte's, a big-time jazz club in North Hollywood, to hear him play with his kid band, the Eagle Rock High School Jazz Band. Brian was playing lead alto and was about as good as I'd ever heard, and I'd heard a few good lead alto players in my day. His jazz solos were incredible, and the experience brought tears to my eyes. He must have been really paying attention when I brought him into the orchestra pit of the Mark Hellinger Theatre and he sat there in his little blue suit and watched the saxophone players.

Big Changes... Ready or Not   215

A special time with father and son during the Alaskan cruise.

He was on the road by the time he was eighteen (sound familiar?) playing with "ghost bands." That is, the Tommy Dorsey Orchestra (without Tommy) or the Glenn Miller Orchestra (without Glenn). Then he met Ray Charles, auditioned, and played lead alto with Ray for about ten years. He married Janice, a beautiful girl and a member of The Raylettes, Ray Charles' back-up singers. They were on the road together for years. But somewhere along the way he learned how to drink and do other drugs. His sisters tell me that he started drinking around age ten, about a year after the family was torn apart by divorce. I don't really know the why or the when, just that it was obvious he needed help and support now.

Karen knew somebody who knew somebody and she set up a family intervention, which was held at our house. Brian walked unsuspectingly up the steps to our Tarzana house and into our living room where he was confronted with a whole room full of family and friends who loved him and wanted him to live. It was a very emotional hour or so, after which Brian was driven straight to rehab, where he stayed a little longer than Britney

Spears could have endured, but not long enough to get clean and sober. Years later, he did it on his own and joined AA. When he was sober, he got lots of gigs working with bands on cruise ships, and worked his way up the chain of command and became a Bandmaster with The *Princess* Cruise Line. He was able to get Marilyn and me family privileges and we went on a ten-day cruise to Alaska via the Inside Passage. He was young, slim, and handsome, the happiest I'd ever seen him, and that ten-day cruise was the longest consecutive quality time I'd ever spent with him since childhood, and I'll never forget it. Like my brother, my son always seemed to be someplace else.

Speaking of Red ... he was now approaching age sixty-five and was looking forward, if that's the phrase, to Medicare. Not a whole lot to look forward to, if you ask me, but to a jazz musician perpetually on the fringe of insolvency with no real health plan, it's a biggie. For many years Red had been taking medication (and certain other substances) for heart pain, shortness of breath, numbness in his arms and every other well-known symptom of heart disease, but had been avoiding a doctor's care (and news he didn't want to hear which he couldn't pay for). He was waiting for Medicare and Social Security, both of which would kick in on his sixty-fifth birthday in the fall of 1992. His wife Diane, an American and one of five children, had a father who owned five houses in Salem, Oregon. Her father decided he'd give each kid a house, which worked out great for Red and Diane, because they were planning to relocate to the States once Red reached that magic birthday. So it was no problem to get here a few months before that and settle into their new home. Red continued to work his same gigs basically all over the world, except he was flying from Salem instead of Stockholm.

When he reached sixty-five on September 20, 1992 he had done the necessary paperwork and was eligible for Medicare and Social Security. Then he went to see the doctor. He was at least seventy-five pounds overweight and didn't look very healthy, and the doctor immediately put him on a treadmill. He collapsed on the treadmill and was rushed to the hospital where it was determined that he needed a quintuple coronary bypass, and soon. The surgery was scheduled and, while in the hospital the night before the operation, he had a massive stroke, from which he never recovered. In my last phone conversation with him I felt as if I were talking to the Rain Man, and that was devastating. He died five days later.

Unfortunately, it gets worse. Lloyd Turner, who'd undergone extensive surgery and treatment for cancer, passed away three weeks after that. I'd lost my older brother and my surrogate older brother all within three weeks. A year and a couple of months later we were moving Mom from her comfortable retirement home to a full-care facility. She now needed supervision twenty-four/seven. As I was packing up her few remaining possessions, Marilyn was giving her a bath. She stopped breathing and died in Marilyn's arms and we cried like babies. No matter how old you are and no matter how old they are, losing your parents is a shock and it knocked me for a loop. And you thought this book would be full of laughs.

Staying in Los Angeles waiting for the non-ringing phone to ring and no one wanting Gordon Mitchell to write anything anymore, dealing with the continuing real estate slump and watching Marilyn's business go more or less down the tubes didn't sound appealing to either of us, so I took an early Writers' Guild retirement, and an early musician's pension. Marilyn sold our Tarzana house and while waiting for escrow to close and a new life to begin, we rewarded ourselves with a trip to Europe. We booked a tour and were headed for London, Paris, and Rome only we never made it past Paris. Marilyn developed an intestinal occlusion, or blockage, and if not for an alert house doctor, might easily have died of peritonitis. She needed emergency surgery, and got her first glimpse of the Champs-Elysees from the back of an ambulance. We went to the American Hospital of Paris, where everybody above floor mopper speaks fluent English. Marilyn was rushed into surgery and then into intensive care. During the ten days of her hospitalization, I dusted off my high school French, got us off the tour we were on, found a place to live near the hospital and dealt with foreign medical coverage and the problem of how to get us home. Marilyn had a wonderful surgeon and

We return to Paris and hang out with the surgeon who saved Marilyn's life, Dr. Jean-Pierre Coquillaud.

the best care, and she recovered beautifully. We estimated that, in America fourteen years ago, the tab for all the service she received would have added up to about $150,000. But the French price tag was $13,000, and my Writers' Guild Health Plan covered it totally. God bless the Writers' Guild of America!

Back home again, we still had a few weeks to get out of the house before we moved to our favorite vacation destination, the Palm Springs area. I'd had enough rejection and bad news to last me the rest of my life, and I expected to do nothing but play golf, feed the pigeons in the park and drool. Wrong again!

Chapter Twenty-Four
The Little Town with a Heart

In *The Wizard of Oz* when Dorothy woke up in Oz the movie suddenly was in full color and everything was beautiful compared to the bleak black-and-gray farm in Kansas she'd just left. And when you drive to the desert from gray, smoggy, overcrowded Los Angeles and get to the other side of the mountain pass and reach the desert, your life is suddenly in color. Less traffic, less noise, less crime, lower-priced real estate . . . it's beautiful. There were no Munchkins around when we arrived in Palm Desert, but from what I hear they were just a bunch of dirty old men anyway.

We picked out a beautiful house on the eleventh tee of a great golf course in a brand-new gated community and we thought we were in hog heaven. As Marilyn got busy turning it into a showplace, I joined the Men's Club, bought a golf car and proceeded to golf, golf, golf. After about a week and a half I made an amazing discovery that every sixty-two year old man should be aware of: THERE'S MORE TO LIFE THAN GOLF. Golf is great when it's your getaway, but not when it's your job and every round becomes a metaphor for your current standing in the universe. Since I was definitely retired and never expected to use my brain again I had lots of time to read and I picked up a locally published four-color slick golf magazine called *Golf News*. I noticed that it was a well-written, award-winning monthly magazine, but that there wasn't a whole lot of humor in it. And if there is a sport that lends itself to humor easier than golf, tell me about it. So I called Dan Poppers, the editor/publisher, told him a little bit about my background and my interest in golf and asked if he'd be interested in a humorous golf column. He said, "Let's have lunch," and before lunch was over I had a deal to write my column, get paid for it, get some perks, some free golf, look for a "hook" that would make a column every month and become a fake sports writer every time a big tournament came to town. Not bad! My column was called *Backspin* and I wrote it for four years, until I got too busy playing music and doing other writing, which I'll talk about later. But probably the main reason for shutting down the column: I really couldn't think of one more funny thing about golf.

About the same time I started writing the column, Marilyn and I went to dinner at a nice place called The Sandbar in La Quinta, one of the desert communities, and I sat in with the jazz trio, playing the bass of Gene Moss, a fellow screenwriter and voice-over guy who'd retired a few years before me and had always wanted to play bass. Once in the desert he bought a bass and an amp, found The Sandbar, declared himself a bass player and played there pro bono with the house pianist for the rest of his life. Gene was a very good joke writer and he and his partner, Jim Thurman, did some of the same gigs that Lloyd Turner and I had done, including writing for Bob Hope one season. But then Thurman went to New York and worked on *Sesame Street* and other similar shows, while Gene stayed in town and became the number one voice-over guy in Los Angeles and made a bundle doing it. The television show that I inherited when I joined the Stan Worth Trio back in the late sixties was the *Moss & Thurman Show*, a local comedy/variety nightly show, and that's where we'd met. He was a big fan of my bass playing, and I would give him little tips and mini-lessons over the years of our friendship. And now Gene was a bass player every weekend and it was great to see him again. After I sat in for a tune or two, I recognized two things: even though I was totally rusty, I could still play and still sounded good … and I enjoyed it.

Then an interesting thing happened maybe the second time I sat in with Gene's keyboard guy Paul Schaffer (the jazz Paul Schaffer, not the rich one). Al Lohman was there having dinner. Al had been half of Lohman

& Barkley, Los Angeles' most successful morning-drive guys on KFI radio for decades, and when Lohman & Barkley got their own television variety show on KNBC-TV (an early version of *Laugh-In)* I was the studio bass player. What are the odds against running into two TV show hosts that I used to play bass for at a small restaurant in La Quinta? Only Mr. Magoo knows. Al was now living in the desert and doing a popular radio show (Barkley had passed on years earlier) and told me about a manager of a radio station who sang and who had a steady weekend gig upcoming at the Hyatt Hotel in downtown Palm Springs. He was putting together a trio and was looking for a bass player. Should he tell him about me? Sure! Even though I hadn't played professionally for about twenty-six years I could tell from my brief sit-ins with Paul Schaffer that it wouldn't take me long to catch up.

I bought a decent relatively inexpensive factory-made bass that looked fabulous and sounded okay, a cheap amplifier (I never used an amp in my first music career) and a cheap tux and I was in business again, playing with the Gene Pietragallo Trio at The Hyatt. The gig lasted about a year; I got my chops back and then some, and ended up playing there with my own trio for a couple of more years. One weekend at The Hyatt, a harmonica player, one of the acts we got friendly with on the *Princess* Line Alaska cruise, came in. He'd just seen Brian in San Francisco, who told him where I was playing, and sent his love to Marilyn and me. I said "Great" and then he added, "Yeah, we went out for a few drinks together" and my heart dropped through the floor. This is not how you stay on the AA program.

Gene Pietragallo, in his position of manager of KPSL, asked me to guest-host one of his talk shows when they had some kind of emergency, and I guess he liked my showbiz-oriented stories and on-air persona and set me up with a radio show once a week. It was a one-hour live interview show with guest celebrities and was called *The Power Lunch*. Marilyn produced the show and we'd have lunch at The Hyatt, giggle a lot, trade jokes and stories and career insights with some high-profile personalities and have a fun radio show and a nice lunch. Because the show was on Friday there were always lots of celebrities around and we had guests like Jack

Jones, Kaye Ballard, Dom DeLuise, Jerry Vale, Wayne Rogers, and even Tempest Storm. It lasted almost two years (a long time in radio) until the station was sold and the new owners had no time for nonsense like that, unless I wanted to buy the time and try to round up sponsors to pay for it. As dumb as I am about business, I didn't need to be told that wasn't such a wonderful idea.

On the radio in Palm Springs.

On the radio with Jack Jones and with Jerry Vale.

Doing the *Power Lunch* at the Hyatt with Producer Marilyn.

At the Sandbar now playing drums with Paul Schaffer and Gene Moss (also pro bono) was George Jerman, a former Capitol Records photographer, recording technician, and big-time jazz fan. George had tape-recorded a lot of the jazz legends in the early days of West Coast jazz, and a nostalgia record company was interested in putting out some CDs based on George's huge collection of tapes. But who could they get with a knowledge of jazz and a reputation in that corner of the music world to write the liner notes? Who indeed! So I ended up writing a total of about fifteen liner notes for George's CDs as well as other local musicians/entertainers personally-produced CDs.

So, let me sum up here. My retirement is a complete failure. I'm in town less than a year, I've got my own radio show and am writing a humor column, I'm also writing liner notes for CDs, and am playing bass at The Hyatt and other places. Drooling and feeding the pigeons in the park will just have to wait.

Meanwhile, back in the big city, we heard from the First Congregational Church of Los Angeles that it was time to dedicate Dad's pipe organ, which, after years of work, had been completely reconditioned and had been added to the church's other pipe organs and was now to have its debut. Some of the world's great organists would be participating in a concert and would we attend? We did, and it was great, and evoked tears on my part to know that Dad's life's work would go on, apparently forever. Lesley, Brian, Karen, and Michele were there and it was an unforgettable day.

Marilyn and I kept on running into people who we'd lost track of who now lived in the desert, and one of the musicians I met early on was Frankie Randall, a helluva jazz piano player/ entertainer/ singer and a protégé of Frank Sinatra. Frank was in semi-retirement at the time, but spent most of his time in the desert where he was very busy with his own golf tournament and his wife's most notable charity, The Barbara Sinatra Center for abused children. I hadn't seen Frankie since we were both young musicians in the New York/New Jersey area and we'd worked together someplace sleazy. Frankie was called Chico Randall back then and was attending college, and his career definitely went onwards and upwards from there.

He got his degree in psychology (which everyone in show business should have) and was hired by Jilly Rizzo to appear with his trio at Jilly's, a bar in New York's theatre district which was a late-night hangout for showbiz biggies including Frank Sinatra, who took a liking to the kid and helped his career immensely. Frankie did it all … recordings, television, nightclubs, and even appeared in a few beach-blanket-bingo-type movies, and became Sinatra's lifelong friend. He was able to return a favor or two to Ol' Blue Eyes when he worked for Steve Wynn and became Vice-President of Bally's Golden Nugget in Atlantic City, New Jersey and booked Sinatra into the place at a then-unheard-of price, which turned out to be good for Sinatra as well as the Golden Nugget.

At the time I ran into Frankie in the desert, he was back to singing and playing piano for a living and after we caught up with each other's news he asked me if I was open on New Year's Eve. I didn't want to say I'd been open on New Year's Eve for about the last twenty years, so I just accepted his offer of a gig, which, of course, led to a lot of other gigs, sometimes at an elegant country club where he was playing, and sometimes a charity party at The Barbara Sinatra Center, as well as the "nightcap party" at the Sinatra Golf Tournament, which, it turned out, was the last one Frank Sinatra attended. Then there was a party at Sinatra's house, which was a thank-you party for the volunteers who'd helped out with the tournament, and Frankie Randall and I were the band. Marilyn was invited and was excited to be there and meet Frank Sinatra. She wondered, "What am I going to say to him?" At the Sinatra house I was setting up my bass and amp and Marilyn was just standing around waiting for some friends to arrive, when Frank Sinatra, in his trademark orange sweater, came right up to her and said, "Can I get you a drink?" and the problem of what to say was solved. After the party was over, Barbara invited a few of us to stay for dinner. We heard a lot of inside stories about their life on and off the road, and it was a fascinating evening.

Marilyn and I were planning a party to celebrate our twenty-fifth wedding anniversary and friends Gene and Carolyn Moss generously offered to host the event at their beautiful Palm Desert home. As a surprise for Marilyn I wrote a song for the occasion, or at least the lyric to a song. I was working with Frankie Randall that weekend at The Springs Country Club. I brought him the lyric and asked him what he thought. He ran right over to the piano and started fooling around with my lyric. The next night he came to work with completed sheet music (from his state-of-the-art music system) and had written a terrific melody to go along with my words, and the song is good enough to be played as a jazz tune. Frankie said he'd sing it at our party if I wanted, and I wanted. But about two weeks before the party he got a booking in Vegas, so I went over to his house where we recorded the tune with piano, bass, and Frankie's voice, and played the disc at the party. The song was a big hit and has had an afterlife. On all my gigs I'd get requests for it, mostly from women, who love the lyric, and since I couldn't convince any male singer within a hundred miles to learn a tune dedicated to my wife called "Marilyn," I had to learn to sing it while playing bass if it were ever to be performed. A few years later when we made a jazz CD, I put the song "Marilyn" in and proved, as if any more proof were necessary, that Mitchells shouldn't sing. My brother had already proven that many times before.

I'd outgrown my factory-made starter bass and a couple of its successors by now, and it was time for a real, hand-carved instrument. When Marilyn and I went on that Alaska cruise with Brian, he and his fellow musicians told us about a bass maker in Larkspur, an arty community just north of San Francisco. We found the guy they were talking about, Pierre Josephs, who had once played bass with Stan Kenton's band. We looked around his shop and there were lots of great basses, but the one that caught my eye was a replica of a very old Bohemian bass that he'd been working on intermittently for nine years. I could have bought the two-hundred-year-old original bass for less money, but it was full of cracks and buzzes and wouldn't have survived life in the desert for very long. I made him an offer on the unfinished replica, which he'd been making for himself and he agreed to finish the bass for me. It's impossible to describe how gorgeous, unique and old-European the bass looks. And it plays even better than it looks. Once I got used to the mensure (the distance on the fingerboard between the notes…every bass is different) I began to play better than I'd ever played in my life. My new bass was the first hand-carved instrument I'd owned since the one that cost fifteen cartons of cigarettes that Red traded to me, which I'd used for most of my musical career, and it was ready just in time for a wonderful gig that came along.

Some local celebrities, people like Jack Jones, Peter Marshall, Kaye Ballard, and Jerry Vale, put their names and a few bucks behind Basin Street West, a new supper club in Rancho Mirage that was started by Lenny Green, a producer, manager, agent, and entrepreneur who had once owned the famous Basin Street showplace in New York. Its desert namesake was a first-class operation with excellent musicians, great food and big name entertainment. Shortly after it opened, I was hired and stayed there (six and seven nights per week) for about three months, making exactly the same amount of money that my bass had cost. It really put me on the musical map working there and I began to get better and better gigs. The

Bassmaker, Pierre Josephs, turning over my brand-new, gorgeous (replica of old) bass.

club folded right at the time of year when it starts to get hot in the desert and the rich folks go back to their more northern and eastern summer locations. There were claims and counter-claims, lawsuits, lots of name calling between the owners of the club and the people running it, but luckily nobody blamed the bass player. What happened, basically, is that some of the big names didn't draw big and the club was spending more money than it was taking in, and there was no oversight committee. Kind of like our government.

Bob Alexander came into our lives and what a welcome development that was. Bob had been a rock 'n' roll producer and concert promoter. He's an excellent fundraiser, and that's a good thing to be. We met because he was putting together a Big Band & Jazz Hall of Fame and thought I might put my talents and my old band pictures to good use in that cause. Bob came to Palm Springs nine years ago to produce a show at the four-hundred-and-fifty-seat Annenberg Theatre called *Sinatra My Way*, starring Frankie Randall, who'd been given many of Sinatra's choice arrangements by Barbara and the Sinatra estate. Frankie, backed by a local big band, sang a lot of signature Sinatra tunes. There were dancing girls and other surprises and it was a good show. Bob has lived in town since that show, and has been busy with his Hall of Fame projects and other ventures, including becoming President of the Palm Springs Walk of Stars when his friend, Gerhard Frenzel, the founder, became too ill to continue.

Bob became interested in yours truly because of my writing credits, because he always has ideas for television shows to develop. But I think the real attraction for him was that I'm the studio bass player on a lot of his favorite rock 'n' roll records, going back to my days in New York in the fifties and sixties, especially "Stand By Me," Ben E. King's big hit. That's me booming out that eight-bar bass solo intro, and I hear it in elevators, in the dentist's chair, at Ralph's Market, and now it's even in greeting cards. That's probably what will be on my tombstone. Remind me not to have a tombstone.

Bob got a bunch of investors interested in his idea of a Dean Martin Roast-type of show called *The Garlic Roast*, which had a twist: all the

On the set, shooting *The Garlic Roast*. Left to right: George Burns, Lucille Ball, Dean Martin, Norm Crosby, Mickey Rooney, Marilyn Monroe, Jack Benny and Ed Sullivan.

"roasters" are impersonators. The host and the "roastee" are alive and well and play themselves, but they're surrounded by Marilyn Monroe, Jack Benny, Dean Martin, Ed Sullivan, George Burns, and Lucille Ball, all impersonated by amazing look-alike, sound-alike actor/performers. During the writing and producing of that pilot no one could figure out why Bob insisted on calling it *The Garlic Roast*, least of all Bob, who would just say "that's what we're calling it." I suspect it had something to do with the slogan which followed and which made Bob giggle every time he heard it, and had at least a grain of logic behind it. The line that followed *The Garlic Roast* was "Tell All Your Stinkin' Friends!" The entire show would be scripted, and Bob asked me to write thirteen episodes, which would be sold direct to syndication.

He had made a deal with Norm Crosby to host the show and had lined up Monty Hall, Mickey Rooney, Carol Channing, Dick Van Patten, and Phyllis Diller, among other celebrities, to be "roastees." I'd written four roasts and we were nearing pre-production on the series when some

Muslim fundamentalist extremists decided things were going too well in America, or maybe they just decided that seventy-two virgins would be nice, but their horrible acts on September 11, 2001 killed just about everything around ground zero and there was and continues to be, collateral damage all around the globe. One of the victims was our little comedy project, because investment money disappeared overnight.

But Bob Alexander can never be counted out. A few years later he put together another investment group and raised enough money to do pilots for the roast and for another show, *Senior Prom*, which was to star Pat Boone and was kind of a Dick Clark's *American Bandstand* for older folks. Lots of meetings with Pat Boone took place in Los Angeles, but he eventually changed his mind and backed out of the show, which now was to star Connie Stevens and Wink Martindale and was called *The Beat Goes On*. I wrote the pilot and rewrote a roast show with Mickey Rooney as the roastee and Norm Crosby as the emcee. Both shows did get produced locally and aired on CBS-TV2, our local affiliate. Both shows took their time

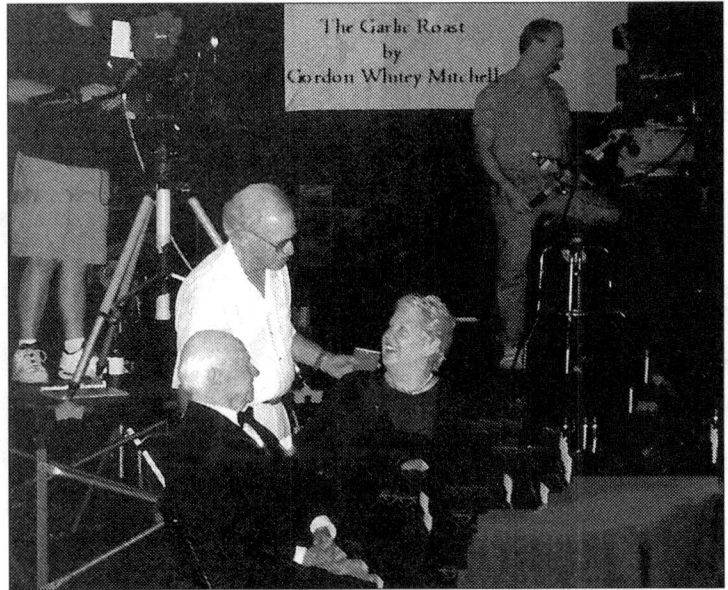

On the set sharing a laugh with Mickey Rooney and his wife Jan.

slots and the roast show in particular is something I'm proud of. Bob was thrilled with our product, because his whole idea was based on the premise that there's nothing for seniors to look at on television and America is fast heading toward being a nation of seniors. But the syndicators didn't pick up either show with the network shorthand explanation "it skews old." Exactly. But Bob doesn't give up easily and is still out there promoting both shows

    I haven't dwelt on my children's scuffles with life because, as painful as they've been to me, they really haven't had much to do with the two careers that unfolded for me and Mr. Magoo. Karen, now married, has three great kids, Will, Joe, and Karlee, and their lives are all on track. Lesley married Terry Clarke, a world-famous musician from Canada, and lives in Toronto with Terry and her two boys, Kristopher and Kyle. She produces music events, writes for jazz magazines, has guided her sons through a lot of acting gigs, and both boys have extensive tape reels and money in the bank for college. You won't be reading about any of these grandchildren in super-

Script reading on the set of *The Garlic Roast*.

Michele did all the hair and make-up for the show.
Here she's doing our Marilyn Monroe.

market tabloids because they're all bright and normal. Michele was briefly married to a smart young man named Alan who had entrepreneurial ability and a million projects, all of which he pursued all at once. When I last heard, he was buying "fixer" houses in close-in neighborhoods, completely renovating them and selling them for profit. And the term "irreconcilable differences" could have been coined with Alan and laid-back Michele in mind. Prior to becoming a real estate mogul, Alan was in his I-want-to-write-direct-and-produce mode, had already made two pilots by the time I met him, and had other projects he was pitching to independent movie companies and networks.

Alan had one not-really-fleshed-out idea in particular that he had verbally pitched to a very young development person at The Disney Channel who liked the idea, such as it was, but felt there was something missing. If he wanted to work on the idea, she'd be glad to hear the newer version. Alan asked if I'd help him and be sort of a silent partner. I said first I wanted to hear the idea. He told me, and I realized that the "something missing" was a premise. What Alan had was a nice place for something funny to happen and a character or two but no reason for them to be together, no motivation on anyone's part to do anything they were doing, and (a Writing 101 taboo) no conflict! In other words: no story. So we spent some hours together, started from scratch and built a story around the characters he wanted to keep, moved them into the same house, made them inter-generational family members (which has built-in conflict) and actually found a premise. I was pleased that, in my opinion, he now had a show he could pitch. I was also pleased that I'd be staying in the desert, playing bass, playing golf, writing my column, working on a play, and wouldn't have to go to yet another network meeting with a young executive who had several important weeks of showbiz experience under her belt. When I heard the report of the meeting, I was delighted. It was proof positive that I no longer should be part of the television industry, as if watching what's currently on weren't proof enough. The young network person hated Alan's revised show and shot it down by saying the worst thing she could think of: "That's so . . . Norman Lear!" I rest my case.

One of the amazing things about my revived music career is that I'm playing so much better than I ever did and seem to keep improving week by week and year by year. In the first half of my life, with a mortgage and a young family to think about, I couldn't be very choosy about the gigs I signed up for: Lester Lanin society parties, rock 'n' roll record dates, bar mitzvahs at Leonard's of Great Neck, Broadway shows . . . none of which had anything to do with jazz. Here in the desert, now that I'm in the third half of my life, I don't have to take any job I don't want to do. And so I don't take any gigs that don't have to do with jazz. The result: I'm playing jazz all the time and getting better all the time. One place I've been working for about eight years is Sullivan's Steakhouse in Palm Desert. It's located on El Paseo, which is the Rodeo Drive of Palm Desert, and they feature jazz music in the lounge three hundred and sixty-five days a year. And that's the fact that jazz musicians have to keep in mind, when sometimes the place gets a little too "corporate" and seems to be run by Suits. They are really nice loyal folks, they never tell anybody what to play (as long as it's jazz) and I get to work with the best musicians in the area. It's become a social base for Marilyn, who comes in with girlfriends and sometimes gets lots of attention from loose males, one of whom invited her to go dancing with him at a well-known pick-up place. I told her "okay" but just don't come home with anyone poor. I guess I'll continue to be there for as long as they'll have me, as long as I'm playing bass, and as long as their corporate business plan remains "Steaks, Jazz, and Martinis."

Several years ago I realized I was the only musician in my circle without a current CD on the market, so Marilyn and I said "wot da hell" and decided to make one. I contacted some of my favorite players and we went into a recording studio and jammed for about four hours. We came up with a straight-ahead jazz CD called *Just in Time*. Marilyn produced the CD and did the cover photography. It's available on line at www.cdbaby.com. In the process I rediscovered what I'd always known: if you pick the right musicians you won't be spending (and wasting) a lot of your time and money on post-production. One of my favorite musicians was Brian, and the idea was to have him on several tunes with a four-man rhythm section, and then do without drums, then piano, and end up with just guitar and bass, one of my favorite sounds.

One of the unexpected bonuses of my rekindled music career was that once again I might have a chance to perform with my musical kids, and that's always a total pleasure. So I was looking forward to recording our organized jam session with Brian and turning it into a CD. I'd already booked him many times before, notably on some Tribute to Benny Goodman shows at the Annenberg Theatre usually starring the late Abe Most, a brilliant studio musician who recreated Benny Goodman's and Artie Shaw's most famous recordings on those great Time/Life albums celebrating the swing/big band era a couple of decades ago. Abe and I had been friends since my earliest days in Los Angeles and whenever he'd come to the desert, I would contract a big band for him made up of mostly older musicians who can play that era's music with some sort of authority. When

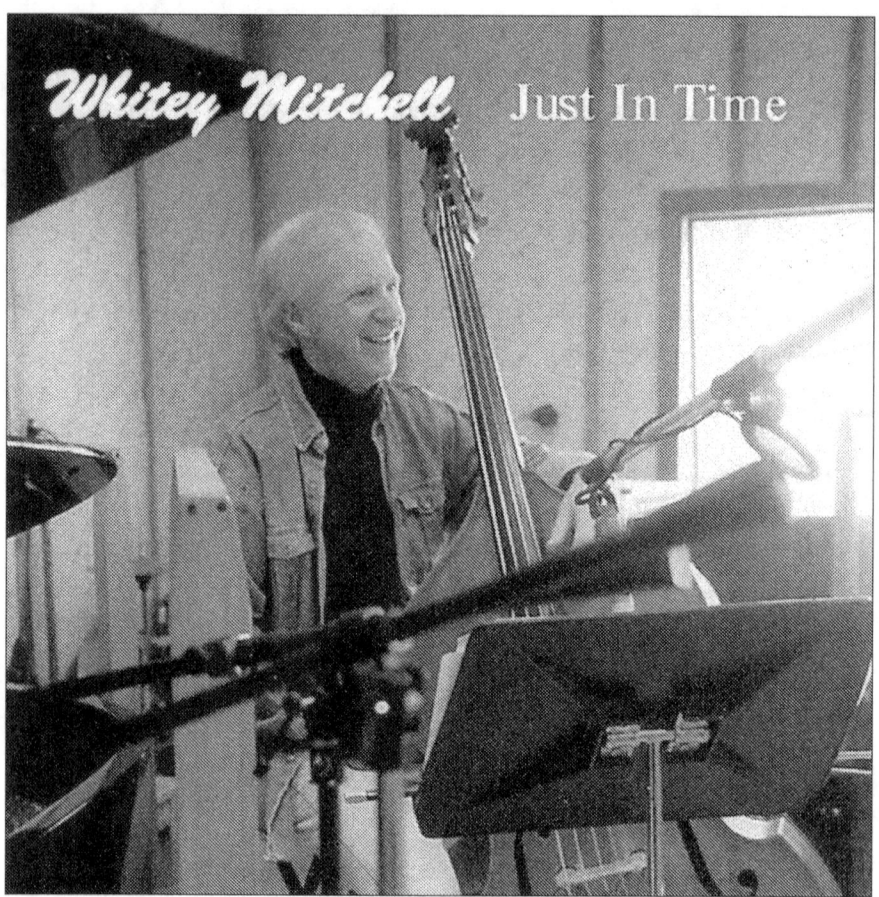

Marilyn's cover shot of my CD.

Abe passed away, some of his bookings went to Ken Peplowski, another wonderful musician and superlative clarinet player, and I contracted for him too.

I had a chance to move Brian into some of those gigs, either on the jazz tenor saxophone chair, or on lead alto, two critical positions in the band. It was amazing to see my kid leading a sax section of musicians perhaps fifty years older than he was, and doing it to universal approval. It was no big gamble on my part because years earlier I'd seen him (and this is one

Brian, me and great local jazz player Yarek Urant, who's enjoying Brian's performance at Pasta Italia in Palm Desert.

of the highlights of my musical life) playing lead alto in a forty-piece orchestra backing Leslie Uggams and Mel Torme in *An Evening With George Gershwin*. So hiring him to just show up with his tenor sax and jam with great musicians made a lot of sense.

Brian showed up forty minutes late, keeping his "clamato juice," which was in a large plastic cup, handy at all times. I noticed Brian's clamato juice was several shades lighter than the small glassful I normally sip while reading the morning paper and it didn't take long to figure out why. He enjoyed the session, but it was far from his best work, and my main concern was "how long has his drinking been affecting his career?" and that it foreshadowed worse things to come. He'd had a good run of jazz gigs here in the desert after I started hiring him for those big band concerts, and after local bandleaders listened to his brilliant work. He worked a lot of venues here, including Sullivan's Steakhouse and the popular Pasta Italia. But it all seemed to dwindle away, and people couldn't (or wouldn't) tell me exactly why. One bit of feedback I was able to get was that Brian was "loud," which I think, sorry to say, was a euphemism for "drunk."

But the CD came out far better than the gloomy scenario I've just described, especially after some judicious editing (including taking out a few bars during which Brian's flask clattered to the floor) and Marilyn created a great-looking cover photo, design, and liner notes and it's only fitting that the song "Marilyn" by Frankie Randall and Whitey Mitchell is right in there. The only drag is that it's Whitey instead of Frankie doing the singing.

One of the benefits of being in showbiz that's not talked about very much is the great number of people you meet and work with in just the normal course of events, and the seemingly high percentage of them who become friends. Case in point: Dave Michaels, our Dean Martin impersonator in *The Garlic Roast*, and the best I've ever seen in that category. Dave's been knocking around for a lot of years and has a great attitude, and certainly did a wonderful job for us. There's a lot of residual love for Dean Martin out there, and our audience willingly suspended their disbelief and loved Dave Michaels as Dean. We've since become friends with Dave and his wife Ann, and they come to the desert every year for a visit and golf (no wonder I like the guy). Out of the blue one day Dave told me he'd always wanted to do a one-man show based on Dean's life, and I'd always wanted to write plays, so we made a deal, and I subsequently wrote *Welcome To My World...An Intimate Evening with Dean Martin*, in which Dean talks about the ups and down of his life, his philosophy (oh, yeah, he definitely had one) and sings some of his greatest hits. Dave took about a year to get that script under his belt and when he was ready, we set up two performances here at a senior center theatre. Both performances sold out, and both audiences gave him a standing ovation. It's a good theory that audiences are never wrong. We had the same guy who directed my two pilots tape both shows and he made Dave a demo DVD he could copy and pass around to theatres, and he's getting some nibbles as this is being written. He just wants to get out of nightclubs and into theatres and do that show for the rest of his life. Which is fine with me, as long as he can still find time to come out here for golfing vacations.

My other playwriting experience grew out of a summer with nothing much to do a few years back. Norman Mark is a radio show host, movie reviewer and a wine columnist, and he and I decided to write a play. We both love showbiz, Norman is funny, we worked well together and, as an unexpected bonus, Norman can type about ten times faster than me. So no time was wasted waiting for my chubby fingers to find the right key. We came up with a play we called *Woody's Last Pitch,* about an irascible Academy Award-winning screenwriter, nearing early retirement age, who needs one more script sale to qualify for his Writers' Guild Pension and medical insurance for the rest of his life. But he's burned so many bridges in Hollywood, which can be an unforgiving town, that the only medium still open to him is television, something he's eschewed his entire career. He has trouble with an ex-wife, with his agent, and with his ne'er-do-well nephew, and has so much financial pressure that he must now pitch to young television development people. It was a wonderful chance to lampoon the industry and at the same time laugh at ageism.

We've had several staged readings of the play locally and in Los Angeles at The Writers' Guild, which sponsors a senior writing program in cooperation with SAG/AFTRA. The Guild picked our play out of many entries and gave us a great venue for our staged reading and SAG/AFTRA gave us a terrific and funny cast. The play (there's no point in pretending to be modest here) was a smash hit, with a standing ovation at the conclusion. A guy could get used to this. Norman and I hope to overcome the problem that there are not enough suitable theatres in our area and mount a production here. We did a staged reading for backers that produced lots of people who would like to throw money at us for this one, and it's one of my dreams that we'll get this one going, even though these days we're both much busier than we were that lazy summer a few years back.

And now . . . something painful.

I knew Brian wasn't doing well, except musically, although his drinking was ruling out some work opportunities. He co-led a very hip modern jazz group called The Jazz Coop and he made a spectacular CD, which he didn't have a chance to get off the ground, and which didn't create much wealth. He was living with his mom in a ground-floor back bedroom of her house in Glendale. He had no car, was not dealing well with a failed relationship with his main squeeze and, like his uncle Red, had no clue about leading a healthy lifestyle. He could quit drinking now and then over a limited time period, but could never stop smoking. We learned later that he'd had a few blackouts, which he attributed to the hot weather, arm numbness and other disturbing symptoms of heart disease. But the big thing Marilyn and I didn't know about was, sadly, he now required about a quart of vodka or more to get through the day. We were busy with our own lives and his reports were always upbeat and optimistic.

He'd lost his cruise line connections years earlier after a physical altercation with the Cruise Director and, with no visible means of support, moved in with his mom, and remained in that situation, with not much light at the end of the tunnel. He'd gained quite a bit of weight, stopped shaving and began to look more and more like the Nick Nolte character in *Down and Out in Beverly Hills*. Marilyn and I feared that, unless radical changes in his lifestyle were made, Brian was not going to achieve the longevity that his genetic make-up promised, but I was not prepared for the worst phone call I'd ever gotten in my life: "Your son has collapsed and is in the hospital on life support." Apparently, Brian and a visiting musician pal were partying a little heartier than usual and Brian blacked out and couldn't be revived. Paramedics came, couldn't get a pulse and took him to the hospital, where he was hooked up to life support. But his brain and other organs had been deprived of oxygen for too long, and he didn't survive. Later we learned that he had a cirrhotic liver, which didn't kill him, and acute cardiomyopathy, which did.

That was five years ago and I still can't really talk about it. How did this perfect and talented child get to the point at age forty-four that he didn't care whether he lived or he died? As Brian was in the hospital in Glendale essentially brain dead and awaiting the pulling of the plug, his sister Karen was upstairs in the neo-natal unit in that same hospital awaiting her prematurely born daughter's condition to improve so she could be released. These two events, an almost simultaneous birth and death, may have given some kind of balance to the universe but that thought didn't help me much. I'm at the point where I'm no longer shocked when people my age or a little younger or a little older start dropping dead, but you don't expect your forty-four-year-old son to die, in effect, from old age. This will take a long time, maybe forever, to stop being a daily source of pain.

A more recent and more acceptable death was that of Don Adams, television's Maxwell Smart, from the show *Get Smart.* He'd been ill and looked poorly four years ago when some *Get Smart* Fan Club members put on a reunion party for the show's cast, crew, production team, and writers. It was held at an upscale restaurant near Universal City and was attended by two hundred or so fans who'd come from all over the globe. In addition to Don, the family of the late Ed Platt, who played Smart's long-suffering Chief so well, was there as well as Barbara Feldon, still looking gorgeous at age sixty-four, Bernie Kopell, who played KAOS' evil genius Siegfried, producer Burt Nodella, Executive Producer Leonard Stern, character actor and former SAG President William Schallert, directors Reza Badiyi and Dick Carson, writers Gerald Gardner and yours truly, among others. Marilyn and I had a fun evening with food, drink, videos and old outtake reels. It was a pleasure just talking to and answering the questions of all those *Get Smart* aficionados who knew every episode, every actor, every director, every writer, and were thrilled to meet anyone connected to the show. Don was using a walker, had little tremors in his hands, and seemed incredibly white and weak. But his mind was still there and it was a fun reunion with him and Barbara.

When Don passed away last year, we went to The Writers' Guild Theatre for a celebration of Don's life, and it was a Who's Who of establishment comedy. His pals Don Rickles and Bob Newhart attended as well as veteran writer (and creator of Don's act) Bill Dana, Hugh Hefner, and Martin Landau, among others. Don's widow, his ex-wives, all of his children, grandchildren, and living siblings were there, and it was a very warm and loving evening. I got Martin Landau aside, congratulated him on his Oscar for playing Bela Lugosi in *Ed Wood*, and ventured the opinion that if anybody in the Motion Picture Academy had seen him in *The Harlem Globetrotters on*

The *Get Smart* Reunion of 2003. Me and Marilyn, back row, center. On my left, Executive Producer Leonard Stern. Front row includes Barbara Feldon, Don Adams and Bernie Koppel.

Gilligan's Island, they would have passed him by. We joked about that movie and both of us promised never to mention it again. Sorry, Martin.

After hors d'oeuvres and drinks in the lobby we went into the theatre and the celebration began. Of course, it was nothing like a funeral, it was more like a roast and it was wonderfully funny, with each speaker getting bigger laughs than the one before. And I noticed something that made me chuckle. Just talking about Don Adams for any length of time makes you start imitating him, if only unconsciously, and every guest who went to the podium at some point was doing his or her version of that nasal squeaky William Powell impression that Don turned into his own trademark. When Lloyd Turner and I were writing the show thirty-something years earlier it was inevitable that, by the end of the day, we were sounding more like Don Adams than Don Adams. The only thing that could follow all those testimonials, some of which evoked tears among the laughs, was a specially prepared video of Don's life that covered his childhood, to his service as a U.S Marine during World War II (he survived some of the worst combat of the entire Pacific theater) and his early struggles as a comedian. The video was excellent and included his trademark routine as the whining *Thin Man* character that he made his own, lots of outtakes from *Get Smart* and other shows that I hadn't seen, and a beautiful video of Don at home shortly before his death. As the camera moved closer he thanked everyone for coming and ended with "Now I don't want you people sitting around weeping and feeling sorry for me. Oh, no... I want you all to put your heads together and figure out a way to bring me back!"

It's evenings like that that make show business such a rewarding career. Even for anonymous writers and even more anonymous bass players. Lucky me...I've already had my Don Adams evening and my fifteen minutes of fame, and I even got to sit there in person while my friends and family gushed on about me at the Walk of Stars dedication.

To say that Marilyn and I have blossomed here in the desert would be

At the Martini Bar on a well-deserved cruise, when
I was a Guest Lecturer on Screenwriting.

a vast understatement. She joined the Palm Springs Women's Press Club, which is made up of ladies with press and entertainment media credits who raise money for scholarships for outstanding journalism students. She had been Vice-President/ Program (and held the same office with Women in Show Business in Los Angeles), which made sense because with our contacts she was able to get great guests for their monthly luncheons. This past year she served as President and was recently re-elected for another term. I serve on the board of The Palm Springs Walk of Stars, write a weekly golf column in *The Desert Entertainer* magazine, play bass at selected jazz joints, and recently completed a book, published several months ago, called *Star Walk, A Guide to The Palm Springs Walk of Stars*. It's a light-hearted collection of mini-biographies of two hundred seventy-five people, everyone who has a star so far. But getting the necessary information to write these whimsical bios was a daunting amount of work and Marilyn was enormously helpful editing, researching, and tracking down living and deceased honorees, or their survivors. These people are not all world famous, but they all deserve recognition, and it was a privilege getting to know them, if only through writing about them.

Marilyn and I have become friends with a hundred people here, or maybe two hundred, or maybe a thousand, I don't know, plus renewing friendships with Los Angeles people who keep on moving here. The Palm Springs area is a place that welcomed both of us with open arms, and it's a place where you can retire if you want to, or find lots to do that's fun if you want to, even if it means making money you never planned on.

I'm grateful for all the help and for all the dumb luck I've had along the way through my two lives, which continues in abundance since moving here to feed the pigeons and drool. I think the two guys from Jersey have had more than their share of fun and rewards, and they'll continue having them as long as Marilyn is at their side and as long as Fred Silverman and Eddie Fisher don't move here and louse things up.

Contracting a 20-piece orchestra for Lainie Kazan at the McCallum Theatre in Palm Desert.

Karen, Marilyn, Lesley and Michele backstage with me at the McCallum Theatre when I played for Rich Little.

Book signing event at Peppertree Bookstore in Palm Springs.

Signing my book, *Star Walk*, during a Palm Springs Walk of Stars Gala.

Arriving for the big Star Day event, greeted by good friend David Mercer

Greeting friends & family.

My list of a few people to thank.

The Little Town with a Heart   249

The actual Star unveiling with my three dear daughters.

Star Day with good friends, Writer-Producer Allan Blye, Marilyn, Me, Writer-Producer Mort Lachman and Director-Producer Bill Asher.

NORMAN LEAR

February 2006

To Whom This May Concern:

And to me that means everyone who has ever enjoyed a good laugh and everyone who understands that laughter adds time to one's life. So large is their number, it is impossible to judge how many people over so many years have been affected in that life-giving way by Gordon "Whitey" Mitchell. It was Whitey's talent and passion for writing about their foibles that helped the audiences he entertained to see the foolishness of their own human condition. Working with Gordon on The Jeffersons, I was one of those people, a member of his audience, and so I join you all in tribute to a terrific human being and mirth-maker par excellance.

Best,

Norman Lear

NL/md

Associated Musicians of Greater New York
322 West 48th Street, New York, NY 10036
Phone 212-245-4802 • www.local802afm.org
Fax 212-245-6389 (2ⁿᵈ fl) • 489-6030 (3ʳᵈ fl) • 245-6257 (4ᵗʰ fl) • 245-6255 (5ᵗʰ fl)

January 11, 2006

Gordon "Whitey" Mitchell
52 Laken Lane
Palm Desert CA 92211

Dear Mr. Mitchell;

    I have been informed that, after your illustrious career as a musician and screen writer, you are to be inducted into the Palm Springs Walk of Stars. Local 802 is proud to have had you as a member, and extends its congratulations and best wishes.

Sincerely,

David M. Lennon
President

MUSICIANS:
We're the US in
MUSIC

February 13, 2006

On behalf of the nearly 8000 members of the Writers Guild of America, west, I offer my warmest congratulations to Whitey Mitchell on the dedication of his star on the Palm Springs Walk of Fame. Many of our members worked with Whitey during his illustrious career as a television writer and producer. Many more, like myself, grew up laughing at his work on such shows as *All in the Family*, *Get Smart*, *The Mary Tyler Moore Show*, and countless others. Now we can all look forward to walking all over him whenever we visit downtown Palm Springs.

Congratulations, Whitey!

Sincerely,

Patric M. Verrone
President, WGAw

Special Thanks

**Here's to these friends…they know me well,
and yet they still like me.**

**I may not have written about these wonderful people in the book,
but they've all touched my life in one way or another.**

Bill Asher, Paul Canzano, Bob Corwin, Neil(Dubee) & Bonnie Dubin, Bill Edelen, Scott Ellsworth, Roz & Burt Feldman, Bruce Fessier, Danny Flahive, Andy Fraga, Richard & Lenore George, Ruth Gibson, Ron Kalina, Steve Kelly, Natalie Lachman, Herb Mickman, Bill & Barbara Marx, Jack Mendelsohn, Johnny Morris, Gene Moss, Tommy Newsom, Ben Ohmart, Darlene & Doug Palmer, Vito Pizzo, Judi Ross, Irwin Rubinsky, William & Lynne Vaughan, Donna & Collin Wade, Judy Wolman …

and especially David & Georgia Mercer.

I am also grateful to The Writers' Guild of America, The American Federation of Musicians, The Palm Springs Walk of Stars, The Palm Springs Women's Press Club, the Management, Staff and Musicians at Sullivan's Steakhouse, and the entire Alta Kocker Caucus.

Finally, thank you to my wife, Marilyn, who thought of lots of ways to make this book, as well as my life, better.

Credits

Creative Consultant, Executive Story Editor or Staff Writer:

Mork & Mindy Garry Marshall Productions; Paramount Studios & ABC
The Jeffersons Norman Lear/Tandem-TAT Productions & CBS (Show-
    runner) Image Award Nomination
Diff'rent Strokes Norman Lear/Tandem-TAT Productions & NBC
Good Times Norman Lear/Tandem-TAT Productions & NBC
Get Smart Talent Associates & CBS
    Writers' Guild Award Nomination
The Bob Hope Show Hope Enterprises, Inc. & NBC
Joe's World Norman Lear/Tandem-TAT Productions & NBC
The Good Life Columbia Pictures Television & NBC
City Mary Tyler Moore Productions & NBC

Episodes:

All In The Family, Mary Tyler Moore Show, Small Wonder, The Twilight Zone, Bustin' Loose, Dark Justice, After MASH, The Partridge Family, You Can't Take It With You, Love, American Style, Maude, Temperatures Rising, The Doris Day Show, My Mother the Car, Gomer Pyle, Tammy Grimes Show, Me & Mrs. C., Get Smart, The Odd Couple, Mama's Family.

Producer/Writer:
Good Times Norman Lear/Tandem-TAT Productions & CBS
Harper Valley PTA Universal Studios & NBC
Billy Martin Celebrity Roast Multiview Productions & NBC (Atlantic City)
The Garlic Roast Hall of Fame Partners, Inc. & CBS
The Beat Goes On Hall of Fame Partners, Inc. & CBS

Television Pilots:
The Garlic Roast Hall of Fame Partners, Inc. & CBS
The Beat Goes On Hall of Fame Partners, Inc. & CBS
Playing House The Shpetner Company & CBS
Handsome Harry's Kaldonia Productions & NBC
Rock Candy The Landers Company (Syndication)
Kid from Left Field 20th Century-Fox Television
Three Way Street Alan King Productions (Las Vegas)
The Pickle Factory Ralph Edwards Productions
Army Brats Universal Studios Television

Movies for Television:
Harlem Globetrotters On Gilligan's Island Universal Studios TV & NBC
Honeymoon Suite Columbia Pictures Television & ABC
Not Now, Norman Metromedia Productions & ABC

Feature Films:
Private Resort Tri-Star Pictures & Unity Pictures
Big Bad John The Unger Company
Horns Up! Jadran Films & Quatroswift, Ltd. (Europe)
The Clubhouse Seven Seas Productions

Stage Plays:
Woody's Last Pitch
An Evening With Dean Martin (A One-Man show)

Books:
Star Walk: A Guide to the Palm Springs Walk of Stars
Hackensack to Hollywood

Instructor:
Television & Screenplay Writing, UCLA, Westwood, CA campus;
Writing for Television, University of California-Riverside, Palm Desert campus
Humor Columnist: *Golf News Magazine; Desert Entertainer*

Radio Talk Show Host:
The Power Lunch, KGAM 1450-AM;
The Natural Golf Hour

Board Member:
Palm Springs Walk of Stars & Star Honoree

Discography:
Whitey Mitchell Sextet, ABC-Paramount
New York Jazz Quartet, Elektra Records
New York Jazz Quartet Goes Latin, Elektra Records
Get Those Elephants Outa Here...The Mitchells,
Red, Whitey & Blue, Metrojazz Records
Three Bones and a Quill, Roost Records
Just in Time, Whitey Mitchell Music

Listed in Six *Who's Who in Music* Books:
Leonard Feather's New Encyclopedia of Jazz
Leonard Feather's Laughter from the Hip
The Penguin Guide to Jazz
The New Grove Dictionary
Jazz-The Rough Guide
The Biographical Encyclopedia

Heading off into the future.

Index

A

Abney, Don, 110
Adams, Don, 9, 117, 121, 241-243
AFM, Local #802, 81, 253
Alexander, Bob, 229-232
Allan, Jed, 189
Allen, Steve, 73, 101
Amateau, Rod, 108
Amos, John, 166
Andrews, Beverly, 194
Andrews Building, 194-195, 198-199, 201, 205, 208
Armstrong, Louis, 36
Army Band, 392nd, 50, 55
Atlantic Records, 83
Aubrey, Jim 96

B

Bacharach, Burt, 83
Barbour, John, 106-109, 111
Barton, Frank, 130-131, 151
Benecke, Tex, 17
Bennett, Tony, 23
Benny, Jack, 9, 12, 106, 149, 156-157, 230
Berra, Yogi, 209

Birdland, 57-60, 75
Blye, Allan, 12, 250
Boone, Pat, 231
Brooks, James L., 121
Brooks, Mel, 132, 151-153
Brown, Les, 106, 111-112
Brown, Ray, 69-72
Bruce, Lenny, 9, 37, 90, 95, 103
Buckley, Lord, 42
Burnett, Carol, 103, 152, 191, 210
Burns, Allan, 107, 114, 121
Busch, Niven, 194

C

Cameo, The, 73-75
Capitol Records, 58, 83, 224
Carson, Johnny, 76, 107, 149, 189, 192
CBS Television City, 148, 150-152
Charles, Ray, 129, 215
Charlie's Tavern, 57
Clarke, Terry, 232
Cohen, Irving, 25, 33, 61
Cole, Buddy, 110
Coleman, Gary, 186
Cosell, Howard, 209

Costello, Frank, 43
Crawford, Broderick, 137
Cugat, Xavier, 98

D

Dana, Bill, 241
Davis, Jerry, 140-141
Dawber, Pam, 170-171
de Cordova, Fred, 107
Decker, Wendell, 52
DeVito, Frank, 100
Dorsey, Jimmy, 42
Dorsey, Tommy, 37, 39, 215
Down Beat Magazine, 69, 89-90, 104
Drifters, The, 58-59
Dubois, Jan'et, 166

E

Eckstine, Billy, 58-59
Eden Barbara, 187-189
Edwards, Duke, 25-26
Eldridge, Roy, 69
Elgart, Les, 97
Ellington, Duke, 36
Ellis, Herb, 69
Embers, The, 75
Evans, Bill, 74-75
Evans, Patrick, 13

F

Faye, Frances, 74
Feather, Leonard, 84, 258
Feingold, Jay, 98
Feldon, Barbara, 121, 241-242
Fields, Shep, 37, 39-41, 43, 45-46, 49
Fields, Freddie, 40
Fisher, Eddie, 9, 79-80, 82, 130, 244
Fitzgerald, Ella, 69-71, 110
Fleming, Peter, 109
Ford, Whitey, 209

Fort Lee, Virginia, 50, 52, 54-55
Francis, Arlene, 54, 146
Freeman, Bud, 65
Frenzel, Gerhard, 229

G

Gallo, Lew, 130-131
Gelbart, Larry, 156
Gibbs, Marla, 160
Gibson, Henry, 129
Gillespie, Dizzy, 28
Gleason, Jackie, 76, 83
Goldberg, Leonard, 138
Golf News, 219, 258
Goodman, Allen, 112-113, 191-192
Goodman, Benny, 9, 33, 91, 98-99, 101, 198, 235
Graham, Bob, 73
Green, Lenny, 227
Green, Urbie, 75, 91
Gregory, Dick, 79-80
Grylic, Rajko, 198
Guillaume, Robert, 167
Guzman, Claudio, 133

H

Hackett, Bobby, 75, 91
Haggis, Paul, 210-211
Hagman, Larry, 135
Hamlisch, Marvin, 103
Hanna-Barbera, 205-206
Harlem Globetrotters, 177, 241, 257
Harper, Valerie, 210, 212
Harrison, Jerry, 207-209
Hawkins, Coleman, 65
Hayward, Chris, 107, 113-114, 116, 128
Hefti, Neil, 75
Hemsley, Sherman, 145, 159
Henderson, Skitch, 73, 98
Henry, Buck, 107
Herman, Woody, 32, 36, 47, 61

Heston, Charlton, 9, 119
Hirsch, Sylvia, 210
Hollywood Hackers, The, 152, 192
Hope, Bob, 8-9, 12-13, 106, 111-112, 121, 123-125, 127-128, 149, 189, 205, 220, 256

I
Igoe, Sonny, 61-63

J
Jackson, Janet, 167
Jacquet, Illinois, 69
Jazz at the Philharmonic, 66, 69-70, 72-73, 111
Johnson, Bruce, 170
Johnson O'Connor Research Foundation, The, 32
Jolson, Al, 80
Jones, Jack, 96, 223, 227
Josefberg, Milt, 156, 168
Josephs, Pierre, 227-228

K
Kalish, Austin, 167
Kalish, Irma, 167
Kanter, Hal, 109, 156
Kaye, Danny, 200
Keller, Sheldon, 106, 192
Kenton, Stan, 58, 63, 227
King, Ben E., 229
King, Carole, 102-103
King, Morgana, 75
Kirby, George, 58
Korman, Harvey, 191
Kostal, Irwin, 154
Kravitz, Lenny, 161
Krupa, Gene, 9, 66-69, 72-73, 91, 133-134

L
Lachman, Mort, 13, 106, 123, 125, 156, 168, 250
Lacy, Steve, 75
Lamond, Don, 77-78
Landau, Martin, 241
Landers Sisters, The, 207-208
Lanin, Lester, 84, 86-89, 234
Larkin, Bill, 106, 125-127
Lawrence, Elliot, 98
Lear, Frances, 161
Lear, Norman, 9, 13, 142, 144-145, 148, 150, 152, 156, 161-163, 167-169, 178, 182, 186, 188, 210, 234, 253, 256-257
Lee, Peggy, 58-59
Leeman, Cliff, 86, 89
Leonard, Sheldon, 96, 139, 205
Letterman, David, 170
Lieber & Stoller, 83
Lohman, Al, 220-221
Lohman & Barkley, 118, 221
Lombardo, Guy, 76
Lompoc Penitentiary, 201-204
London, Julie, 73
Lowe, Mundell, 35, 60
Lynde, Paul, 107

M
Manhattan School of Music, 56-57
Mantle, Mickey, 209
Mark, Norman, 239
Mark Hellinger Theatre, 214
Marlow, Ric, 66
Marquette, Peewee, 60
Marshall, Garry, 169-170, 256
Marshall, Peter, 227
Martin, Billy, 209, 257
Marx, Groucho, 109, 149
Maxwell, Marilyn, 141
McKenna, Dave, 61-63
McRaven, Dale, 170-171
Mensch, Homer, 78, 110
Mercer, David, 247, 255
Mercer, Georgia, 255
Michaels, Dave, 238
Miller, Glenn, 17, 40, 215

Mills, Donna, 135, 137
Mitchell, Blue, 84
Mitchell, Brian, 83-84, 97, 129, 183, 214-215, 221, 225, 227, 235-240
Mitchell, Grace J., 5, 15
Mitchell, Karen, 13, 84, 95, 129, 183, 215, 225, 232, 240, 245
Mitchell, Keith "Red," 15-16, 19-23, 25, 27-28, 32-33, 47-48, 55, 69, 77-78, 84, 98-102, 104-105, 115-116, 134, 146-148, 183, 216, 227, 240
Mitchell, Lesley (Clarke), 13, 75, 84, 96, 129, 131, 183, 189, 225, 232, 245
Mitchell, Marilyn, 5-6, 12-13, 133-136, 139, 152, 154-155, 160, 165, 173, 178, 183, 186-192, 200-201, 203-204, 206, 210-213, 216-221, 224-227, 230, 235, 238, 240-245, 250, 255
Mitchell, Michele, 13, 84, 133-134, 155, 162, 173, 178, 183, 201, 210, 225, 233, 245
Mitchell, William D., 14
Mittleman, Rick, 195
Modernaires, The, 17
Moss, Gene, 220, 224, 226, 255
Most, Abe, 235
Moye, Michael, 167

N

Nabors, Jim, 96
Newhart, Bob, 241
Newley, Anthony, 96
Newport Jazz Festival, The, 84-85
Newsom, Tommy, 191-192, 255
Nicholl, Don, 143, 148, 161-162
Norvo, Red, 47, 116

O

O'Bannon, Rockne, 200
O'Connor, Carroll, 148, 150, 168
O'Day, Anita, 84-85

P

Palm Springs Walk of Stars, 11, 229, 243-244, 246, 255, 258
Palm Springs Women's Press Club, 244, 255
Palmer, Don, 62, 65
Paramount Theatre, 17
Parker, Charlie "Yardbird," 28, 130
Parker, Johnny, 89
Parker, Ray, 205-206
Peplowski, Ken, 236
Perlmutter, Sam, 173
Peterson, Oscar, 69, 71
Philbin, Regis, 191
Phillips, Flip, 69, 71
Pietragallo, Gene, 221
Previn, Andre, 9, 76-78, 101, 104
Prowse, Juliet, 79-80
Puma, Joe, 75

R

Radburn, New Jersey, 14-17, 22
Randall, Frankie, 13, 60, 225-226, 229, 238
Ray, Rick, 133, 138-139
Reiner, Rob, 142
Rhine, Larry, 156
Rich, Buddy, 9, 69, 72
Richmond, Bill, 105
Rickles, Don, 241
Roker, Roxie, 160, 164
Rolle, Esther, 166, 169
Romoff, Colin, 82
Rosen, Mike, 198, 200
Ross, Mickey, 148, 156, 161, 165
Rugolo, Pete, 58-59, 63

S

Sandrich, Jay, 123
Sanford, Isabel, 145
Schiller, Bob, 168
Schwartz, Elroy, 149

Schwartz, Lloyd, 176-177, 207
Schwartz, Sherwood, 149, 176-177
Schwarzenegger, Arnold, 9, 179, 181
Scott, Bobby, 57, 66-68
Scott, Tony, 57
Setlowe, Richard, 195
Shaughnessy, Ed, 102-103
Sherry, Elinor, 36
Shriver, Maria, 180
Shu, Eddie, 66, 68
Silverman, Fred, 176-178, 187-189, 192, 197, 244
Sinatra, Barbara, 225-226
Sinatra, Frank, 9, 13, 60, 189, 225-226
Skelton, Red, 149, 156
Slade, Bernard, 140, 204
Smith, Kate, 40-41
Spillane, Mickey, 44
Spivak, Charlie, 98
Stapleton, Jean, 9, 150, 168
Starr, Ringo, 103
Stern, Leonard, 241-242
Streisand, Barbra, 83
Struthers, Sally, 142, 148
Styne, Julie, 103
Sullivan's Steakhouse, 234, 237, 255
Syracuse University, 29

T

Tadman, Aubrey, 189, 195, 208-210, 214
Tartikoff, Brandon, 192
Thomerson, Tim, 201
Tolkin, Mel, 156
Torme, Mel, 73, 129, 237
Trevino, Lee, 174
Trikonis, Gus, 200-201
Troup, Bobby, 73, 107
Turner, Darlene, 154-155
Turner, Lloyd, 114, 116-121, 123, 128, 131, 149-152, 154-158, 160, 164-165, 168-170, 174, 178, 206, 217, 220, 242

U

Unger, Tony, 179-180

V

Van Dyke, Jerry, 107
Van Patten, Dick, 208, 230
Ventura, Charlie, 61-63, 65
Viola, Al, 73

W

Walker, Jimmie, 166
Ward, Helen, 101-102
Ward, Jay, 107, 113-117, 121, 150
Wayne, David, 135, 137
Webster, Ben, 65
Weiskopf, Bob, 168
West, Bernie, 148, 161
Williams, Andy, 73, 82
Williams, Robin, 9, 169-171, 173
Winding, Kai, 58
Women in Show Business, 190-191, 244
Worth, Stan, 112-113, 116-117, 121, 220
Writers' Guild of America, 109, 117, 138, 182-183, 205, 218, 254-255

Y

Young, Lester, 69, 71

Z

Zagreb, Croatia, 198-199
Ziegfeld Theatre, 157
Zolnekoff, Allan, 146-147, 184

BearManorMedia

Can you resist looking at these great titles from Bearmanor Media?

We didn't think so.

To get details on these, and nearly a hundred more titles—visit
www.bearmanormedia.com

You'll be sorry!

...if you miss out.   P.S. Don't be sorry.

www.ingramcontent.com/pod-product-compliance
Lightning Source LLC
Chambersburg PA
CBHW062008220426
43662CB00010B/1276